Soviet Jewry in the 1980s

Soviet Jewry in the 1980s

The Politics of Anti-Semitism

and Emigration and the Dynamics of Resettlement

Edited by Robert O. Freedman

Duke University Press   Durham and London 1989

© 1989 Duke University Press
All rights reserved
Printed in the United States of America
on acid-free paper ∞
Library of Congress Cataloging-in-Publication Data
appear on the last printed page of this book.

This book is dedicated to Fabian Kolker
in tribute to his long years of service
on behalf of Soviet Jewry

Contents

Tables and Figures

Tables

Figures

Preface

The issue of Soviet Jewry has occupied an important place in the struggle for human rights for more than two decades. Beginning as a small trickle in the mid-1960s, the exodus of Soviet Jews became a major wave in the late 1970s, only to fall sharply in the early 1980s, but to rise again in 1987 and 1988. More than 275,000 Soviet Jews have succeeded in leaving the USSR, with most resettling in either Israel or the United States, albeit not without difficulty.

As the issue of Soviet Jewry rose in importance, the Center for the Study of Soviet Jewish Emigration and Resettlement was established at Baltimore Hebrew University. It has sponsored a series of conferences to analyze the question of Soviet Jewry in all of its aspects. The first conference, held in 1976, analyzed the "mental baggage" the Soviet Jews who were resettling in the United States brought with them to America. The second, held in 1980, examined the problems in the resettlement process in the United States. The third conference, held in 1981, examined the politics and process of the emigration movement during the 1971–1980 period and the nature of resettlement in both Israel and the United States. The proceedings of this conference were published by Duke University Press under the title *Soviet Jewry in the Decisive Decade 1971–1980* (edited by Robert O. Freedman). With the precipitous decline in Soviet Jewish emigration in the first half of the 1980s, the center decided to hold a conference in May 1986 to ascertain the causes of this dramatic decline and to analyze alternate strategies that might be employed to reverse it. A number of basic questions were asked. First and foremost, was it foreign policy considerations—specifically the deterioration of Soviet-American relations—or internal Soviet politics which led to the decline? Second, if foreign policy considerations were in fact the main cause, what actions should be taken? Should the Jackson-Vanik Amendment, for example, be dropped or modified? If this action were to be taken, who is to make the decision to urge the change on the U.S. Congress, the American Jewish community, or the State of Israel? In the American Jewish community, should the lead come from the National Conference on Soviet Jewry or the Union of Councils for Soviet Jews or both, acting cooperatively? If the decision is to be made in Israel, should it be done by the Israeli government or should recently released refuseniks, with their specialized knowledge of the Soviet system, be allowed a major role in the decisionmaking? To seek to answer these questions, invitations were sent to scholars and government officials throughout the world. Representing the United States was Ambassador Richard Schifter, assistant secretary of state for human rights. Representing the American Jewish organizations with primary responsibility for Soviet Jewish affairs were Jerry Goodman, then executive director of the National Conference on Soviet Jewry, and Dr. Mark Epstein, then executive director of the Union of Councils for Soviet Jews. Representing the State of Israel was Yehoshua Pratt of the Israeli Embassy. Also speaking at the conference were three former Soviet Jews, a refusenik now living in Israel (Anatoly Khazanov), an émigré now living in Canada (Yaakov Rabkin), and another now living in the United States (Ilya Levkov). Scholars from the United States (Dr. Zvi Gitelman, Dr. Sidney Heitman, Dr. William Korey, Dr. Marshall Goldman, Dr. Steven Feinstein, and Dr. Robert Freedman), from England (Dr. Howard Spier), and from Israel (Dr. Theodore Friedgut) also spoke at the conference, as did Mr. Fabian Kolker, cofounder of the American Council for Soviet Jews, a predecessor of the National Conference on Soviet Jewry.

As might be expected, the debate at the conference was a spirited one, and this book, which is the outcome of the conference, reflects the spirited debate. The book has been organized in such a way that it both discusses the main developments in the Soviet Jewry movement in the 1980–87 period and also contains a chapter dealing with alternative strategies for the Soviet Jewry movement to pursue, with the contributors, where necessary, revising and updating their chapters to reflect the rise in emigration that began in 1987.

I would like to thank a number of individuals for their help in making the conference, and this book, possible. First and foremost, I would like to thank Dr. Leivy Smolar, president of the Baltimore Hebrew University, who has given his wholehearted support for the series of conferences on Soviet Jewry held at the college. Second, I would like to thank Mrs. Raquel Schuster-Herr of the Baltimore Jewish Council for her help and that of the council in cosponsoring the conference. Third, I would like to thank my secretary, Mrs. Elise Baron, for her excellent work in typing the manuscript and my research assistant, Mrs. Elaine Eckstein, for helping me to keep my files on Soviet Jewry up to date.

A special expression of gratitude is due Fabian Kolker who for more than twenty years has been active in the struggle to aid Soviet Jewry and whose generous support made the conference possible. It is to Fabian Kolker that this book is dedicated.

Robert O. Freedman
Baltimore, Maryland
December 1988

Introduction

The fate of Soviet Jewry in the 1980s has not been an enviable one. While in 1979 a record 51,320 Soviet Jews emigrated from the USSR, in 1986 the number of émigrés had dropped to only 914. At the same time the Soviet government tightened its pressure on Jews living in the USSR who attempted to study Judaism. Hebrew teachers were arrested and imprisoned, and informal Jewish study groups were broken up and their leaders threatened. The advent of Mikhail Gorbachev in March 1985, and his much-heralded policy of *glasnost* (openness), initially did little to help Soviet Jews. While such famous refuseniks as Anatoly Scharansky and Eliahu Essas were allowed to emigrate during the first two years of Gorbachev's rule, emigration remained very low (1,140 in 1985 and 914 in 1986); there was an increase in the number of Prisoners of Zion (those arrested for trying to emigrate to Israel); there was a further crackdown on Jewish culture inside the Soviet Union; and a highly restrictive emigration decree was enacted. In 1987 the situation changed: there was a sharp increase in emigration (8,155), all of the Prisoners of Zion were released, and a number of prominent refuseniks were allowed to emigrate. However, whether the changes in 1987 mark a new trend or are merely an aberration is not yet clear.

This book, which analyzes developments relating to Soviet Jewry in the 1980–87 period, is divided into four major sections. The first deals with internal politics in the USSR as it relates to the question of Soviet Jewry. The second section deals with linkage between Soviet foreign policy and Soviet Jewry. The third section examines alternate strategies for promoting the release and resettlement of Soviet Jews. The fourth section of the book discusses, from the vantage point of almost two decades, the resettlement of Soviet Jewry in both Israel and the United States.

In the first chapter of the book Theodore Friedgut of the Hebrew

University of Jerusalem attributes the decline in emigration in the early 1980s to a combination of three factors: the demise of détente, the growing economic crisis in the USSR, and the increase in social tension there. He notes that while Brezhnev sought to establish a policy of "neither anti-Semitism nor Zionism," the Soviet leader's policies were not successful. This was due in part to the endemic anti-Semitism pervasive in the USSR and in part to the continued efforts by the Soviet Jews themselves, armed with detailed information from abroad and encouraged by the support of Western governments (especially the United States), to develop Jewish culture in the USSR so as to keep up their national consciousness until the opportunity to emigrate was again available. Friedgut then notes that in the Gorbachev period there is increased hope for Soviet Jews to emigrate, and he considers that the new emigration decree, "however flawed," is a step in the right direction.

One of the most important domestic political developments relating to Soviet Jewry in the 1980s was the establishment of the Soviet Public Anti-Zionist Committee in April 1983. The Anti-Zionist Committee is described in detail by Dr. William Korey of B'nai B'rith. Korey asserts that not only did the committee in its peak period of activity (1983–85) try to dissuade Soviet Jews from emigrating to Israel, but also that its central theme, the similarity of Zionism and Nazism and their collaboration before and during World War II, reflects the virulent anti-Semitism that continues to pervade the USSR. Korey also highlights the roles of Soviet "Court Jews" like David Dragunsky and Samuel Zivs and analyzes the Soviet media attention given to such anti-Semitic authors as Yuri Kolesnikov (a vice-president of the Anti-Zionist Committee) and Lev Korneyev to demonstrate the severity of the problems faced by Jews living in the USSR.

The arrival of Gorbachev and his policy of glasnost, while perhaps encouraging Soviet intellectuals, some of them Jewish (especially after Andrei Sakharov was allowed to return to Moscow from exile), nonetheless brought with it some additional problems for Soviet Jews. In particular, the easing of restrictions on the expression of ideas led to the growth of Pamyat, a grass-roots organization which, while ostensibly devoted to preserving Russia's cultural monuments, is actually an anti-Semitic organization which blames the Soviet Union's problems on the so-called Zionist-Masonic conspiracy. Howard Spier of the Institute for Jewish Affairs in London analyzes this organization in chapter 3 of this book and notes that it closely resembles the anti-Semitic Union of the Russian People, an organization that existed in czarist times and which promoted the anti-Semitic slander *The Protocols of the Elders of Zion*. Spier also notes that a number of prominent anti-Semitic propagandists have been attracted to Pamyat, including Vladimir Begun and Evgeny Evseev. While the Soviet leadership has now come out in opposition to Pamyat and has severely criticized the organization, Spier warns that it has some support in the Soviet public and may also have at least tacit support in some circles of the Soviet government as well.

While the establishment of the Soviet Public Anti-Zionist Committee and the emergence of the anti-Semitic Pamyat organization were important domestic developments in the Soviet Union affecting Soviet Jewry during the 1980s, foreign policy issues also had their impact. The State of Israel, one of whose central priorities is the ingathering of Jews from all over the world, continued its active interest in the plight of Soviet Jewry. In chapter 4 Robert O. Freedman, Peggy Meyerhoff Pearlstone Professor of Political Science and dean of graduate studies at Baltimore Hebrew University, analyzes the issue of Soviet Jewry as a factor in Israeli foreign policy. He asserts that despite a great deal of rhetoric, the issue of Soviet Jewry was a relatively unimportant factor in Israel's relations with the USSR, with Middle Eastern political considerations a far more important factor. Indeed, argues Freedman, at least until the spring of 1987 the issue of Soviet Jewry was far more important to Israeli-Diaspora relations (particularly the clash over the "drop-out" issue) than it was to Israeli-Soviet ties. Nonetheless, he also notes that the efforts of Israeli Prime Minister Shimon Peres to tie an increase in the exodus of Soviet Jews to the inclusion of the USSR in a Middle East peace conference raised the salience of Soviet Jewry both in terms of Israel foreign policy and in Israel's domestic politics. Freedman concludes, however, that Israel by itself appears to have had little influence over the Soviet leadership's decision to allow Jews to emigrate or in the ultimate destination chosen by recent emigrants, with the United States playing a far greater role in both decisions.

If the United States has played a major role in getting the USSR to open its gates to Jewish emigration, the states of Western Europe, despite their rhetoric, have played a far less influential role. In chapter 5 Howard Spier, presenting a Western European perspective, suggests that the West European states, whether singly or jointly, had relatively little leverage in relation to the USSR's Jewish policies; moreover, they were not seeking confrontation with the USSR but desired a return to the détente of the 1970s.

While world attention has centered on the plight of Soviet Jewry, Moscow has also allowed two other groups, Soviet Germans and Soviet Armenians, to emigrate, albeit with a minimum of publicity. In chapter 6 Sidney Heitman, professor of history at Colorado State University, compares Soviet policy toward the three emigrating groups. He notes that in many ways the status of Soviet Germans resembles that of Soviet Jews, although that of Soviet Armenians was very different. Thus the Soviet Germans, like the Soviet Jews, were an unassimilated, dispersed, and alienated national minority with strong traditions and ethnic consciousness which had a history of persecution and discrimination under both the czarist monarchy and the Soviet regime. Moreover, while the numbers of Soviet German emigrants (who were clearly influenced by the Jewish example) rose sharply in the 1970s, the number of Soviet German emigrants fell in the 1980s, again paralleling the Jewish experience. Nonetheless by 1985, 105,000 Soviet Germans had succeeded in emigrating. By contrast, the situation of Soviet Armenians seeking to emigrate was unique. Although the number of emigrants rose and fell in the 1970s and 1980s in tandem with Soviet Jewish and Soviet German emigration, only the special group of 200,000 Armenians who had come to the USSR at the close of World War II at the invitation of Stalin to help rebuild the Armenian Republic were allowed to apply to emigrate. Heitman notes that 50,000 of these Armenians, disillusioned with life in the USSR, have so far emigrated.

As Jewish emigration dropped sharply in the 1980s, a number of policy alternatives were suggested to influence the Soviet government to resume large-scale emigration. In chapter 7 of this book Marshall Goldman, associate director of the Russian Research Center of Harvard University, argues that the Jackson-Vanik Amendment, "which has outlived its usefulness," should be eliminated. He also contends that the American Jewish community made a major mistake in not making concessions on Jackson-Vanik in 1979 when Moscow allowed a record 51,320 Soviet Jews to leave. Indeed, asserts Goldman, had the Soviet Union achieved Most Favored Nation (MFN) status in 1979, the USSR might not have invaded Afghanistan, and he asserts that with the arrival of Gorbachev it is time for the American Jewish community to change its policy in order to encourage Jewish emigration from the Soviet Union.

While the issue of emigration has received primary attention, the issue of Soviet Jewish resettlement, and its problems, remains an important one. In chapter 8 of this book Zvi Gitelman of the University of Michigan, in comparing the patterns of emigration to the United States and Israel, notes that the typical Soviet Jew who made aliyah to Israel came from one of the outlying republics of the USSR (primarily from the Baltic Republics, Soviet Georgia, or Central Asia) where there was a long tradition of religion and/or Zionism. By contrast, he states, the typical Jew who emigrates to the United States is a third or fourth generation Soviet citizen from the interior where religion has been more effectively stamped out. Gitelman concludes that Soviet émigrés in both Israel and the United States seem to be fundamentally satisfied and well resettled, although the Soviet Jews who immigrated to Israel from Central Asia seem to have had the greatest problem in resettlement.

A special case of resettlement is presented by Steven Feinstein of the University of Wisconsin who describes the resettlement in Israel of Soviet Jewish artists. While he notes that many had already experimented with Jewish themes while still in the Soviet Union, it was not until they settled in Israel that their work could fully reflect the Jewish tradition and become more reflective of contemporary trends in international art.

In sum, these chapters reflect the dynamics of Soviet Jewish affairs in the period 1980–87. These years witnessed a sharp decline in Soviet emigration and in 1987 the beginnings of a resumption of a large-scale exodus. Both the formation of the Soviet Public Anti-Zionist Committee and Gorbachev's glasnost affected the Soviet government's treatment of its Jews, while Soviet-American, Soviet-Israeli, and, to a lesser degree, Soviet–West German relations also had their effect. The period was also notable for the sharp debates among World Jewry both as to the most expeditious way to get the Soviet government to release more Jews and as to where their ultimate place of resettlement should be. Finally, during the 1980s those Jews who had succeeded in emigrating from the Soviet Union continued the process of resettlement in their new homelands, often making a major contribution to their new host societies.

It is hoped that this book, which analyzes developments relating to Soviet Jewry in the 1980s, will make a contribution toward the understanding of their lives and fate during this critical period in their history.

Part One

**The Impact of Internal Politics in the
Soviet Union on Soviet Jewry**

1. Passing Eclipse:
The Exodus Movement in the 1980s

Theodore H. Friedgut

Introduction

The 1970s had been years of triumph for the Jewish exodus movement in the USSR. During this decade nearly a quarter million Jews had been permitted to emigrate. The renaissance of Jewish national and cultural identity had been firmly established as a phenomenon with which to be reckoned inside the USSR and had rallied widespread sympathy and support the world over.

For the first time since the 1920s the Soviet regime had granted recognition to emigration of such dimensions and duration that it could not be concealed from the public at large. The fact that this emigration centered around such a historically sensitive minority as the Jews and that the emigrants' announced destination was Israel, a country with which the Soviet Union had demonstratively severed its relations, could only magnify the impact. In addition, a "demonstration effect" soon became evident as the Jewish emigration was followed by similar movements of another nonterritorial minority, the Germans, and a large-scale emigration of Armenians, who not only had their own Union Republic, but who had, a generation earlier, campaigned for the return of the Armenian diaspora to the Soviet Armenian motherland. In the numerous analyses of the Jewish exodus movement published to date, there has not been adequate examination of its importance as a factor in Soviet domestic politics and society.

This decade of achievement was not, however, without its shadows. The large-scale emigration far surpassed all early projections as to its potential, but it soon became evident that a large group of activists was being denied the right to leave. A community of long-term refuseniks became a festering issue, their continuing imprisonments, exiles, and harassment overshadowing tens of thousands of joyful family reunions. The refusenik issue became an embarrassment to the Soviet authorities by focusing attention on the ugliest features of the Soviet political system.

By the mid-1980s the freeing of Prisoners of Zion and of long-term refuseniks became the benchmark by which the entire movement's progress or retrogression was measured. For some time these dramatic personal fates very nearly overshadowed the basic issue of the freedom of Jews to leave the USSR. When the glasnost emigration began in the spring of 1987, this overshadowing was a source of anxiety to many refuseniks who feared that the release of a few prominent figures might be a Machiavellian trick of the Soviet authorities to diminish public pressure for a return to an unimpeded exodus.

A second problem that darkened the last half of the 1970s was what became known as the issue of dropouts—those Jews leaving the Soviet Union with visas for Israel but en route changing their destination for other countries. The political and moral complexities of this problem and suggestions of how to deal with it are treated elsewhere in this volume. In this overview of the movement's development we will only note its psychological and operational effects. The overwhelming majority of activists who have organized the cultural and political activity of the exodus movement do so in the name of aliyah, immigration to Israel, as Zionists devoted to their people's return to its homeland. These Zionist activists take upon themselves the burden of public leadership of the movement, thus exposing themselves to regime reprisal and repressions. It was, therefore, with frustration, and even anger, that these leaders saw a growing proportion of the precious quota of exit visas (always granted in numbers smaller than those wishing to leave) going to people who had no intention of attempting a new life in Israel. Even the total commitment of these exodus activists to the principle of freedom of choice as a part of their revulsion from the compulsions of Soviet society did not ease their discomfort at the moral problem created by the dropouts' exploitation of Zionist efforts. In the already unbearably tense atmosphere of Soviet Jewish life this simply added new strains.

A similar splitting of forces was evident both within various Jewish communities and in the worldwide movement for assisting Soviet Jews. Israeli institutions and personalities accused the U.S. government as well as certain American-Jewish public organizations of unfairly "tempting" Soviet Jews to come to America. These accusations became the focus of internal recriminations that threatened to diminish the unity and effectiveness of the Soviet Jewry movement in a number of countries. In addition, what was seen as an Israeli attempt to coerce the Soviet Jews to come to Israel against their will was rejected as inhumane and antidemocratic, thus tarnishing Israel's image. The government of Israel, which had originally responded to the Soviet Jews' struggle for exodus by urging, inspiring, and coordinating much of the international effort now found that it had no control and a diminishing measure of influence over this effort. A major reassessment of approach was called for but was painfully slow in emerging.

The Turn of the Decade

In the final two years of the 1970s hopes were generated that a permanently high plateau of Jewish emigration might have been reached. In the early months of 1979 it appeared that the exodus would easily surpass the magic number of 60,000 postulated in earlier years as a proof of virtual free emigration. The continuity of the movement seemed assured, for as the wave of emigration grew, the number of those requesting a *vyzov* (an invitation from relatives abroad) grew in parallel, with new thousands of Jews taking the decision to leave. Thus a constant backlog of potential emigrants came into being.

Yet by the summer of 1979 careful observers of the exodus movement were already sounding the alarm. Even as the wave of emigration was growing, the granting of new exit permits slowed, and in the second half of 1979 this began to be reflected in a declining monthly rate of emigration. For those who saw only the overall figures, the record-breaking exodus of 51,547 appeared to be a crowning peak to a decade of successful struggle. The following years of decline—21,471 in 1980, 9,400 in 1981, 2,692 in 1982, and figures that hovered around the thousand per year mark from then to the end of 1986—quickly erased the optimistic sense of achievement dominant in the 1970s. Ignoring the vociferous protests of thousands trapped in the limbo status of refuseniks, Soviet spokesmen blandly declared the emigration chapter in Soviet Jewish history closed, stating that no more Soviet Jews were applying to leave, that over 90 percent of applications had been approved, and that only a small number of persons, refused for legitimate reasons of Soviet state security, were denied emigration.

What caused the change? Why did the Soviet government suddenly close the gates in midyear, after appearing to have accepted the principle of free exit? Numerous explanations have been suggested. Some of these have little apparent connection with Soviet interests or actions and therefore little credibility. Such, for instance, is the claim that the growing percentage of emigrants heading for North America, rather than to Israel, caused the change. This claim, which has obvious relevance to the Israeli establishment's efforts to use administrative methods in putting an end to the drop-out problem, fails to take account of two important pieces of evidence. The first is that Soviet authorities had repeatedly pushed dissidents into exile with visas for Israel when it was clear (particularly in the case of non-Jews) that they would not go to Israel. In such cases it is hard to argue convincingly that the emigrants' ultimate destination was of any importance to the Soviet regime. Of even more importance is the fact that at the same time that Jewish emigration was cut off, emigrations of Germans, who had no drop-out problem, and of Armenians, who were leaving their homeland and creating a new diaspora, were also stopped. In 1987, when the Jewish emigration began to increase again, these two emigrations also resumed. There can be little doubt, then, that destination was not the determining factor.

Attention should therefore be focused on possible reasons which can be related to problematic policy areas in Soviet domestic and international affairs. It would appear that the closure of emigration was related to three main factors: détente, economic crisis, and social unrest. Any one of these alone might have engaged the attention of one or more of the Soviet leaders, and yet might have been insufficient to rally the political support necessary to bring what was then an aging and conservative leadership to change a well-established policy. However, when all three policy areas became problematic simultaneously, a coalition of attention supporting suspension of emigration could easily be formed.

In the field of détente it became clear in the summer of 1979 that the Carter regime's confidence in the USSR as a partner in the relaxation of tensions was rapidly cooling and that the SALT II treaty would not be brought before the United States Senate for ratification. In addition, as the 1979 wave of emigration rose, signaling a year-end possible total of 60,000 or more, there was no responsive signal from the U.S. government or from any of the political or social groups supporting Soviet Jewry, suggesting a quid pro quo in the form of expanded credits, freeing of technological aid and trade, or activation of the review clause in the Jackson-Vanik amendment. In December came the Soviet invasion of Afghanistan, followed in 1980 by the growing political crisis around the growth of the Solidarity movement in Poland. Détente, at least for the near future, was dead. Jewish emigration, as a bargaining element in the détente process, had lost its value.

At the same time the Soviet Union was sinking into economic stagnation. The predictable problems of a mature economy operating in a suffocating bureaucratic environment in conditions of hypertension and shortage were compounded by a seven-year run of adverse weather that nearly destroyed the lagging agricultural sector. The seriousness of the difficulties was clearly apparent when Brezhnev found it necessary to state repeatedly in high Communist party forums that the inability of the regime to maintain a consistent food supply for its industrial centers had become the highest-priority political and economic problem facing the regime.[1] The short-term plan by which the Soviet leaders hoped to alleviate their economic problems involved numerous measures of resource conservation and belt-tightening, but in keeping with time-honored Soviet methods the core of the program centered around a campaign for greater effort, more work, and tighter work discipline. Local officials might well have complained to the center that it was difficult to try and convince rank-and-file citizens of the need for such efforts while tens of thousands of Jews, Germans, and Armenians, many of them highly trained and relatively sober and hardworking, were streaming out of the country. Continuing emigration was thus very probably viewed as an impediment to overcoming the economic crisis.

The stagnation and crisis of Brezhnev's latter years brought with it a wave of growing social tensions. The spread of alcoholism, the rise in infant mortality, and other alarming social symptoms were clearly seen by analysts of Soviet society. In addition, there were growing tensions between Great Russians and other Soviet nationalities.[2] On the background of these tensions the emigrating minorities, who were seen as having been prominent in the making of the revolution, were accused of deserting a sinking ship and of leaving the Russians to clean up the mess left in the wake of the revolution's failures. Only now, under Gorbachev's recent policy of freer discussion and criticism are we able to see the full extent to which corruption, stagnation, and demoralization were felt in the grass roots of Soviet society.[3]

One of the symptoms of the demoralization in Soviet society was a general emigration fever that affected whole sections of the Soviet scientific, cultural, and technical intelligentsia. These were the very groups central to any Soviet effort to overcome economic difficulties and speed the country's transition to modernity. They were also the people who, due to their professional placement, were most aware of the true dimensions of the Soviet crisis and of the regime's inability to cope. In addition, they were generally in close contact with many of the emigrants, particularly the Jews, whose socioeconomic achievements had clustered them in this stratum. As the Soviet crisis became sharper at the end of the 1970s, many non-Jewish members of the intelligentsia began to shift their attention from their nominal work to a concentrated effort to get themselves and their families out of the USSR. Failing that, many opted for "internal emigration," that state of apathy to society and surroundings familiar in the annals of the Russian intelligentsia. While other elements of the plan to rally society, such as the anti-alcoholism campaign or the efforts to improve public health and workers' productivity, could have real impact only over a long period of time, the regime was both able and willing to cure the emigration fever and concentrate the intelligentsia on its production tasks by slamming the gates with such a resounding bang that an unmistakable message would be transmitted.[4]

The decision to end emigration is best seen, then, as a complex of three factors, containing both domestic and international elements. As changing circumstances and the changing perceptions of a new Soviet leadership influence regime priorities, the prospects for the continuation and growth of the renewed emigration stream will also change. This, too, is likely to be determined by a complex of domestic and international factors.

A New Policy: Neither Anti-Semitism nor Zionism

The enunciation of the Soviet regime's new policy toward its Jewish minority came only in 1981 at the 26th Communist Party Congress. Speaking in the context of the need for the smaller national minorities to take on more of the burden of economic development hitherto borne disproportionately by the Great Russians, Brezhnev began to talk of national relations in the USSR. He stated that every nation's dignity should be protected and that no deviations from this norm would be tolerated. "We will tolerate neither chauvinism nor nationalism—for example, neither anti-Semitism nor Zionism." As though to emphasize the promise to the Jews implicit in these words, the elections to the leading Communist party bodies at the close of the party congress raised Jewish representation to a level unknown since World War II. Six persons publicly known to be Jews were allotted places in the Central Committee and Central Auditing Commission.[5]

Brezhnev's formulation of neither anti-Semitism nor Zionism expresses the essence of the policy formulated by his regime for the Jews of the USSR in the 1980s. The Jews were to forget about emigration, live "normal Soviet lives," and submit to isolation from other Jewish communities of the world. In essence, they were to revert to the situation in which they had lived in preemigration years. Here and there they would be permitted some crumbs of Sovietized Jewish culture. An occasional concert or play on a Jewish theme might be presented. From time to time a Russian-language book with material of Jewish interest might be published. Some of these items would be displayed in Soviet society with sufficient prominence to signal to the public the legitimacy of this controlled Soviet Jewish culture. Yet little more than this was in prospect to satisfy the new sense of national identity that had grown up among Soviet Jews in the 1970s. If the Jews would accept this, renouncing Zionism (and the Communist party version of Zionism as enunciated by Brezhnev included abandonment of any interest in and contact with foreign Jews unless initiated by the Soviet authorities in support of state interests), then Brezhnev seemed to be promising a cessation of discrimination, both public and professional. Not only would propaganda of an anti-Semitic nature be kept out of the press, but educational and occupational discrimination that had grown steadily over the years was to be decreased, if not wholly eliminated.

At the end of 1979 a samizdat document had already reported the existence of a government instruction ordering officials to ease the existing restrictions on the hiring and promotion of Jews as well as on their acceptance into higher education.[6] In 1983 the acceptance of the children of a number of refuseniks into medical school in Leningrad created a stir. In the autumn of 1986 the Moscow refusenik community was abuzz with the story of five Jewish families who had petitioned the Party Committee in Moscow to guarantee their children a fair entrance examination at Moscow State University, the Soviet Union's most prestigious and exclusive institution of higher education. This petition came in the wake of refusenik publication of evidence that Jewish applicants were being given near-impossible problems in entrance tests, particularly in the mathematics and physics departments. All five applicants were said to have been subsequently accepted to the university. There were also scattered reports of offers by the regime to reinstate and even promote refuseniks who would sign an act of contrition renouncing and regretting all intentions of emigration.

The Failure of the Brezhnev Policy

Despite these dramatic steps, the new Soviet policy was a near-total failure. There were numerous reasons for this. First of all the rapid closure of emigration had trapped a large number of Jews who had already submitted their applications for an exit visa or who had so committed themselves to emigration that there was no turning back. As fast as people were getting out in 1979 and 1980, new applications were being submitted, and, as we have already noted, new invitations were being asked for by families caught up in the emigration snowball.[7] This phenomenon was not new. The rise and fall of demand for *vyzovy* and for exit visas has always had a strong correlation with the ease with which people were actually leaving the country at any given time. However, due to the lag between a change in policy and the awareness of that change in the community, a temporary mismatch may appear. Thus the number of invitations applied for in the years 1980–84 actually outran the number of exit visas granted. The rapidity with which emigration was closed off thus increased tensions within the Jewish community at a time when official policy was aimed at making the Jews feel more comfortable. This discomfort was not limited to a small part of the community. The reserve pool of those who at some time have applied for a *vyzov* but have not emigrated is about 380,000 people.[8] Of more immediate importance is the refusenik community, those who have applied for their exit visa and been refused by OVIR—the department of visas and registration of the Soviet Interior Ministry. At the end of 1986 the refusenik community was thought to number about 11,000 people, an estimate that has since then proved too modest by half. For these people, whose whole existence is now entwined in the effort to leave the Soviet Union, there can be no such thing as reversion to normal Soviet life. There is a whole generation that has grown up as refuseniks, and thousands of teachers, engineers, and scientists have been excluded from their professions, their careers destroyed in a manner that no reversal of policy can mend.

In addition, whatever the directions given by the authorities in 1979, there is abundant evidence that discrimination in hiring and in educational admissions persists. Three factors can be discerned that account for the persistence of such discrimination. First is the natural conservatism and caution of the Soviet bureaucracy. As the emigration wave grew, most persons in responsible posts in the Soviet Union needed no formal instructions to keep them from hiring or promoting Jews. The position of director of any significant Soviet institution, scientific, cultural, or economic, is as much a political post as it is administrative. High schools, factories, research institutes, or government offices can only be headed by a member of the Communist party, screened by the local Party Committee. In addition, if the institution is large, or important, there is a local party functionary charged with overseeing activity at the institution and a representative of the security police who busies himself with the political orthodoxy of the entire staff. It was clear that the regime regarded emigrants as tantamount to traitors. Therefore any director who wished to avoid possible future charges of political immaturity or of consciously harboring unreliable elements, simply continued not to hire or to promote anyone who might conceivably consider emigration at some future date.

This persistence in narrowing opportunities for Jews was assisted by a supplemental factor. From the mid-1960s the number of applicants for higher education had begun to outrun the number of places available, and it was possible to find a sufficient number of qualified candidates for Soviet universities without accepting more than a minimum number of Jews. At the same time demographic processes and the emigration of a large number of university-age Jews thinned the ranks of Jewish applicants, while a Soviet "affirmative action" nationality selection policy restricted the number of Jews accepted into higher education even where a specific anti-Jewish discrimination did not exist. As the number of university graduates grew rapidly in the 1970s, a rising wave of non-Jews available for hiring and promotion submerged the declining numbers of Jews, partially screening the persisting patterns of discrimination. A third factor with which we will deal separately, and at greater length, is the presence of crude anti-Semitism, encouraged to show itself when official propaganda supports it and maintaining its presence even after the authorities' use of anti-Jewish slogans subsides. Popular anti-Semitic feeling has multiple and deep roots in tradition, in jealousy of the socioeconomic prominence attained by Jews, and perhaps even more importantly today in a backlash of renascent Russian nationalism.

Certainly the renewed prominence of officially inspired anti-Semitism during Israel's invasion of Lebanon in 1982 and 1983 set to naught any formal promises the regime had made. The prominence with which such hatemongers as Lev Korneev were published in all the central organs of the Soviet press left no Soviet Jew untouched. Moreover, it appeared clear that this line of propaganda was supported within the highest levels of the Soviet leadership. Sporadic and private disavowals of this anti-Semitism, even when they came from authoritative circles, could do little to dissipate the anxieties of a Soviet Jewish community that felt itself terribly exposed and vulnerable. The brief prominence of the Soviet Public Anti-Zionist Committee added to this unease, for in its publications and press conferences the committee subscribed to the theories of a worldwide Jewish conspiracy, thus intensifying the existing mistrust of even the most vociferously loyal or protectively assimilated Soviet Jew.[9] A complete vicious circle of mutual rejection and mistrust had been created in which normalization of the lives of Soviet Jews was all but impossible.

The attempt to isolate Soviet Jews from other Jewish communities failed as badly as did the attempt at normalization. In the first place the more than 270,000 Soviet Jews who have left the Soviet Union over the past twenty-five years generate a flow of uncensored communication that is probably the greatest single source of free information to reach any group of Soviet citizens. The letters, photographs, and telephone calls chronicling the daily lives of individuals and families provide firsthand, perfectly credible testimony as to the texture of life outside the Soviet Union. Using this unprecedented wealth of reliable detail, the Soviet citizen now has not only a new scale on which to measure his own life, but is better equipped to evaluate the Soviet version of the outside world. This new access to information is one of the important political and social effects of the mass emigration of the 1970s. Even were the effects of this information flow to be restricted to the immediate communities of emigrants—and this does not appear to be the case—the Soviet authorities would still have lost a major dimension of control over important groups of citizens. In the summer of 1987 this new informational contact took on an additional aspect. The Soviet authorities began permitting a few emigrants to return to visit parents or other relatives still in the USSR. Should this continue, the direct testimony of these people who have succeeded in establishing themselves in their adopted countries would create a new and unprecedented dissonance with the almost unrelieved picture of doom and disaster that is the supposed lot of the emigrant given in the official media.

The failure to isolate Soviet Jews is not an outgrowth of private communication alone. The success of the exodus movement in the 1970s was in part due to the broad political support it was able to enlist in various countries of the world. Jewish communities, political leaders of both left and right, church groups, and scientific and cultural organizations were all moved by the plight of the refuseniks and by the courage they showed in facing up to the power of the Soviet state. The result was that Soviet representatives, whether visited in their homeland or visiting abroad, found that the repression of emigration was a constant source of critical comment and political embarrassment. One of the important successes of the public movement to aid Soviet Jewry has been its ability to convince leaders in many countries that there is a large, active, and concerned political constituency that regards the welfare of the exodus movement as an important political issue as well as an unimpeachable moral position.

One of the signal successes of the effort to maintain the subject of Soviet Jewry on the public agenda came at the summit meeting at Reykjavik in October 1986. The American secretary of state, George Shultz, who had agreed earlier to Israeli requests that freedom of emigration be seen as the litmus test of any human rights agreement, insisted that human rights be included in the summit agenda. The Soviet delegation realized that the emigration issue had to be faced rather than denied when the Americans offered to present them with an Israeli-compiled list of names, addresses, and dates of refusal for the entire known refusenik community. This recognition of the importance of Jewish emigration was reinforced and surpassed when the joint communiqué issued by the American and Soviet governments announcing the date for the December 1987 summit publicly included the matter of human rights on the agenda.

The Refusenik Community in the mid-1980s

Mikhail Gorbachev was formally elected general secretary of the CPSU in March 1985. The first year of his incumbency, however, showed no trend toward easing the policy of isolating Soviet Jews. Throughout 1985 and early 1986 concerted regime attempts were made to stifle the autonomous activities of the refusenik community. A number of Hebrew teachers were arrested and the KGB harassed the scientific and Jewish culture seminars in Moscow and Leningrad. There were also several well-publicized cases of expulsion of foreign visitors who had attempted to visit the refuseniks. Most notable among these was Israel's former president, Professor Ephraim Katzir, an internationally known scientist, who was prevented by physical force from visiting refuseniks while in the

USSR at a scientific conference. The publication in June 1986 of a virulent anti-Jewish book as a bibliographic handbook for agitators appeared to bode ill for the Soviet Jews. This tract connected the rise of the Jewish religion with cannibalism, denied any historical claim of the Jews to Israel as a homeland, and propagated the legend of a Freemason-Zionist plot to control the world, linking Zionists and Kerensky (as a Freemason) as part of this plot to anti-Bolshevik activities from 1917 on.

To put this period into proper perspective we should examine some of the unanticipated consequences of Soviet emigration policy for the structure and intensity of refusenik activity. Communities of refuseniks vary greatly in numbers, educational profile, and sophistication of activity. Nevertheless, the current situation has produced numerous common features. First of all, the closing off of emigration gave the movement a stability and continuity of leadership that it had never had before. Though a number of long-term refuseniks had always been prominent, many of them, particularly after exile or jail terms, had been more symbols than active leaders. The organizing of political and cultural activities was always passed on to new persons so that the charges against and surveillance of the incriminated persons would not taint the entire movement. With the closing off of emigration, organizers of teaching and of other activities enjoyed longer tenure, gathering experience. This is reflected particularly in the teaching of Hebrew, which has come to be organized with multi-year curricula, special training for teachers, and a wealth of texts and audiovisual aids previously undreamed of. This stability has also assisted the spread of teaching in smaller outlying communities. While intercity contacts have always existed in the exodus movement, they could now be based on longer-term interpersonal contact that builds confidence, understanding, and a stronger coordination of effort.

The cutoff of emigration presented refusenik families with a new and serious problem regarding their children's education. Faced with an almost certain long-term wait to get out, tens of thousands of children were literally born and brought up in refusal. The activist parents met this by organizing kindergartens, Sunday schools, and holiday camps. Here, the children, free of the duality and social pressure under which they live in the general Soviet schools, cultivate a knowledge of and pride in their general Jewish identity. There are, of course, considerable dangers and difficulties in bringing up young people in such a fragmented psychological world. This added an extra burden to the refuseniks' already tense environment, in which uncertainty has such a prominent part. The result, however, is that children who enter adolescence after years of home study of Hebrew and of Jewish culture and history have the basis for a strong self-image and, most important of all, a clear understanding and sharing of their parents' values.

The independent founding by the refuseniks of a yeshiva (theological seminary) with a growing number of full-time students following an organized curriculum was an entirely new dimension of religious activity. The creation of this institution in Moscow was the achievement of Eliahu Essas who was permitted to leave for Israel at the beginning of 1986. The activity of the yeshiva continued despite the departure of its charismatic founder. In similar fashion Itshak Kogan of Leningrad had also become a devoutly observant Jew and had begun instruction of people from a number of other communities in the laws of Jewish ritual and the observance of the festivals. Before leaving for Israel at the end of 1986, he gathered his pupils together for final instruction and examinations and then sent them out to become independent propagators of the faith. As more and more visitors from abroad and more information reached the refusenik community, new groups and outlooks, both religious and secular, began to crystallize. For the first time since World War II the Soviet Jews were able to savor something of the ideological pluralism in which the non-Soviet Jewish community lives.

The Moscow refusenik scientists' seminar was a well-known phenomenon even before the cutoff of emigration. In the 1980s it too has adapted its activities to the new conditions. The number of scientist refuseniks has continued to grow steadily, and the seminar has branched out into sections by disciplines. No international scientific congress is held in the USSR without some of its participants coming to lecture before the refuseniks. Expulsion from the Soviet scientific community, and the loss of their laboratories, blights the careers of many Jewish scientists. The refusenik science seminar compensates in some measure, maintaining the intellectual vitality of these highly motivated and talented people.

Gorbachev: Restructuring Soviet Policies and Reality

From the beginning of his incumbency Gorbachev has announced the intention of introducing qualitative changes into Soviet society and the Soviet economy. As noted, the initial impact of the change in the Soviet leadership on the exodus movement was not encouraging. Yet by mid-

1986 a prospect of change for the better was in the air. Arrests had ceased and harassment had eased, although it had not stopped. By the autumn there was a clear anticipation of change, reined in by the long-tested skepticism of the veteran refuseniks. There was also a clear realization that political support for Gorbachev's restructuring was as yet perilously thin in the Soviet establishment. Some of the new leader's opponents are philosophically opposed to even the most limited steps of democratization, including, of course, emigration. Others have personal and institutional power interests that would be harmed by the restructuring. A large number, particularly in the middle and lower levels of the state and party bureaucracies, are simply incapable of understanding the new values that Gorbachev forces upon them. A long-term refusenik asked why he should not be given his exit visa, since the secretary general had publicly stated that holding people back because of state secrets should be limited to no more than five to ten years. He was answered by the head of the local visa office who said that with all due respect to Gorbachev's immense energy and talents, the secretary general could not possibly be personally involved in all the thousands of enterprises and institutions of the Soviet Union, and most particularly he had no knowledge of the complex problems faced by OVIR officials in that city.[10] As more and more Soviet Jews reported their bureaucratic encounters during 1987, it became clear that the authorities were in considerable confusion, with promises of one agency denied by another, and the refuseniks caught helplessly in the middle.

One of the first indications that Gorbachev was including emigration in his restructuring of Soviet society came with the announcement of a decree of the Council of Ministers dated August 28, 1986.[11] This decree made public for the first time the precise regulations governing application for emigration from the USSR. It contains no recognition of the right of any citizen to leave his country or to return to it. In this it falls far short of the criteria posited in international conventions on human rights and of any generally accepted standards of a democratic society. Furthermore, the decree restricts those who may apply for emigration to people with first degree (parent, spouse, or sibling) relatives abroad. This criterion, if applied, would exclude thousands of those who were already refuseniks at the time the decree was published as well as tens of thousands of potential applicants. Insufficient closeness of the relatives sending a *vyzov* had been invoked with increasing frequency from 1979 on as a reason to reject applications for emigration. This had been, indeed, one of the earliest signs of the attempt to close off emigration in 1979. Publication of this rule as a publicly announced restriction appeared to presage an attempt at future restriction of the number of applicants for emigration. The new decree came into force on January 1, 1987, and in the first five months after was evidently applied with high consistency. Refuseniks monitoring the dynamics of the exodus movement reported that even as the number of exit visas began to grow, OVIR was refusing to accept the papers of many new applicants for lack of first degree relatives abroad. This, however, changed toward the end of May when a number of applicants whose papers had been turned back to them were invited to resubmit their applications. Reports of a renewed strictness in the application of this clause began to come from Moscow in November, following the setback to Gorbachev's power involved in the dismissal of his Moscow appointee, Boris Eltsin.

In the summer of 1987 children over eighteen years of age who until then had been tied to their refusenik parents' requests to emigrate were invited to apply independently (even when they had no first degree relatives in Israel) and in July and August 1987 the first of these were already leaving the Soviet Union, creating a legitimate basis for the granting of their parents' exit visas. The long-term development of this phenomenon will be an important indicator in the future development of Soviet emigration policy.

In addition to kinship restrictions the decree also contained a clause denying right of application to persons judged to hold state secrets. State secrets are a vast category in Soviet life. In Stalinist days they included all ongoing medical research, and to this day the level of Soviet gold production is considered a state secret. As other reasons for denying the right to emigrate were put into disrepute and slowly abandoned, the Soviet spokesmen drew the cloak of secrecy tighter around themselves as something that would be understood in the international community and by its very nature could not be exposed and explained. However, like other polities, the Soviet Union does have clear regulations as to various degrees of security clearance, and as the matter of secrecy became more and more prominent in the discussion of the right to emigrate, leaders of the exodus movement made it the central tactical target of their efforts. The refuseniks' goal was to extract from the Soviet authorities a clear public definition of time limitation for each category of access to secrets. To the end of 1987 no accommodation on this point was forthcoming, despite continuing pressure from the refuseniks and from many international sources. In November 1987 a long-prepared conference of refuseniks took place in Moscow attended by more than a hundred people whose emigration was being delayed on grounds of state secrecy. At this conference the refuseniks systematically examined the difference between Soviet law and the law of other countries in the matter of restrictions on citizens' rights to emigrate on grounds of state secrecy. Here was a direct challenge to Gorbachev's policies. Falling on the eve of his visit to Washington, the Moscow secrecy and emigration conference received considerable attention in the American media thus injecting the question into the human rights section of the summit agenda.

In addition to kinship and security, the decree contains a number of other restrictive clauses under which applications are not entertained. The one clause that carries a potential for broadening rather than restricting emigration is the final article in the decree stating that "Questions of entry and exit from the USSR on private affairs may also be regulated by bilateral agreements between the USSR and other states."[12] This creates a potential solution to questions of Jewish emigration that is fraught with political ramifications that are clear, but too complex to be considered here, as they spill over into the area of Soviet-Israeli relations.

Whatever the shortcomings of the new decree, it has one virtue. Where previously the application for emigration was governed by administrative regulations known only to officials, the new decree makes these regulations public and reasonably precise. At least the ambiguities and peril points of this legislation are in the open today. Thus there is a solid basis from which the refuseniks can build a campaign for further development of their right to leave. In the Soviet Union where so much of law is hidden, and of little use to the citizen in shaping his life, such public and precise legislation, however flawed, should be regarded as a step forward.[13]

Other than this point, the major merit in this decree appears to be its potential in solving the drop-out problem mentioned earlier. No restriction of destination of the emigrant appears in the text of the decree. Thus relatives may send a *vyzov* from France, Canada, Australia, Israel, or whatever country the emigrant may request, and only those actually intending to settle in Israel would leave the Soviet Union with a visa for Israel. In July 1987 the head of the All-Union OVIR, Rudolf Kuznetsov, stated in an interview in the Soviet weekly *New Times* that former Soviet citizens, now citizens of other countries, could send *vyzovy* to their relatives for purposes of visits or emigration.[14] Kuznetsov's statement has been followed by the granting of a few visas for emigration directly to Australia as a sort of testing of the waters for this new policy. Whether in the long run the Soviet authorities will in fact discriminate among different countries of destination in the granting of visas remains to be seen.

At the time it was published, the decree on emigration appeared to signal an openness in acknowledging the existence of a problem of Jewish emigration more than any tendency toward liberalism in its solution. A new frankness, but only the most grudging and hard-won concessions, became apparent in contacts with Soviet officials. These contacts ranged from businesslike discussions between lower levels of officials in the Soviet delegation at Rejkjavik and relatives of Jewish refuseniks who had come to demonstrate there, all the way up to a cordial and extended conversation at the United Nations between then Prime Minister of Israel Shimon Peres and Soviet Foreign Minister Edward Shevardnadze in September 1986.[15] Despite the gestures of courtesy and openness, emigration figures remained low and the problem of the Prisoners of Zion remained unsolved. The year 1986 ended with only 914 Jews allowed to leave the Soviet Union, as compared to 1,140 the previous year.

Year of Turning, 1987

It was only at the beginning of 1987 that evidence began to accumulate indicating that the question of emigration was receiving higher priority in Gorbachev's policies. It was reported that an extraordinary commission had been formed to supervise and speed up the granting of visas by OVIR.[16] A strong follow-up was provided in a *Pravda* article signed by the newspaper's chief editor, Central Committee member V. G. Afanas'ev.[17] He blamed unjustified bureaucratic delays in the granting of exit visas for giving the Soviet Union a bad image abroad, thus impeding the success of Soviet foreign policy. Afanas'ev's article not only gave implicit public recognition to the legitimacy of emigration, but admitted that there had been unwarranted obstructions and delays in granting permission to leave. A few days later the director of the newly formed Department of Humanitarian and Cultural Affairs in the Soviet Foreign Ministry stated in an interview that there would be a "drastic increase" in the number of Soviet citizens allowed to emigrate in 1987.[18] Near the end of January, Samuel Zivs, one of the leaders of the Anti-Zionist Committee of the Soviet Public stated that five hundred exit permits had been granted in January, a figure later repeated by the spokesman of the Soviet Foreign Ministry. In addition Zivs stated that as many as 10,000 cases of would-be emigrants were under review, raising the prospect that virtually the entire refusenik community might be granted reconsideration.[19] Yet the promises were not quickly backed up by deeds. The numbers announced by Zivs and Gerasimov were false, for only 98 Jews emigrated in January and 148 in February.[20] Perhaps they were referring to the number of cases reviewed and recommended for the granting of visas in future months. Indeed, emigration rose to 470 in March, 717 in April, and 879 in May.

The earliest significant change was the release from prison of three Prisoners of Zion, Roald Zelichonok of Leningrad, Zakhar Zunshain of Riga, and Iosef Begun of Moscow. For the refuseniks this was of the greatest importance. The welfare of the prisoners had been one of their central concerns in their activities. More to the point, the Soviet authorities in charge of "the Jewish question" had been attempting to draw some of the refusenik leaders into a dialogue with the aim of convincing them that new winds were blowing and that the level of noise made by the exodus movement should be reduced. The Jewish activists had demanded that the regime prove its good faith by immediate release of five of the Prisoners of Zion and a promise to release the remaining prisoners quickly and to allow all of them with their families to emigrate without harassment. The release of the first three was indeed followed by the release of all the others and permission to most of them to emigrate. At the same time, refusal of emigration and a continuation of harassment by local authorities was particularly worrisome to Zelichonok and to Alexei Magarik, last of the prisoners to be released, both of whom were threatened with being pushed out of their places of residence and with rearrest as parasites if they refused to accept the menial jobs assigned them.[21] In this way the authorities maintained a high level of anxiety and uncertainty in the refusenik community.

Despite the hope kindled by the prisoners' release, many mixed signals continued to come out of the Soviet Union, reflecting the slow and uneven development of Gorbachev's program of glasnost. As might have been expected, large numbers of Jews crowded the OVIR offices at the beginning of January to see how application of the new decree on emigration might affect them. For the great majority the enquiries ended in disappointment. Numerous long-term refuseniks across the USSR heard the standard bureaucratic phrases that their emigration would endanger the state security of the Soviet Union and was therefore denied. To emphasize this, OVIR officials in Moscow published the names of eight Jews who, they claimed, could not be allowed to emigrate because they had been privy to state secrets. Significantly, no period or final date was mentioned in connection with this ban. It was understood as permanent.[22] The bureaucratic confusion was compounded when Gerasimov, who must be regarded as speaking for the Gorbachev establishment, stated that the reconsideration of refuseniks' cases would include many of those who were considered in the past to have been privy to state secrets. He hoped aloud that the review would produce results satisfactory to all sides. Toward the end of 1987, with a summit in the offing and frequent visits of high-ranking Soviet and American dignitaries in each others' capitals, many of the prominent long-term "secrecy refuseniks" were released, but of the eight mentioned previously seven were still held in Moscow, along with hundreds of others whose connection to anything secret was tenuous at best. As the November 1987 Moscow refusenik conference on secrecy and emigration demonstrated, there can be no solution of the problems of refuseniks without a publicly defined categorization of time limits for secrecy refusals.

In the second half of 1987 a new cloud appeared on the horizon for the Jewish activists. The Gorbachev policy of glasnost had eased the way for Jewish activists to express their demands and advertise their conditions. However, many other trends and ideas were also emerging into the light of day. Among them was the ultranationalist and anti-Semitic Pamyat group. They spread their ideas openly in Leningrad and demanded recognition and registration in a meeting with the head of the Moscow Communist party organization. When Jewish activists requested the right to hold a public meeting in Moscow to protest the propagation of hatred for Jews by this group, permission was refused and the leading organizers detained for several hours so that they could not hold an unofficial meeting. Though many previously hidden social tensions are now openly recognized and debated in the Soviet press, anti-Semitism remains a taboo subject. Repeated attempts to turn public attention to the danger posed by the Pamyat group were frustrated by the authorities who warned that there would be harsh retribution against anyone trying to claim that anti-Semitism existed in the USSR. In Leningrad the Jewish activists' anxieties were sharpened by the murder of seventy-year-old Naum Nemchenko. Although not himself a refusenik, Nemchenko had taken part in Jewish cultural activities in Leningrad, and at a Holocaust memorial meeting organized by the refuseniks, had spoken publicly of the danger to the Jews posed by the emergence of Pamyat. Nemchenko was murdered just when he had intended to travel to Moscow to take part in the meeting against anti-Semitism. The Leningrad refusenik community believes that neo-fascists of the Pamyat sort committed the murder. The police claim that the murder was committed as part of a break-in and robbery, and two persons were later convicted on such charges. The possibility of a wave of popular anti-Semitism whether ignored or encouraged by any part of the regime haunts the consciousness of every Soviet Jew, far outweighing small gestures such as the opening of the kosher restaurant or other promises of concessions to religion that were made to American Jewish leaders.

As these lines are written in December 1987, the prospects for the exodus movement and in particular for the refuseniks, appear brighter than even the most optimistic observer would have predicted a year earlier. In October and November emigration hovered around the nine hundred mark, each month equaling the emigration of the whole previous year. Even so, the 7,143 who emigrated in the first eleven months of 1987 fell far short of the promises by Soviet officials of ten to twelve thousand emigrants. Yet even for the emigration-minded part of Soviet Jewry, though their lot may be eased over the next five years, their basic problem will remain unsolved. The phrasing of the August 1986 decree on application for emigration remains a Damocles' sword dangling over the long line of those waiting to apply. Soviet spokesmen have repeatedly emphasized that they are opposed to the concept of free emigration.[23]

Then too, the confidence that Gorbachev will continue to promote even a limited freeing of emigration is as yet weak. The sources of public support for Gorbachev's reforms are as yet severely limited. Economic payoffs that might earn broad public support are still in the distant future. Gorbachev has been increasingly frank in acknowledging the extent of the public resistance to his programs, to the point of stating in a recent speech that opposition included not only state bureaucrats and Communist party officials, but "work collectives," that is, the mass of Soviet people.[24] Should Gorbachev decide that he can attract public support by espousing a more Russian and nationalist stand in the spirit of Pamyat, this would undoubtedly reinvigorate those elements in the party who have in the past been the supporters of official anti-Semitism of Korneev's type. In addition, emigration-inclined Jews appear to be one of the pawns in the battle between Gorbachev and his opponents in the party and state bureaucracies. As the demotion of one of Gorbachev's key appointees has shown, he does not have things all his way in that battle. The pugnacious tone adopted by Gorbachev in a presummit interview, while answering a question about Jewish emigration, rejecting any need for further concessions, may indicate his having conceded something on this subject to his opponents.[25]

The secretary general and his entire retinue consistently and belligerently stonewalled the issue of human rights throughout the summit. This stood in stark contrast to the impressive political fact of over two hundred thousand Americans, Jews and non-Jews alike, from all parts of the continent who demonstrated in Washington the day before Gorbachev's arrival for the summit. The central theme of the demonstration was that the freeing of Jewish emigration was the litmus test by which Soviet credibility on other sensitive issues such as arms control would be measured. The lack of progress on the human rights agenda at the Washington discussions was reflected in the postsummit communiqué. The best that could be claimed was that the two sides had agreed to disagree. This summation, postponing the issue while promising a later continuation, was a source of bitter disappointment to the Soviet refuseniks as well as to their supporters. In the longer term it would appear that the cost to Soviet foreign policy of continuing the earlier restrictions and harassments would outweigh the domestic advantages that might be culled. However, the domestic costs to the Soviet regime of freeing emigration even slightly, should not be ignored.

Gorbachev, as a relatively young leader, has a long view and is capable of taking a half-step back on the way to making long strides forward. He is aware that slow change over a lengthy period will be necessary for the introduction of any meaningful reform and has openly stated that changing the political culture of the Soviet administration will take generations.[26]

At present there is no indication that Gorbachev would be inclined to allow unchecked emigration even were he to have a perfectly free hand. The most authoritative statements of Soviet officials to date indicate a policy of gradual and limited renewal of emigration to reduce the salience of the refusenik community as an international irritant. This has been of particular importance in the period leading up to the Washington summit of December 1987, with the overall emigration numbers rising gradually and the most prominent long-term refuseniks released. The imminent prospect of a Moscow summit in 1988 promises that the leverage offered here will continue. The calculation of the Soviet side appears to be that at the present rate the veteran refusenik community would have emigrated by the time this next summit takes place. The Soviet authorities would then most probably attempt to keep pressures at a low level by screening new applicants carefully, upholding generally, if not absolutely, the demand for first degree relatives, while avoiding generally, if not absolutely, spurious security-based refusals.

Nonetheless, it is expected that the release of refuseniks, even if spread over a relatively long period, will generate a new wave of applicants from among the 380,000 *vyzov* holders. This is, in fact, already happening. Today new applications come in almost at the rate that emigrants leave. This in turn would bring on a new weighing of future plans in the ranks of the hitherto silent majority of Soviet Jews. Although the latter may not yet have made any overt move to join the exodus movement, they cannot help but be aware of its existence and of the influence it reflects onto their lives. The success of the refuseniks in reopening the gates of emigration only increases the proclivity of this mass to consider emigration as a feasible option when faced with the spectre of possible resurgent anti-Semitism, the discomfort of living in an environment of increasing Russian nationalism, the persistence of limitations in the professional sphere, and other factors that block the assimilation process.

The only factors which can divert a continuing stream of Jews from applying for emigration would be a full success in improving the Soviet economy and the creation of a radically new social and political climate for Soviet Jews as well as for the rest of the citizens of the Soviet Union. In such a case Gorbachev's reform programs, and the new reformist institutions that would spring up around them, could become the focus for some of the energy now poured into dissidence and emigration.[27] This was the case among many Jewish intellectuals in the immediate post-Stalin thaw period and when the democratic movement came to its peak in the late 1960s. Indeed, Gorbachev's innovations in cultural and journalistic freedom attracted excited interest during 1986 and 1987 even among veteran refuseniks whose entire attention had been bent for years to the task of leaving the Soviet Union.

As Soviet Jews move toward the last decade of the century, they must view the future with mixed emotions. They are a community in decline, dwindling in numbers and in importance. Discrimination and demography have combined to remove them from the forefront of many areas of Soviet life. Whatever Gorbachev's reforms, there is no indication that they include any effort at a revival of a meaningful Soviet-Jewish national or cultural presence. Indeed, one of the premises of the policy of freedom in isolation launched by Breznev appeared to be the supposition that the Jews would soon cease to have any significant organized presence in the life of the Soviet Union.

For the exodus movement, however, there is a more cheering prospect. The eclipse that overshadowed its activities in the first half of the 1980s appears to be passing. The Prisoners of Zion are free and most of them are already in Israel. As the veteran leaders leave Moscow and Leningrad, a new generation is assuming the responsibility for the teaching of Hebrew and of Jewish history and tradition. If the exodus goes at its present slow and controlled pace, the current teachers will educate a new generation of activists attracted by their curiosity as to their own roots in a Soviet environment that has denied them Jewish knowledge while propagating increased awareness of other ethnic backgrounds. The more it speeds up, the more it makes the emigration option real to less committed Soviet Jews. Either way, the pressure for emigration within the Soviet Jewish public will be maintained until the last Soviet Jew wishing to emigrate has exercised this right.

2. The Soviet Public Anti-Zionist Committee: An Analysis

William Korey

The Soviet Public Anti-Zionist Committee came into existence on April 21, 1983, and until 1986 served as the primary voice of the Kremlin on Jewish questions, often using Soviet Jews as its spokesmen. At regular intervals, its voice was heard through the press or in broadcasts abroad channeling the Kremlin's special propaganda to various publics, both within the Soviet Union and abroad. Over time the committee assumed an increasing number of functions and played an especially important role as the apologist and articulator of the Kremlin's propaganda policy on Zionism, which not only incorporated elements of anti-Semitism but also verged on the politically obscene by, at times, equating Zionism with Nazism.

Using prominent Jews as the instrument of the totalitarian state to perform functions of control and propaganda with reference to the Jewish community as a whole is, of course, not new. The Nazis perfected the technique of utilizing existing Jewish Councils (*Judenraete*) or creating new ones initially to manipulate and control the Jewish community, and the USSR has not been averse to exploiting specially created Jewish mechanisms. When Stalin was planning, during the era of the Doctor's Plot in early 1953, to evacuate en masse the Jews of the major urban areas of western Russia to Kazakhstan in Central Asia, he arranged for prominent Jewish establishment figures to prepare a large-scale petition signed by them specifically requesting the almost Nazi-type evacuation for alleged humanitarian purposes—to rescue Jewry from public hostility.[1] The man who became head of the Anti-Zionist Committee, General David Dragunsky, was reported to have been among the first leading Jewish figures to sign the draft petition in early 1953. This was noted by Paul Novick, the editor of the Yiddish newspaper *Freiheit,* in recalling his conversations with Ilya Ehrenburg.[2]

More nearly similar, particularly in its anti-Zionist focus, was the press conference held fifteen years ago, on March 4, 1970, at the so-called House of Friendship with the Peoples of Foreign Countries.[3] The conference officially dealt with "questions relating to the situation in the Middle East." A group of prominent "citizens of the USSR of Jewish nationality"—a newly created designation—was paraded at the conference in order to perform two functions. The first was to denounce Zionism, or more specifically Israel. "The crimes of the Israeli military," it was said, "revive memories of the barbarism of the Nazis." The overt aim here was to appease the Arab countries in the Middle East and to rally the Soviet general and Jewish public behind Moscow's Middle East foreign policy, a policy whose popular support was somewhat less than enthusiastic.

The second purpose was implicit: to deny the validity of a growing demand, made clear in extensive and large-scale petitions reaching the West, that Soviet Jews sought to emigrate and be reunited with their kin in Israel. Speakers at the press conference formally declared that Jews were not subject to any discrimination or anti-Semitism and, presumably, were equal in rights to all others "in the 240-million Soviet family."[4] And for the first time in a quarter of a century they spoke of the services presumably rendered to Jewry by the Soviet motherland. A collective declaration incorporating these views was signed by fifty-two leading establishment figures.

The Soviet mass media, following the press conference, mounted a major campaign in which thousands of "citizens of Jewish nationality" took part through letters or statements almost daily in *Pravda,* as well as in other Soviet newspapers.[5] The peak was reached in late March and early April 1970 and then gradually dropped off, although it continued, at a much lower level, for nearly an entire year.

The campaign against Zionism afterward dropped the Jewish component and took on a virulent anti-Semitic character which helped spur the growing and massive exodus movement among Jews. Critics within the Soviet institutional establishment, particularly among academicians, found fault with the overt anti-Semitism and recommended returning to the technique of the March 4, 1970, press conference. This approach was articulated at a conference in February 1976 held by various institutes in the humanities of the Soviet Academy of Sciences in Moscow.[6] The conference was oriented to improving methodology for combating Zionism.

The main aim was to halt the exodus movement among Jews. The chairman of the conference, B. G. Gafurov, emphasized that a principal task of anti-Zionist propaganda was to counter the emigration of "youth and talent" from the USSR.[7] Gafurov served as director of the Institute of Oriental Studies of the USSR Academy of Sciences and chairman of the Permanent Commission in the Institute for research into the exposure and criticism of the history, ideology, and practice of Zionism.

One strategy that was recommended was to use Jews for the "unmasking" of Zionism instead of the crude anti-Semitism then masquerading as anti-Zionism. This view was advanced by the chief editor of the journal *Narody Azii i Afriki,* who stressed that the "unmasking of nationalism should be tactical."[8] In early 1983 the recommendation was to find expression.

Announcement of the Anti-Zionist Committee's formation was preceded by preliminary public disclosures in a large-scale media effort designed to prepare the general community. *Tass,* on March 31, 1983, stated that eight prominent persons (all known to be Jews of the establishment) had appealed for the creation of a "Soviet Public Anti-Zionist Committee" in order to aid in exposing "its anti-people and anti-humanitarian nature for diversionary propaganda and policy of Zionism." *Pravda* and *Literaturnaia Gazeta* the next day carried the lengthy text of the appeal and the signatures.[9]

The appeal took on a sharp anti-Zionist tone: "In its essence, Zionism is a concentration of extreme nationalism, chauvinism and racial intolerance, justification of territorial seizure and annexation, armed adventurism, a cult of political arbitrariness and impunity, demagogy and ideological sabotage, sordid maneuvers and perfidy."[10] The founders also asserted that imperialism used international Zionism extensively as one of its shock detachments in the assault on Socialism.

If details of how the anti-Zionist campaign would unfold were not specified, the intentions of the authorities were nonetheless made clear. Not only was Zionism to be directly attacked, but also the Jewish emigration would be taken off Moscow's agenda. The appeal observed, in a formulation heretofore not used, that "the Jews, citizens of the USSR, are part and parcel of the Soviet people." Implicit was the notion that they could not be induced to emigrate. Explicitly condemned was "Zionist propaganda," the alleged purpose of which was "to interfere in their (Jews') life" and which is filled with "falsehood and slander against the socialist homeland." The appeal rejected any perception that there is such a thing as a "Jewish problem" in the USSR.

Yet a third intention could be read into the language and formulations used. By emphasizing the oneness of Soviet Jews with the Soviet public, the Kremlin was signaling a determination to break all links and contacts with Jewry on the outside—"international Zionism." The media campaign against Zionism was already emphasizing that Soviet Jewish contacts with visitors could be construed as "subversive."[11]

The eight signatories were Col. General David Dragunsky, Lenin Prize laureate Martin Kabachnik, writer Genrikh Gofman, law professor Samuel Zivs, film maker Boris Sheinin, history professor Georgy Bondarevsky, philosophy professor and editor Genrikhas Zimanas, and writer Yuri Kolesnikov.

A striking feature of the appeal's authors and of the committee leadership, once created, was that none of them had participated in specifically Jewish life or activity in the USSR. Missing was the name of Aron Vergelis, the editor of the Moscow Yiddish monthly, *Sovietishe Heimland*. Nor were any of the journal's staff mentioned nor even of the editors and staff of the Yiddish newspaper in Birobidzhan, the *Birobidzhaner Shtern*. Nor did the list include any of the one-half dozen rabbis in the USSR, especially the chief rabbi of Moscow, Yakov Fishman.

When criticism of the committee began to mount in the West that it was merely a tool of the authorities, and a not very Jewish tool at that, Moscow must have entertained second thoughts and prevailed upon Rabbi Fishman to join. In a Hebrew language broadcast beamed to Israel on April 28 by Moscow Radio Peace and Progress, he was cited as declaring that "as a Soviet citizen . . . I do my duty by joining the Soviet Public Anti-Zionist Committee."[12] He went on to attack "Jewish capitalists" who "use others, boys and girls, whom they lure into their nets. So-called Zionists are rich persons who do not go to live in Israel but rather build factories to exploit the 'poor Jews.' " Rabbi Fishman was scheduled to appear at the committee's first press conference on June 6, which was a Monday. But on the previous Saturday, *Tass* reported that he had died of a sudden heart attack at the age of seventy.[13] No prominent member of the active Jewish community has replaced him on the committee.

According to the *Pravda* announcement of the committee's creation on April 21, what presumably sparked the decision was an "enthusiastic" public response to the appeal and a "meeting of representatives of a number of public organizations" held that day.[14] No names of "representatives" were listed, but they came from special organizations including the All-Union Central Council of Trade Unions, *Novosti* (the important external Soviet instrument used for propaganda abroad), and the Soviet Committee for Solidarity with the Peoples of Asia and Africa. One can speculate on the basis of who were chosen as officers that *Novosti* was especially interested. Named as a deputy chairman was Mark Krupkin, a deputy director of *Novosti*. Another deputy chairman was Igor Belayev, a non-Jew (and apparently the only one on the committee), who is the Middle East expert for *Literaturnaia Gazeta*. The third vice-chairman was novelist Yuri Kolesnikov, about whom more will be said later. Zivs was chosen first deputy chairman.[15]

That David Abramovich Dragunsky would be chosen chairman was scarcely surprising. Twice awarded during wartime the prized Hero of the Soviet Union medal, the seventy-two-year-old general had been frequently utilized by the Kremlin over the years as its "court Jew" to respond to charges of anti-Semitism. The number of Jews in high positions in the armed forces declined and disappeared during the late forties, and they were no longer admitted into higher military schools. Dragunsky was a rare Jewish survivor. Equally significant, he continued to render important military service to the state, and in the mid-1980s administered the Vysstrel Military Academy which trained officers of Third World armies.[16] Among graduates bearing Dragunsky's approving signature is at least one PLO military official.[17] A U.S. intelligence official observed: "He doesn't just propagandize against Zionists; he trains people to kill them."[18]

Shortly afterward, the structure of the committee took shape. It was comprised of thirty-seven members, some non-Jews, including the editor of *Yunost,* a "poultry farmer" and a political correspondent for *Izvestia.*[19] Among the committee members was the Jewish writer Tsezar Solodar, whose articles are full of anti-Semitic hysteria. From the membership a presidium of thirteen was chosen, including the officers. One presidium member was a deputy to the Supreme Soviet identified as a "factory worker" whose name suggested that he was non-Jewish.

Initially, ambitious plans were projected. Dragunsky and Zivs, in an interview with a Vilnius newspaper on May 6, said that branches were to be set up in each Union Republic with additional branches in Moscow, Leningrad, Novosibirsk, and Birobidzhan.[20] Scholarly, artistic, and literary works along with films, plays, and paintings were to be produced for the committee. Candidates for state prizes in the field of anti-Zionism would be put forward. Finally, it was hoped to create a working group of specialists on Zionism to assist in shaping opinion everywhere.[21] But that was for the future. The present was to be taken up with a massive propaganda display.

It was on June 6, 1983, that the Kremlin's purposes in setting up the Anti-Zionist Committee were made transparently clear.[22] Propaganda on a major scale from a central platform and directed to a variety of audiences—this was the overriding aim. Neither public policy nor public activity was a primary concern. The committee, according to *Izvestia* in early June, had acquired an address—Fruzenskaya Naberezhnaya 46—but visitors to the site found few occupants and limited activity.[23] An announcement was made about the preparation of a booklet on the "enthusiastic" public response to the establishment of the committee.

On June 6[24] a major press conference was staged for the committee in which star billing was made for Dragunsky and, especially, Zivs, with a minor, though significant and ominous part played by Kolesnikov. The date chosen—June 6—was deliberate. It was to mark the anniversary of Israel's offensive into Lebanon in 1982. Israel, together with "international Zionism," were to be the targets.

Yet, surprisingly, the major focus turned out to be the Soviet Jewish emigration issue. Clearly the outcry in the Western world had not been stilled and, indeed, was continuing to find expression at Madrid where the ongoing conference of Helsinki Final Act signatories ineluctably called upon the Soviet Union to adhere to the provisions of the act. Basket Three of the accord had made "reunion of families," that is, Jewish emigration, a cardinal concern. And Soviet Jews still clung to the hope that they ultimately might obtain exit visas. In fact, the number being permitted to leave had declined precipitously.

The USSR was determined to end both the internal and external clamor for emigration. Zivs, a specialist on international law, was assigned that responsibility. He said that "the considerable decrease" in the number of people emigrating from the USSR was the result of the fact that the process of family reunion flowing from World II had been "basically completed."[25] It was as if an objective and unalterable fact had been revealed. Soviet policy or decisionmaking had nothing to do with the drastic drop in emigration. The families that needed reuniting had found that already largely consummated.

Novosti, reporting on the conference the next day, gave the presumably objective point worldwide attention: "Some Western correspondents insistently tried to find out why emigration of persons of Jewish nationality from the USSR has now fallen off so sharply. They were told that the people who had left were mainly those whose families had been split up during World War II. The process of reuniting families is, for the most part now completed."[26] It was a neatly contrived myth to justify previous Soviet emigration policy. The facts, of course, were quite different. The Kremlin had been prompted to allow Jewish emigration for a variety of reasons totally unrelated to families presumably split by World War II.[27]

Equally fallacious was the argument that the reunion of families had been completed. Solid evidence existed that some 400,000 Soviet Jews still in the USSR had requested and received from relatives in Israel a so-called *vyzov,* or affidavit assuring the kinship affinity.[28] Acquisition of the *vyzov* was the first step in the emigration process for a Soviet Jew. Moreover, some 10,000 Soviet Jews were known to have formally applied for an exit visa and had been refused, frequently more than once.[29] There is solid speculation that the actual number of refuseniks may be twice or three times this total.

Zivs and the committee, however, preferred to suppress the truth and to adhere to a myth that contained a solid humanitarian element. But after elaborating the seemingly objective fact of the completion of the reuniting process, Zivs felt compelled to add a subjective factor which weakened his argument. As noted by Zivs, the influence of Zionist propaganda upon Jews had diminished, thereby inhibiting a desire to emigrate. Novosti reported that many earlier emigrants had written letters to the committee—which were then read out at the press conference—which disclosed how they had been deceived by Zionist propaganda to believe in "a life in paradise" in Israel.[30] Instead, their fate has been one of trauma and tragedy. In their letters they condemned the Zionist "snarer of souls."

If the process of reunion was objectively completed, what was the point of arguing that Zionist propaganda was no longer enticing? It suggested the reality that the USSR did play an active role in discouraging emigration. The myth was threatened with being totally punctured. Still, the Kremlin felt it essential to develop the line that Zionist propaganda must be vigorously combated in order to bring an end to the emigration aspiration. Indeed, this became a major program of the committee, expressed both in policy statements and newly published works. The thesis of a completion of a reunion process would soon be dropped. It was too feeble an argument to uphold.

Besides, there existed the critical anti-Zionist and anti-Israeli objective of the committee spelled out in its very name and in the selection of the date for the holding of a press conference. At the conference the committee framed the Zionist issue in the East-West context.[31] The United States, under President Reagan, was waging "psychological war." "International Zionism" played a vital part in that war. Jewish political power in the United States and Israel—as perceived by Moscow—was an integral and vital part of the presumed global assault upon the USSR and Communist East Europe.

If Israel and "international Zionism" were subjected to critical commentary, nonetheless the criticism was restrained. First, the priority emphasis was given over to justifying the cutback in Jewish emigration. Secondly, the virulence of the typical anti-Zionist diatribes in the media, often accompanied by anti-Semitic stereotypes or blatant Judophobia, was absent. If Zionism was criticized, Zivs tried to place it in the context of the emigration issue. The committee's role, he said, was "to explain and help Soviet citizens understand the false and venomous nature of Zionist propaganda."[32]

Indeed, Zivs, whose comments largely dominated the proceedings, made a determined public effort to assume a negative and critical posture vis-à-vis overt Soviet anti-Semitic books, especially with their canards about alleged Nazi-Zionist collusion. One such book had acquired international notoriety in 1983. It was Lev Korneyev's *The Class Essence of Zionism,* one of the most vicious books ever published in the USSR, yet praised by *Izvestia* and *Sovetskaia Kultura.*[33] Angry commentary about the book in the Western world and particularly among left-wing circles could be expected to impact negatively upon various circles in the USSR who, in their contacts with the West, might feel a sense of embarrassment.

Zivs very much fit this category. Earlier, in an interview with Novosti, he spoke of the need for high quality academic works of an "ideologically principled character."[34] The initial appeal of the committee referred to "reasoned criticism" of Zionism as its aim. At the press conference on June 6, therefore, Zivs sought to disassociate himself and his committee from Korneyev and similar Judophobes. Referring to such works, Zivs emphasized that the committee would "struggle against improper expositions (about Zionism) in such books which unfortunately do appear." Significantly, this telling public comment of Zivs was not recorded in the Soviet media. (The *New York Times* correspondent, who was present at the press conference, reported them the next day.)[35]

In sharp contrast were the comments of Kolesnikov. While Zivs hoped to avoid an all-out criticism of Zionism that could spill over into anti-Semitism, Kolesnikov opened up with a vituperative barrage directed against Zionism which, during the Hitler period, had deliberately failed to protect Jews.[36] "On the contrary," Kolesnikov went on, the Zionists "had betrayed them by conspiring with the Gestapo and ss leaders." The canard was followed by a politically obscene allegation. If Eichmann, after his trial, was hastily executed by the Israeli authorities, it was, said Kolesnikov, in order to prevent "the sacred secrets" of Nazi-Zionist collaboration from becoming public.[37]

It was the Kolesnikov line, even if only a minor theme in 1983, that would ultimately prevail in 1984 and 1985. By 1984 a vicious anti-Semitism, involving Kolesnikov's own personal writings, would be in full bloom.

As early as the late summer and fall of 1983, it had become clear that the Kremlin would use the committee as a propaganda instrument directed both to the Jewish world *and* the Arab world in dealing with Middle East issues. For Jews, both within and without the USSR, the committee provided an automatic sanction for the Soviet Union's anti-Israel, pro-Arab policies. For the Arab countries it offered a demonstration of how far Moscow was prepared to go in its propaganda to promote the Arab cause.

Thus, the Anti-Zionist Committee issued public statements appearing in the Soviet press condemning Israel's actions in Lebanon and the occupied territories.[38] The Israel-Lebanese withdrawal agreement of May 1983 was denounced and the attack on the Islamic college in El Khalil in early August in which several students were killed was sharply censured. Articles by top committee members, such as Dragunsky and Mark Krupkin, appeared in leading Soviet press organs, markedly highlighted.[39] These were devoted to the condemnation of Israel and Zionism. In addition, the committee took part in Soviet Hebrew-language broadcasts beamed to Israel.[40]

Particularly instructive was an interview with Dragunsky by Radio Damascus in late October.[41] The general sought to impress his Arab listeners with the impact of the committee's pro-Arab activities. He related that it had already received 10,000 letters of which 1,250 came from outside the USSR, including Israel. He referred to "important" articles for which the committee was responsible which had appeared in the Soviet press. He boasted that the committee had become organizationally stronger. Finally, he acknowledged that the committee had developed "close and extensive relations with the Arab world," especially Syria. Syria, of course, was among the most militant "Rejectionist" and anti-Zionist states in the Middle East. Its 1980 Friendship Treaty with the USSR specifically targeted Zionism as an enemy that had to be controlled.

As initially conceived by the Soviet leadership, the Anti-Zionist Committee was to function on a defensive, propaganda level, justifying Kremlin policy primarily on the Jewish emigration cutback and secondarily on militant anti-Zionism. Besides the press conferences, newspaper articles and special broadcasts abroad, the committee produced at the end of August and early September 1983, two brochures, both attractively packaged and published by Novosti.[42] The first focused upon the June press conference and was titled *The Anti-Zionist Committee of Soviet Public Opinion: Aims and Tasks*. The second constituted a collection of letters received by the committee alleging nationwide support, particularly among Soviet Jews, for it.

Significantly, the committee was deprived of positive functions which might show a commitment to Jewish tradition and Jewish culture. Clearly, the Kremlin had no intention of creating another Yevsektsiia (Jewish Sections of the party which had been active in the twenties),[43] or another Jewish Anti-Fascist Committee (active from 1943 to 1948)[44] both of which did promote multifaceted, if politically circumscribed, Yiddish cultural and literary programs and works. Both institutions had been destroyed in keeping with the party aim of facilitating the forcible assimilation of Jews. It was hardly conceivable that the Kremlin would now wish to foster in a systematic way Jewish culture or identity. For that reason, the few Soviet Jews officially involved with Jewish culture and religion were not originally included in the committee.

Precisely because the Kremlin's intention was to avoid Jewish identity, apparent restraints were placed upon the expansion and extension of the committee's structure, despite initial promises along this line. Little was reported in the Soviet press about the creation of new local branches.

In November rumors appeared in the West that branches had been set up in the Latvian cities of Riga and Daugavpils.[45] Later, it was noted in the West that Zivs had sought to set up branches in Lithuania.[46] However, corroboration of these rumors have not appeared in the Soviet media.

A second limitation on the Anti-Zionist Committee was more technical and related to how it would function in the international political sphere. It was perfectly appropriate for the committee to be the tough, hard-line anti-Zionist advocate, but supposing the Kremlin wished to send a message to American or Western Jews on détente? Dragunsky told an Arab foreign interviewer in October 1983 that the committee was "now preparing an appeal to the Jews of the United States, exposing Israeli genocide actions against the Arabs."[47] This appeal never appeared.

Instead, the following month—November—saw the publication in *New Times* of Moscow of an "Open Letter" to U.S. Jews from fifty-three "Soviet citizens of Jewish nationality."[48] It concentrated upon détente, an end to the arms race, and a freeze on nuclear weapons. Such steps, when realized, would mark "the beginning of the road that should lead to disarmament." The committee may have been instrumental in conceiving the idea and in advising as to who ought to be the signatories—at least one half were associated with the committee—but to sponsor the appeal would be inconsistent with the group's hard-line purpose. At the same time, however, the committee no doubt had a hand in a secondary point made in the "Open Letter"—that the raising of the issue of "concern for Soviet Jews" in the United States was allegedly harmful to détente. Finally, the "Open Letter" contained a call to American Jews to challenge the alleged aggressive policy of Israel which posed "a threat to the very existence of that state." This, too, revealed a committee purpose. Yet the broad aim of the "Open Letter" made it essential to sever any direct linkage to the committee.

From the beginning of 1984 the committee's anti-Zionist propaganda function took on a much sharper form, indeed, becoming its dominant feature. The character of the new stress was, however, established elsewhere. On January 17, 1984, *Pravda* published an obviously pace-setting article on Zionism by one of its top commentators and a specialist on anti-Zionist questions, Vladimir Bolshakov. The Bolshakov thesis, patently echoing the new Kremlin thrust, made Zionism the moral and political equivalent of Nazism.[49]

The equation was expressed and would continue to be expressed on three levels. First, Zionism was said to have been the active supporter and partner of Nazism in the latter's climb to power and in its repressive policies, including the destruction of Jewry. The absurdity of the charge was less consequential than its moral heinousness. Second, the purposes of Zionism and Nazism were said to be the same, establishing a particular ethnic group as the "chosen people," as superior to and dominant over all others. Hitler, it was argued, had actually borrowed his ideology from Theodor Herzl. Finally, Israel was declared to be following a bellicose foreign policy line, especially in Lebanon, that was similar to the Nazis and prompted by a motivation similar to the latter's.

Two days later, on January 19, *Tass* reported that the Anti-Zionist Committee had held a press conference which condemned Israel (as well as the United States) for "barbarous aggression" in Lebanon.[50] It was the beginning of a year-long effort linking Zionism and Israel with Nazism and Nazi-like policies.

The climactic express of the new emphasis was an elaborate and re-markable press conference[51] held by the committee at the press center of the USSR Ministry of Foreign Affairs and heavily reported in the press (especially in *Literaturnaia Gazeta* on May 23, 1984) and on radio broadcasts. Moscow Radio, in its domestic service, underscored the committee's preeminent objective: "The main thing in the work of the committee is to expose the reactionary activity of contemporary interna-tional Zionism. At the press conference, the provocative role of inter-national centers of Zionism was demonstrated convincingly."[52]

Dragunsky played the leading role in establishing the Zionist-Nazi equation. "We expose," he said, "the methods borrowed (by Israel) from the arsenal of Nazi war criminals such as concentration camps, keeping people in custody in unbearable conditions, summary beatings and mur-ders, and Israel's institutionalization of terror as its state policy." De-nounced, too, was the Israel-Lebanon peace agreement which, he said, had been imposed upon Lebanon and which violated its sovereignty.

But Zionism was not only portrayed as a Nazi-type aggressive power. It was also described as a Nazi-type subversive ideology striking at the Soviet Union itself through the "spurious slogan" of "defending Soviet Jewry." "International Zionist centres and their emissaries" are presented as responsible for the campaign and for inveigling President Ronald Reagan into it. The U.S. president has joined the campaign of slander, said Dragunsky, in order to cover up U.S. violations of human rights and in order to win support among Jews "whose great-grandfathers fled the pogroms against Jews under the czarist regime to seek refuge overseas."[53]

The fascinating turn in the committee's press conference came as no stunning surprise. Sharp criticism of the Kremlin's anti-Jewish practices in a variety of areas—education, culture, and emigration—was being echoed everywhere in the Western world. Some kind of response was obviously thought to be essential. And the press conference was staged in such a manner as to present a flow of witnesses to deny allegations about Soviet anti-Semitism and to link the allegations—the "slander"—to international Zionism.

Since discrimination against Jews in Soviet universities has become a major public issue in the West, the committee brought forth a young woman named Nataliya Grindberg studying at the mechanics-mathematical department of the University of Moscow. She asserted: "Western propaganda claims that young Jews are barred from higher education are lies." No statistics were offered, and aside from her "personal" testimony, little of substance was advanced.

On the cultural level the committee was able to summon the assistance of Aron Vergelis from *Sovietishe Heimland* and Leonid Shkolnik, editor of the *Birobidzhaner Shtern*. The impact was greater than that offered by the Moscow student. Vergelis is accustomed to offering a version of Jewish cultural life that to the uninformed may appear impressive. Shkolnik described plans to commemorate the fiftieth anniversary of the establishment of the Jewish Autonomous Region. He failed to note the anomaly, however, that only some 6 percent of the region's population is Jewish.

The major emphasis was on the emigration issue where the argument was now made that Zionist propaganda was the source of the problem and of personal tragedy. Several persons told harrowing tales. A Kishinev resident, Yefim Lecht, related how the Zionists induced his wife, who had a grave illness, to emigrate to Israel together with their young children. There she died shortly after attempting suicide. Lecht told the press: "The Zionist emissaries are mean and vindictive. I have found this out from my own experience. I know quite a few cases where, after failing to prod people into leaving for Israel, Zionists floated foul rumors to compromise the families of these people, sow suspicion and provoke conflicts."

A second witness, Ilya Tolmassky, related how his wife had emigrated to Israel and how she had failed to adjust to life in the Jewish state. Eventually she became ill and died. Tolmassky concluded that Soviet Jews must "fight against Zionism and lay bare the true essence of its propaganda."

A third witness, Gavriel Ilyaev, had just returned to the Soviet Union after living in Israel eleven years. Now seventy-five years of age and from Tashkent, Ilyaev related how he had to live in a damp basement in Jerusalem despite his asthma, how he never acquired sufficient money to buy more than the minimal basic foodstuffs, and how he had to start a new career—bookbinding—in his old age.

The point of these "horror" stories was to demonstrate the evil of Zionist propaganda and how it no longer was effective. Zivs, in contrast to his previous posture, which justified the emigration decline in objective terms, now stressed exclusively the failure of Zionist propaganda. But inherent in the argument was the need for more "horror" stories and more "witness" demonstrations at press conferences so as to convince the uncertain and the doubtful. If the number of Jewish emigrants had drastically dropped, said Zivs, it was due to the fact that "the numbers of those who have understood their mistake and abandoned their intentions have been rising over the past year."[54]

Zivs could have added that the past year was one marked by massive publication of the supposed "horrors" of living in Israel. The Anti-Zionist Committee had been active in this endeavor. In any case Zivs made it unmistakably clear that "the process of reuniting families has practically ended." Both Soviet Jews and Jewry abroad had to learn emigration was no longer a legitimate option. It was Zionism which was the enemy and which was responsible for the delegitimization of emigration. Indeed, 1984 marked the lowest point by far since 1970 in the Jewish emigration pattern.[55]

Illuminating the dominant ideological trend of the committee oriented to an overall assault upon Zionism was the role assigned to Yuri Kolesnikov, an otherwise obscure novelist who, though Jewish, had written a particularly virulent anti-Semitic book, *The Curtain Rises,* published in 1979 by the strongly nationalist Military Publishing House in Moscow.[56] A detailed summary of the work with appropriate citations is essential to appreciate its character. This will be done shortly. Here it need only be noted that, when published, it received but one major review—in *Pravda*—and then seemed to disappear from public view.

The review which appeared on September 5, 1979, was written by General Dragunsky.[57] It was one of his rare published articles prior to 1983. Hailing the novel as "one of the first artistic works exposing that dangerous and current phenomenon—Zionism," Dragunsky indicated that it had established on a "documentary foundation" a linkage between "Nazi crimes" and the "Zionist top clique." That alleged linkage was scarcely "accidental," said Dragunsky, since both Nazis and Zionists "put the purity of the race higher than anything else."

For the next four years nothing further was reported about the work. But once the Anti-Zionist Committee was created, and Kolesnikov made its vice-chairman, the Kremlin went to inordinate lengths in order to focus national and international attention upon both the author and his book. The reason was made patently clear. Soviet authorities, through massive promotion efforts, were underscoring the predetermined function of the committee.

First, the Kolesnikov book was reissued in serial form in two numbers of the literary weekly, *Roman-Gazeta* (13–14, 1983). Then, in 1984, it was translated into several foreign languages, including English and published by "Progress Publishers." Finally, the book was lavishly praised by the Soviet press with *Ogonyok,* the popular weekly published by *Pravda* in an edition of two million, devoting an unusual large-scale tribute to the book. The review appeared on May 19, 1984, just four days after the committee's press conference in which Kolesnikov himself would appear.[58]

The *Ogonyok* reviewer, Valentina Malmi, established at the beginning the principal theme of both the book and her review: "Italian Fascism, German Nazism, Romanian nationalism—and everywhere, everywhere, everywhere—the skillful and bloody strides of Zionism." She went on to emphasize that the main point of the author and, indeed, the "lesson of history" is that "the marching songs of the Fascist and Zionist youth were clearly similar." But if Fascism and Nazism were treated with scorn and sarcasm, Zionism was presented in more serious and deadly fashion. For Zionism at its "essence" is "misanthropic" which ineluctably "calls us to vigilance to be prepared to rebuff [it]."

Beyond the anti-Zionist obsession and undoubtedly undergirding it was Judophobia itself. The typical Soviet anit-Jewish stereotype was given special emphasis by the reviewer. The Jewish characters were interested only in business; "Commerce was life itself." And they exploit war for business, for "cash only." The stereotyped Jewish businessman bought and sold "his own life 'for cash only.' "

The Kolesnikov book recalls the writings of Nazi Germany. The Nazi propagandist Julius Streicher could hardly have been more obscene. A leading Jewish character, who was from Bessarabia, Haim Volditer, is introduced as a "halutz" during the late World War II period whose task it was to buy Czech machine guns from Romanian whores with American Jews' money in order to kill Arabs. He is brought into contact with the central character of the novel—Rabbi Ben Zion Hagera—the head of the local Jewish community in Limossol, Cyprus, and an "extremely influential member of the Zionist Action Committee."

Rabbi Hagera is the very embodiment of evil even as he incorporates within himself every negative Jewish stereotype. Described in sinister terms as "the spitting image of Rasputin," he is rich and gross and simultaneously miserly and money-grubbing. A monumental hypocrite, this religious leader, who is also the community banker, is the joint owner of a local brothel with an unscrupulous police officer. The identification of Judaism with prostitution resonates throughout the book.

Crude anti-Semitism of the Nazi variety was made explicit in the discussions of the Zionist Action Committee. A key courier from the Zionist "Centre" arrives to explain: "It is no secret that some of our coreligionist financial magnates hold the destinies of other people in their hands. In any case, their power to influence the policies of the rulers of these people is tremendous. That is why, by remaining in the countries of the Diaspora, they can and do render priceless aid to our cause." Here is made clear the "conspiracy" of the international Jewish financiers. Nazi Germany and the countries the latter dominates are, of course, an exception, notes the courier. But, he then observes that it "is our duty to save those well-off and influential people . . . until the time comes when they will again be able to say their weighty word in Germany." The last point is designated to clarify a secondary theme running through the book as to why, allegedly, the Zionist leadership frequently allowed poor Jews to be slaughtered while the rich were supposedly rescued.

Emerging in the discussions of the committee and in the unfolding of the plot is the book's major theme: Zionist-Nazi collaboration. The courier is asked how the Zionist "Centre" regards "the anti-Semitism of

Herr Hitler." The answer takes the form of an enthusiastic endorsement: "To put it bluntly, if this Adolph Hitler were not here today, then we Beitarim Zionists would have to invent him!" He goes on to explain that "Yes, we Zionists are interested in encouraging anti-Semitism!" In this way Jews are not allowed to forget "who they are" and thereby motivated to become *halutzim* (pioneers) in Palestine.

The Nazi-Zionist linkage is drawn in precise, if somewhat absurd, terms. The German intelligence chief, Admiral Canaris, is portrayed as operating in the United States during World War I as a Jewish business-man with the name "Moishe Meyerbeer." The high-level Nazi official Reinhard Heydrich is shown to have descended from a Jewish grand-mother. Especially stunning is the "revelation" that Adolf Eichmann, an agent of the Jewish agency, was deliberately infiltrated into the Nazi movement as far back as 1932.

Later, Eichmann secretly visits Palestine in the guise of a correspon-dent for a Berlin newspaper. He meets with three agents of the Hagana special operations service. The following discussion is then offered to the reader:

> The Hagana men then say that it is high time for the parties to get down to business. "Now, both of you and us can achieve a lot. But, for that, we need arms! And we want you to help us get them." Eichmann's spirits soared . . . the deal was fully in line with the purpose of his mission in Palestine. . . . It was then that a deal of tremendous international significance was struck between the SS Fueher and the Sherut le Israel representative . . . the Nazis were establishing a "fifth column in Palestine to operate against the British; the Zionists were doing their utmost to bring closer the day when they would speak with the Arabs, and partly with British, in the language of machine-gun fire."

At approximately the time the Kolesnikov book was being given extraordinary attention in *Ogonyok,* the author was offered a broadly national and international platform to express his views. On May 15, 1984 (four days prior to the *Ogonyok* essay), at the Kremlin stage-managed press conference for the Anti-Zionist Committee, Kolesnikov was given special attention. A correspondent from *Nedelya*—the week-end insert in *Izvestia*—put to him the following loaded question: "What can you say about the dirty methods used by the Zionists?" The novelist was succinct in his response: "The reactionary activity of international Zionism and the aggressive policy of the ruling circles of Israel toward the Arab peoples have been denounced by the world public as expansionist, terrorist, and racist." He went on to condemn "noisy gatherings" organized by the Zionists which use "falsehood and blackmail, bribes and promises, threats and even violence in order to continue enticing Jews out of the Soviet Union."

Even as the vitriolic anti-Zionist campaign with its anti-Semitic overtones was being pursued, the committee sought to cloak itself in some kind of Jewish garb, if only to provide it with a sense of legitimacy. The committee sought to take on more specifically Jewish functions as time went on. Nonetheless, the additional roles did little to hide or minimize the seamier aspect of the Dragunsky group, so closely linked to the Kremlin's broader ideological and propaganda objectives regarding Zionism and Israel.

In late February 1984 the presidium of the committee met and concerned itself largely with preparations in the USSR for the 125th anniversary of the birth of Sholom Aleichem, the Yiddish writer,[59] who has remained throughout Soviet history the solitary example and focus of public attempts to demonstrate the Kremlin's interest in things Jewish. While some cultural programs did emerge from the discussions, including a special evening on June 4 at Moscow's Central Actor's Building, it is significant that the Soviet press coverage given to the presidium meeting was limited.[60] In addition, the meeting found it politic to couple its cultural discussion with a condemnation of the Jewish Defense League for an alleged attack upon the Soviet Mission to the United Nations.

Similarly, the committee at its May 15 press conference, directly involved for the first time both Vergelis and Shkolnik, two key figures in what remained of Yiddish culture in the USSR.[61] Both played prominent roles at the press conference and sought to document a certain vitality to Jewish culture in the USSR.

However, the next press conference of the committee was given over almost entirely to a single issue—alleged Zionist-Nazi collaboration. The press conference was held on October 12, 1984, and largely focused on plans to commemorate in the USSR the fortieth anniversary of the victory over Nazism.[62] The significance of the press event lay in the fact that it constituted a harbinger of developments for 1985 and, especially, of such developments as would affect the public perception of Jews in the context of a great patriotic ceremony.

Dragunsky opened the proceedings by contending that Zionists have made every effort to diminish the role of the Soviet Union in the historic destruction of Nazi Germany. Documentation for this malicious charge was not produced. The committee chairman added that it was "the victory of the Soviet Union that saved the Jews from total annihilation."[63]

From the obviously political perspective of Dragunsky, it was convenient to distinguish between the actions of non-Zionist Jews and of Zionists during World War II. The former had fought against Nazism in the Red Army, the Allied armies, and in the partisan and resistance movements. In contrast, Zionists avoided fighting Nazism altogether and, instead, collaborated with the Fascist enemy.

In his presentation, Dragunsky had ignored the massive documentation of the prominent and often key role of Zionists in the Warsaw Ghetto uprising, in the various resistance and partisan movements and, of course, in the Jewish Brigade itself raised in Palestine. Instead, he and his colleagues on the Committee, including Zivs, Bondarevsky, and Rybalchenko, during the press conference, pointed to various instances that, appropriately packaged and distorted, might bolster the argument of alleged Zionist-Nazi collaboration. Their contention was supported by two outside "experts"—Yulian Shulmeister, a senior lecturer at the University of Lvov, who is known for his virulent anti-Zionist writings, and Yevgeniya Finkel, characterized as a resistance fighter during the Nazi occupation.[64]

Among the examples offered of the Zionist-Nazi collaboration were the "transfer agreement" of 1933 and the various contacts between representatives of the Gestapo and the Hagana. Presumably, too, Zionist leaders of the Jewish Councils were described as having betrayed the Jewish communities. The officials of the press conference also presented as a witness someone described as an Italian historian—Massimo Massara—who sought to demonstrate that Zionism and Italian Fascism had a close affinity.

A corollary of the thesis that Zionism had an ideological affinity with Nazism and collaborated with it was the argument that Israel conducted itself as Nazi-like, particularly in Lebanon. At the press conference this theme was articulated by two Scandinavian members of the so-called International Commission of Inquiry into Israel's Crimes against the Lebanese and Palestinian People. The use of non-Russians, even when they may not be recognized as independent and distinguished experts, was designed to provide an aura of objectivity. Additional "evidence" of the supposed Nazi-like character of Israel was offered by Mark Krupkin, the Novosti executive, who cited the election of Rabbi Meir Kahane to the Knesset in July 1984.

The press conference of the Anti-Zionist Committee was to exert an impact on later media accounts oriented to emphasizing the heroic role of the Red Army in the war against Hitler.[65] *Komsomol'skaia Pravda*, on October 31, carried a response to a query about attempts made by "Zionist" propaganda to denigrate the Soviet contribution to the victory over Nazism. A. Aleksandrov reproduced passages from the October 12 press conference and went on to claim that "a criminal alliance of the Zionists and Nazis" had led to the massacre of six million Jews.[66] He added that the Zionists were only concerned with Jewish victims of the Nazis and not with other nationalities, including Soviet citizens.

The last point was made again in *Izvestia* on January 13, 1985, by the deputy chairman of the Novosti agency. The article, which referred to the committee's press conference, claimed that Israeli school textbooks on recent history made virtually no reference to the Soviet contribution to the defeat of Hitler.[67]

That the Anti-Zionist Committee theme on Zionist-Nazi collaboration would become the dominant perception in the media was underscored when *Tass* on January 17, 1985, published the text of an interview with the Soviet Union's most virulent anti-Semitic propagandist—Lev Korneyev.[68] Much of his earlier writings were devoted to the collusion theme. More recently, in 1982, Korneyev went so far as to question the Holocaust itself in terms of the number of its Jewish victims. He speculated that the published figures exceeded by as much as three times the actual size of the Nazi massacre of Jews.

For over a year little was heard from Korneyev in the media, suggesting that the Kremlin leadership had been sufficiently embarrassed by his anti-Semitism in the outside world as to warrant his being kept out of the major press organs. Only several mild and inconsequential articles had appeared from his pen. Now, Korneyev had returned with his usual vitriol. In the interview he accused Zionist-Jewish bankers and industrialists of financing the Nazis.[69] He also charged—as he had earlier—that Zionists prevented Jews from joining the struggle against Fascism and that they shared responsibility for the Nazi extermination of Jews.

That Korneyev would return with his anti-Semitic canards was hardly surprising given the kind of propaganda line that was being intensively pursued by the "Jewish" Anti-Zionist Committee and especially by its vice-chairman, the "Jewish" writer, Yuri Kolesnikov. The committee had assumed a pacesetter role in an area which, ironically, carried anti-Semitic overtones.

To divert attention from this malodorous function the Anti-Zionist Committee sent a telegram to the United States Congress condemning anti-Semitism in the United States: "It is a feeling of great concern that moves us to appeal to you, members of the U.S. Congress. We have learned from an Associated Press report that 715 cases of anti-Semitic acts of vandalism, insults, threats, attacks on individual Jews and Jewish organizations were registered in your country in the past year."[70] The solicitousness was accompanied by a demand that American legislators "do everything possible to stop the growth of anti-Semitism in the USA [since] it is a disgrace to civilized society."

In the late summer and fall of 1985—strikingly on the eve of the Reagan-Gorbachev summit—the Kremlin's anti-Zionist campaign sharply intensified. Inevitably, the Soviet Anti-Zionist Committee was called upon to play a central role in the campaign with its prominence now reaching unprecedented levels of public visibility. Especially important was the committee-sponsored publication in August 1985 of a 300-page book of photos, illustrations, and documents entitled *White Paper*.[71] Designed to be an authoritative statement on the "evils" and "horrors" of Zionism, it was published in an edition of 200,000 copies and given extensive public attention in the media.[72]

Some background to the publication of the *White Paper* is particularly pertinent and throws light on the Kremlin's determination to make the Anti-Zionist Committee the point man in its broad political campaign against Zionism. An earlier and smaller *White Paper* on Zionism had appeared in 1979.[73] It was published in an edition of 150,000 copies by the principal legal group of the USSR—the Association of Soviet Lawyers, which is similar to the American Bar Association. The book was heavily publicized in the media, and vast numbers of copies were distributed to Communist party cadres, bureaucrats, police, and military officials.

The perspectives of the two major contributors to the 1979 volume throw light upon the character of the *White Book*. One of the writers was Lydia Modzhorian, a specialist on international law who worked for the Institute of Oriental Studies of the Soviet Academy of Sciences. Her books and articles were clearly anti-Semitic. The other principal writer was E. D. Modrzhinskaia, who worked at the Institute of Philosophy of the Academy of Sciences. A prolific writer of anti-Zionist articles, she was the principal backer at the Academy of Sciences of the notorious anti-Semite, Yevgenii Yevseev.

On August 15, 1985, a *Tass* broadcast announced publication of a new *White Book,* published jointly by the Association of Soviet Lawyers *and* the Anti-Zionist Committee. Unquestionably, the moving force in this effort was Samuel Zivs, a key figure in both organizations. For the committee it meant a significant upgrading of its status and prominence. The *Tass* broadcast provided an insight into the character of the book. "Zionist leaders," it said, "are responsible for the deaths of thousands of Jews annihilated by the Nazis. It is precisely the Zionists who assisted the Nazi butchers by helping them to make up the lists of the doomed inmates of the ghettoes, escorted the latter to the places of extermination and convinced them to resign to the butchers."[74] Another *Tass* broadcast later in August spelled out that the new book focused on "the subversive activity of Zionist centres."[75]

The new *White Book,* considerably enlarged from the older one with the addition of further documents, is considered by the Kremlin as authoritative. Published in a huge edition of 200,000 copies and designed for a "wide circle of readers," the book was highly praised in the media, reprinted in part in the periodical press, and given to anyone within and without the USSR who might raise questions about Jews.[76] (Thus, when Professor Nathan Glazer of Harvard University discussed the plight of Soviet Jews during the Helsinki-sponsored Cultural Forum in Budapest in November 1985, the one who gave the Soviet rejoinder offered Glazer the *White Book* as well as several additional booklets so that he might learn the "truth.")[77]

The introduction to the new volume characterized the book's purpose. What it was intended to do is reveal "the subversive activity of the Zionist centres," expose "the treacherous methods used by them," and show "the tragic fate of people who fell into the trap of propaganda." The work was perceived as "an awesome accusation" against Zionism which demonstrates the "irrefutable basis for a public verdict on the guilt of Zionism in tragic crimes."

A major segment of the book details how Soviet Jews had been "lured" by mischievous, deceitful, and "blackmailing" Zionists into an "odyssey of torment and suffering." Another important segment allegedly documents the "collaboration" of Zionism with the Nazis. And a final segment picks up the most recent theme of the Anti-Zionist Committee concerning the supposed raging anti-Semitism in the United States and the West. Clearly, the official intent was to strive to discourage and halt the emigration drive within the USSR, but the crudeness and the distortions of the "documentation" bordered on open bigotry which could only reinforce virulent anti-Semitism.

To strengthen the raised status of the Anti-Zionist Committee, Soviet authorities have arranged for the translation and promotion of General David Dragunsky's *A Soldier's Memoirs* with an introduction written by, not surprisingly, Samuel Zivs.[78] If the Zivs introduction is designed to portray Dragunsky as a characteristic "son" of the Jewish people while the memoirs illustrate his patriotism and heroism, an afterword written by Dragunsky reveals his mind-set as well as the real aim of the memoirs.

In the afterword Dragunsky discloses "the very first time I had come face-to-face with Zionism." Supposedly it happened in 1956 in Paris at a ceremony to commemorate the victims of Nazism. At the very moment of the ceremony Israel, together with Britain and France, "launched their aggression against Egypt." Dragunsky then relates that he was approached by Israel's minister of education, Zalman Shazar. According to the Soviet general, Shazar "with off-hand impatience said to me: 'Mr. General, why does the Soviet Union oppose our lawful rights? We need land. We are crowded'—There before me stood one of the leaders of international Zionism. What could I have expected from him. All I could say was: 'Mr. Minister, what you have just said echoes the old Nazi claim of *Lebensraum*. Have you forgotten the price of Hitler's adventure?' " Dragunsky's flight of imagination is equaled only by his malice.

The heightened status of the Anti-Zionist Committee also found expression in foreign broadcasts over Radio Moscow, in frequent citations in the Soviet press, and in the massive distribution of the committee's booklets as well as the *White Book*. Foreign tourists visiting the Moscow synagogue in 1985 received from a congregation official a free gift of four committee booklets published by Novosti.[79] In their contents they described "the foul role of Zionists as accomplices of the Nazis in exterminating millions of working Jews" and how "Zionism threatens to destroy the world's nations along with human culture and civilization." An indication of the committee's importance was the power extended it to invite foreign experts as its guest. The first prominent committee guest is remarkably revealing—Alfred Lilienthal, the well-known anti-Zionist propagandist. In an interview in the journal *Argumenty i Fakty* in November 1985,[80] Lilienthal established his credentials by noting that the "Zionist" lobby in Washington has "influence over the president [Reagan] too." Two months earlier, the journal carried parts of the *White Book*.

The Soviet Anti-Zionist Committee could be trotted out when appropriate to fulfill Kremlin aims. Thus, Samuel Zivs, the committee's preeminent spokesman, would appear publicly wherever and whenever an official Kremlin response to Western concern about Soviet Jewish policy was needed. As Moscow's "court Jew" he showed up with the Soviet delegation in Bern in May 1986 at a Helsinki-sponsored conference on "human contacts"; in Geneva in March 1987 at sessions of the U.N. Commission on Human Rights; in Vienna in the spring of 1987 at meetings of the Helsinki Review Conference and, finally, in Washington in December 1987 at the summit discussions. Zivs would be called upon to articulate the Kremlin "line" on the Soviet Jewish question at public meetings or press conferences or privately. Apologetics was its distinguishing character.

Andrei Sakharov, in an analysis in the *New York Review of Books* (July 21, 1983) of Zivs's major human rights work which had been devoted to a violent assault upon Amnesty International, commented about the author in this way: "There is no question that Zivs' entire book had been written as a KGB assignment. The information Zivs had at his disposal was used in the most dishonest and biased manner, and thus his book is a cunning tissue of malicious lies and slander joined by thin threads of half truth." Sakharov's indictment since then has never been challenged.

Such an evaluation, together with the very nature of the Anti-Zionist Committee activity, inevitably limited the impact of the committee upon Jewish communities abroad. None took the Soviet group and Zivs himself as anything more than mere Kremlin puppets. None would enter into formal or even informal dialogue with them. The total isolation of the committee had become so sharply apparent by the time of the 1987 Reagan-Gorbachev summit that, according to an American government official reported in the *New York Times* (December 8, 1987), Moscow has already decided upon its abandonment. Zivs declined to confirm the report but said "there is a possibility" for this eventuality. A Soviet official in Washington at the time pointed out that Moscow would be establishing a new group that would deal with broad human rights issues, and, he suggested, the Anti-Zionist Committee would be absorbed into the new group.

The last word was offered by leading and longtime Soviet refuseniks who had just been released a few weeks before the summit. Ida Nudel called the reported initiative a mere "cosmetic move." Viktor Brailovsky observed: "It proves only that the [committee] members are puppets and nothing more."

With the dialogue between the Soviet Union and the United States now deepening and embracing a whole variety of areas—arms control, trade, and cultural exchange—the very operation of the Soviet Public Anti-Zionist Committee became increasingly anomalous. Its existence ran counter to the themes of détente and responsibility which the new general secretary of the Soviet Communist Party Central Committee, Mikhail Gorbachev, has sounded. Consequently, from the high point of its activity in 1985 it fell in Soviet strategy to the point of near dissolution by the end of 1987.

Nonetheless, the Anti-Zionist Committee did function effectively as a propaganda instrument of Soviet totalitarianism from 1983–85. Where the Kremlin found it embarrassing to deny that Soviet Jews seek to emigrate, the committee performed that task without hesitancy. In the area of anti-Zionist propaganda it became the leading spokesman for the USSR, even when anti-Zionism was merely a cover for anti-Semitism.

While Gorbachev's reordering of Soviet priorities led to the diminution of the role of the Soviet Anti-Zionist Committee, and may indeed lead to its dissolution, this analysis of its activity in the 1983–86 period serves as a useful case study of the Soviet government's ability to manipulate the issue of Judaism and Zionism for its larger political purposes. Indeed, should Gorbachev fail in his efforts at perestroika, or lose his position of leadership in the Soviet Union, the return to prominence of the Soviet Anti-Zionist Committee—or an organization very much like it—cannot be ruled out.

3. Soviet Anti-Semitism Unchained: The Rise of the "Historical and Patriotic Association, Pamyat"

Howard Spier

The rise to prominence under Gorbachev of Pamyat (Memory) and a number of closely linked chauvinistic and anti-Semitic bodies is a development of considerable significance. The fact that these self-styled historical and patriotic associations have been bitterly attacked by important organs of the Soviet media would seem to indicate that they have struck a chord in the Soviet public. An analysis of the character and aims of Pamyat raises questions which are fundamental to the nature of Soviet society.

The May 6 Rally and Meeting with Boris Eltsin

The informal, that is, unregistered and tolerated, organization Pamyat first came to prominence after an apparently spontaneous demonstration in a central Moscow square on May 6, 1987. The approximately four hundred demonstrators who took part in the rally marched toward the Moscow City Soviet, bearing slogans demanding a meeting with General Secretary Gorbachev and Moscow party chief Boris Eltsin, condemning the "saboteurs of *perestroika"* (restructuring) and calling for official recognition of Pamyat.[1]

In deciding whether or not to meet with the demonstrators, Eltsin may have found himself faced with a serious dilemma. As a particularly close associate of Gorbachev,[2] he may well have hesitated at bestowing any degree of legitimacy on those who espoused some highly questionable views, to say the least; yet he could not easily dismiss those who claimed genuine concern with the preservation of the city's historical and cultural heritage and with a host of environmental matters.

In any event the report of the meeting (which lasted over two hours) between the demonstrators and Eltsin and Valery Saykin, chairman of the Moscow City Soviet, which appeared in the weekly *Moscow*

News was to some extent ambivalent. While the report attacked the demonstrators' extremism, anti-Semitism, and "absolute intolerance" of the opinions of others, it did not fail to point out that much remained to be done in the Soviet capital in such areas, for example, as combating bureaucracy, stepping up the drive against alcoholism, and coping with the problem of overpopulation. In one intriguing and remarkable reference to the meeting, *Moscow News* reported that "It was noted that thought would be given to the registering of the Pamyat Association."[3]

It seems that Eltsin's career may not have been helped by his decision to meet with the Pamyat demonstrators: his action was implicitly criticized by the Soviet government newspaper *Izvestia*,[4] and he failed, contrary to expectations in some quarters,[5] to be elected to the Politburo at the June 1987 plenum of the Communist Party of the Soviet Union (CPSU) Central Committee. In contrast, Aleksandr Yakovlev, one of Pamyat's principal targets of abuse, was promoted to full Politburo membership.

The Rise of Pamyat

The events of May 6—seemingly a deliberate attempt by Pamyat's organizers to take advantage of the new opportunities presented by the policies of "democratization" and glasnost—appear to have been the final straw for the Soviet authorities—or at least some elements among them. A decision was taken to focus media attention on the new phenomenon in Soviet society, and since that occasion a succession of vituperative attacks on Pamyat has appeared in some leading organs of the media,[6] although there have been notable exceptions.

In fact, the "historical and patriotic association 'Pamyat' " has not always assumed its present form. Pamyat was founded in 1980 by a number of employees at the USSR Ministry of Aviation Industry.[7] The aim of the new organization—to strive to prevent the destruction of Moscow's historical and cultural monuments—was apparently a highly popular one, and it would appear that there was a widespread view that the task was being neglected by the powers-that-be.[8] It seems that thousands of people flocked to the various functions organized by the new body.

It appears that the objectives Pamyat's founders had set themselves began to change as the leadership of the association was increasingly penetrated by people "with nothing in common either with the aviation industry or history"; instead of devoting itself to "real" problems, it became preoccupied with "mythical enemies." Pamyat left the aviation ministry for the Gorbunov Palace of Culture, but not for long; unimpressed by its activities, the local party committee resolved to eject it from its premises. But although it no longer had premises of its own, Pamyat was, it seems, able to hold a number of meetings in various establishments by hiding its true purpose, a ruse which worked successfully on at least one occasion. By autumn 1985 Pamyat had, it appears, acquired its current identity.

The following account of an aborted meeting seems not untypical of Pamyat's modus operandi. In February 1987 the organizers of Pamyat made an attempt to hold a function in the conference hall of Moscow's Yunost Hotel. In a letter to the local party official, V. V. Egiazorov, director of the Republican Trust of Monumental and Decorative Art of the RSFSR Artistic Fund, guaranteed that the fund would pay for the rental of the hall. As it turned out, almost at the last moment the meeting did not go ahead "for technical reasons." Whatever these "technical reasons" may have been, they were evidently found wanting by supporters of Pamyat, who could be pacified only by the appearance of the first secretary of the party's district committee and his suggestion that they discuss together, on the committee's premises, any problems of concern.

The ensuing debate clearly ended in farce. The party official had invited a number of prominent scholars specializing in Russian history and culture for the purposes of discussion; one of those who took part was V. L. Yanin, a corresponding member of the Soviet Academy of Sciences and one of the leading authorities on Russian antiquity in the country. These erudite scholars, it was reported, were confronted by Dmitry Vasilev, the principal organizer of Pamyat, who "ignorantly held forth on historical subjects."

The Character of Pamyat

As mentioned above, members of Pamyat place great emphasis on their concern with the preservation of elements of Russia's cultural and historical past, such as national monuments and churches. This concern, as even their detractors point out, is a perfectly legitimate and honorable one. But Pamyat and its associated groups also operate on a second, more overtly political level. They are, in reality, an extreme Great Russian nationalist group and, moreover, extol the Russian Orthodox faith in sharp contradiction to Soviet ideology. While many members of the group may sincerely support *perestroika*—after all, it presents them with the opportunity to operate more openly—objectively they may be manipulated and used by those disaffected with and profoundly opposed to the program of reforms currently being introduced by the Soviet leadership. While their slogans may point elsewhere, many supporters of Pamyat are in fact among the true "saboteurs of *perestroika*."

Members of Pamyat have found an appropriate scapegoat for the problems that have beset Soviet society—namely the tried-and-tested "Zionist (that is, Jewish)-Masonic conspiracy" against Russia and the Russian people. This notion has deep roots in Russia. It was the rallying cry of the Black Hundreds organization, the Union of the Russian People, a reactionary monarchist and anti-Semitic body that fought against the planned reforms following the 1905 revolution. After the Bolshevik Revolution and the routing of the White forces, this creed, in particular its most notorious manifestation, *The Protocols of the Elders of Zion,* was "exported" to the West where it was subsequently adopted with great enthusiasm by the Nazis.

In the 1970s and early 1980s the theme of the *Protocols* emerged, sometimes explicitly but more often implicitly, in writings of Soviet anti-Zionist and anti-Semitic propagandists. Indeed, some of these propagandists have resurfaced in Pamyat after an interval of several years' oblivion. "Veteran" anti-Semitic propagandists and activists who are known to have associated with Pamyat are Vladimir Begun, Valery Emelyanov, and Evgeny Evseev (see Appendix 4). Recent Soviet media accounts of Pamyat's activities have commented on the many similarities between the creed of the Union of the Russian People and that of Pamyat, including their common acceptance of the authenticity of the *Protocols*. One Soviet newspaper has even gone so far as to claim that the works of the "veteran" anti-Semitic propagandists have proved "beneficial to the West"; the reason given for this charge was the publication and distribution by the Institute of Jewish Affairs in 1975 of translated excerpts from Vladimir Begun's book, *Creeping Counter-revolution*.[9] In fact, there is a certain irony in the Soviet media's criticism of Pamyat's activities, for it is to a great extent the anti-Semitic excesses of the anti-Zionist campaign of the 1970s and early 1980s which planted these seeds.

Pamyat activists claim to detect symbols of Zionism and Freemasonry virtually everywhere. Thus, a newspaper, if held up and read against the light, is said to reveal a signal between secret forces;[10] design competition entries for a historical monument on display in a Moscow exhibition hall are said to contain "Masonic-Zionist and even fascist symbols";[11] the Order of Lenin sign on the cover of the staunchly anti-Russian nationalist weekly *Ogonyok* has, for some allegedly sinister purpose, been omitted since the beginning of the year;[12] the Soviet press is inundated with "coded menorahs and six-pointed stars . . . set squares and compasses are masonic symbols";[13] and so forth. At the same time certain Soviet officials and prominent cultural figures are alleged to be agents of Zionism and Freemasonry. This is the case, for example, with Aleksandr Yakovlev, the Politburo candidate member who in 1972 fell into disfavor for his opposition to the Russian nationalists but was promoted in June 1987 to full Politburo membership.[14] Academician D. S. Likhachev,[15] chairman of the USSR Culture Fund and a Russian Orthodox believer, is also a "Zionist accomplice" as is the well-known artist Ilya Glazunov[16] and the director of the Moscow Arts Theatre, Oleg Efremov.[17] The prominent poet Andrey Voznesensky received, apparently from Pamyat, an unsigned letter, which contained "a sort of death threat."[18] Moreover, two individuals are singled out as responsible for the drastic decline in the number of Moscow's churches—Lazar Kaganovich, the only Jew in Stalin's Politburo, and Emelyan Yaroslavsky (originally Gubelman),[19] the chairman of the Militant Atheists. Pamyat members are generally careful not to criticize Gorbachev directly, but one activist went as far to describe him as the puppet of Georgy Arbatov, his Jewish adviser on foreign policy and head of the Institute of the United States and Canada of the Soviet Academy of Sciences.[20]

Whatever one thinks of the views held by Pamyat members, there is no doubt that they have won the backing of party officials at various levels. A number of meetings have been held in party premises, a fact which has given Soviet media critics of the extreme Russian nationalists great cause for concern. Kim Andreev, the chairman of the council of Pamyat, is himself a party member. One can speculate endlessly about the patronage from influential quarters that Pamyat activities may have received. It cannot be without significance that, at the time of writing, no references whatever have been made to Pamyat and its associated organizations in *Pravda,* the daily organ of the CPSU Central Committee, and *Sovetskaya Rossiya,* the daily organ of the RSFSR Supreme Soviet and Council of Ministers.

As far as can be ascertained, meetings of Pamyat appear to be well attended, with the presence of many young people, despite the lack of advance notice in the press. The meetings have, in some cases, been conducted on the lines of a secret society, with demagoguery and oratory used to whip up the passions of the audience. In Dmitry Vasilev, a journalist and photographer, Pamyat seems to have found a formidable, even charismatic, leader. There is evidence that speeches by Vasilev in particular are being recorded on tape and copies speedily distributed around the country.[21]

Conclusion

It is very difficult to assess accurately the importance of the phenomenon of Pamyat in the contemporary USSR. In purely organizational terms Pamyat is known to have branches, or closely linked groups, in Leningrad, Sverdlovsk, and Novosibirsk, aside from its center in Moscow. Since the May 6 rally Pamyat has received exceptionally wide coverage in the Soviet media, a reflection of the importance ascribed to it by the party authorities. (Indeed, the term Pamyat—memory—is a highly emotive word in Soviet conditions, evoking as it does all manner of associations with the sacrifices of the Russian people in the Great Fatherland War.) At the same time one can expect such publicity to increase the Soviet population's awareness of the existence of the organization. It must be held to be an asset to Pamyat that it has a central leading figure in the person of Dmitry Vasilev.

The Soviet media accounts to which we have referred are, without exception, highly critical of Pamyat, dismissive of its fanatical Russian nationalism and contemptuous of its activities. The media do not fail to point out, however, that genuine problems do indeed exist in today's USSR. Vasilev and his coactivists (perfectly understandably in Soviet conditions) pay lip service to Marxist-Leninist ideology and the leadership's current policy of perestroika; indeed, they stress their attachment to these values and objectives. However, there can be no doubt that their strident nationalism and extremism are entirely at variance with the current objectives of the Soviet leadership. The party's call for democratization and glasnost has revealed the existence not only of Pamyat but of other, equally anti-Western and illiberal tendencies such as the so-called Lyubery—Moscow street gangs who inflict physical violence on alien (that is, perceived Western) elements in Soviet society such as hippies, punks, and rock music enthusiasts. There is some evidence of the existence in the USSR of youth groups who don Nazi regalia and make Hitler

salutes; recently, they were reported to have vandalized a Jewish cemetery in Leningrad on Hitler's birthday.[22] All of these organizations are
evidently profiting from their newfound notoriety. At the time of writing
the party leadership seems to be disinclined to tackle these bodies; presumably, there is no desire to provide more ammunition than necessary
to the critics of glasnost.

Pamyat is in many respects a grass-roots movement of the disaffected; as yet, it does not appear to have attracted any persons of prominence to its ranks. One can, of course, speculate endlessly over which
forces may lie behind it, but what is certain is that at a time of great flux
in the USSR the significance of the Pamyat phenomenon should not be
underestimated.

Part Two

Linkages between Soviet Foreign Policy and the Exodus of Soviet Jewry

4. Soviet Jewry as a Factor in Soviet-Israeli Relations

Robert O. Freedman

One of the most intriguing aspects of Israeli foreign policy since the creation of the State of Israel in 1948 has been its relationship to the Soviet Union in general and to the Jews of the Soviet Union in particular. One of the central elements of Israel's ethos has been the ingathering of Jews from all over the world, particularly from places where they are physically threatened. The concept of "never again," that is, never again will Jews be left to die because there is no refuge available to them, as during the Holocaust, remains a powerful concept in Israel, one that unites both Ashkenazim and Sephardim. In the case of Soviet Jewry there is an additional factor of importance. Many of Israel's original leaders came from czarist Russia, and at the time of the Communist seizure of power in October 1917 there were some 300,000 Zionists, organized into 1,200 local groups.[1] Given the limited number of Jews in Palestine at the time, the hope that many of the Russian Jewish Zionists would come to Palestine was a powerful one among Zionist leaders, not least of them Chaim Weizman who, himself, was born in czarist Russia. Indeed, the hope that most of the remaining 3,000,000 Soviet Jews may yet come to Israel remains an important consideration in Israeli foreign policy to this day.

Unfortunately for the hopes of the Palestinian Zionist leadership, the new Soviet state soon cracked down on Zionism, considering it both a "tool of British imperialism" and a device for diverting Jewish workers from the class struggle. As a result, very few Soviet Jews were able to leave the USSR for Palestine; the notable exceptions were Chaim Bialik, Saul Chernikowskii, and a few other Hebrew writers and poets, along with the Habimah Theatre Troup who left in the early 1920s.[2]

Compounding the problem for Soviet Jewry in the interwar period was the rise to power of Joseph Stalin. It is not possible to present a detailed examination of Stalin's attitude to Soviet Jews here. There is, however, one important element to note. A number of Stalin's top rivals in the Communist party were Jews (Trotsky, Kamenev, and Zinoviev), and he was involved in a power struggle with them until the late 1920s when he was able to assert his full control over the Soviet state and eventually eliminate them (and other Jews) from positions of power. To what degree memories of this power struggle influenced him later in life is impossible to determine.[3] However, he did dissolve the *Yevsektsiia,* the Jewish section of the Communist party, in 1930, at least in part because of "Jewish nationalist tendencies."[4] As a result, there was no central Soviet-Jewish organization until the Jewish Anti-Fascist Committee was formed in 1942.

In the early stages of the German attack on the Soviet Union in World War II, Stalin was desperate for Western assistance, and the Jewish Anti-Fascist Committee was one outgrowth of his quest for Western aid.[5] As Yehoshua Gilboa has stated in his study of Stalin's policy toward Soviet Jewry, "Soviet authorities attached great significance to the influence of world Jewry in shaping general public opinion in the West, whose support in the war against Germany was considered vital."[6] By organizing the Jewish Anti-Fascist Committee and sending its top leaders (Solomon Mikhoels, director of the Moscow Jewish State theater, and Yitzhak Feffer, a noted Soviet-Jewish poet) on a tour of Jewish communities in England, Canada, Mexico, and the United States, Stalin hoped to gain increased Western (and Jewish) economic aid, increased military assistance, and also the early opening of a second front against the Germans on the continent of Europe, thereby relieving some of the German pressure on the Red Army.

Interestingly enough, however, while Stalin's aim in establishing the Jewish Anti-Fascist Committee was to gain Western support, the committee soon developed a life of its own and served, albeit informally, as an organization of Soviet Jews during World War II. Indeed, there were a number of Soviet Jews who wished to greatly expand the domestic role of the committee. As the poet David Hofstein stated: "The Jewish Anti-Fascist Committee must become the center of Russian Jewry, and not merely an agency for raising funds in the United States."[7] Nonetheless, while Stalin permitted a rise in Soviet-Jewish consciousness through the establishment of the Jewish Anti-Fascist Committee, as well as through the production of a large number of Jewish wartime literary works, many of which were infused by specifically Jewish themes, the end of World War II and the onset of the Cold War were to bring about a major change in his attitudes.

In the aftermath of World War II the Soviet Union, under Stalin's leadership, sought to consolidate its security through the acquisition, either directly or by proxy, of regions contiguous to its borders. Thus, the Soviet Union took hold of Eastern Europe, strengthened its position in Outer Mongolia, and endeavored to control China's Sinkiang and Manchurian territories. The latter two areas, however, were lost to Soviet control when the Chinese Communists secured power in late 1949. The Middle East, another area contiguous to the Soviet Union, did not escape Soviet efforts at control, as the Soviet Union sought military bases and territory from Turkey, as well as a section of northwest Iran. As in the case of Sinkiang and Manchuria, however, the Soviet Middle East efforts proved abortive. Indeed, to overall Soviet policy, they may be seen as counterproductive in that they helped precipitate the Truman Doctrine and the Turkish-U.S. and Iranian-U.S. alignments.

The British were also highly apprehensive at the Soviet territorial demands in the Middle East, a region England sought as its sphere of influence in the postwar period, and the newly elected Labor government sought to create a bloc of pro-British Moslem Arab states, stretching from Egypt to Iraq, to both stop Soviet penetration of the region and to enhance the British position there. With military bases in Egypt, Jordan, Palestine, and Iraq, the British evidently hoped to establish a sphere of influence of their own at a time when East and West Europe were being divided between the two superpowers. Although most Arab states were far from enthusiastic about the British scheme, the primary regional opponent of the British plan was the Jewish community of Palestine, which by this time was actively opposing British efforts to curb Jewish immigration to Palestine from the Holocaust-devastated Jewish communities of Europe. Similarly opposed to the British plan was the Soviet Union, which, cognizant of the tremendous development of military technology during World War II, saw the British base system in the Middle East as posing a threat against the Soviet Union. A coincidence of interests, therefore, placed the Soviet Union and the Jewish community of Palestine on the same side during the diplomatic activity at the United Nations in 1947 and the Arab-Israeli war of 1948–49. Indeed, while the United States was taking what might be called today an "evenhanded" (if not vacillating) position toward the Arab-Israeli conflict during this period,[8] the Soviet Union actively aided Israel by sending it extensive military aid (via Czechoslovakia) and giving it diplomatic support as well. Indeed, in light of current Soviet policy toward Israel, it is most interesting to read the Soviet press during this period as it strongly condemned the Arabs for invading Israel, while praising the newly established Jewish state. Thus, on May 30, 1948, two weeks after the Arab invasion of Israel, *Pravda* stated: "The Arab states in attacking the State of Israel, have entered a path fraught with dangerous consequences. The unprovoked aggression against the young Jewish state will encounter the harshest judgment of the people of the Soviet Union and progressive peoples of the whole world."

Stalin's decision to aid in the establishment of the State of Israel and to grant the new state both diplomatic and military support would appear to have been based on his evaluation of the geopolitics of the region. An independent Jewish state would split the bloc of Moslem Arab states the British were seeking to establish while also depriving the British of the excellent harbor at Haifa and of bases in the Negev desert. Indeed, an examination of the material in the archives of the Jewish Agency in Jerusalem indicates that this was the primary Soviet concern, as the only element the Soviets seemed to want as a quid pro quo for their support of Israel was that the Israelis would not grant military bases to any foreign power.[9] While there may well have been other, more secondary, Soviet motivations in deciding to aid the Israelis in the 1947–49 period, the available information indicates that strategic considerations played the most important part.[10]

Unfortunately both for Israel and for Soviet Jewry, by 1948 Stalin had become paranoid,[11] and while he was willing to aid the State of Israel, he was unwilling for any manifestations of Jewish nationalism within the borders of the USSR. As might be expected, the scene of tens of thousants of Soviet Jews spontaneously greeting Golda Meir, Israel's first ambassador to the USSR at Rosh Hashana services, and chanting "Am Yisrael Chai" (The People of Israel Lives) could only reinforce Stalin's increasingly negative attitude to Soviet Jewish nationalism.[12] The ties Soviet Jews had with their coreligionists abroad, which had been an asset for Stalin's strategy during World War II, now became a major liability for the Soviet Jews themselves when the United States and Britain became Russia's Cold War enemies. Stalin's destruction of Jewish culture during the 1948–53 period, and his murder of top Jewish poets and writers are, unfortunately, too well known to have to be described in detail.[13] Essentially, the leader of the Jewish Anti-Fascist Committee, Solomon Mikhoels, was murdered; the committee itself was dissolved; all Yiddish publishing houses were closed down; Jewish books were removed from Soviet libraries and bookstores; Jews were accused of being "cosmopolitans" and eliminated from many areas of Soviet life, including the foreign service and foreign trade ministry; Jews were accused of "economic crimes" and made scapegoats for Soviet economic difficulties in the early 1950s; and in 1952 twenty-four leading Jewish writers were murdered as Stalin evidently sought to destroy the Jewish cultural leadership of the Soviet Union. An even more serious action against Soviet Jewry seemed in preparation in early 1953 with the announcement of the Doctor's Plot where so-called "doctor murderers tied to Joint Distribution Committee, that international Jewish Zionist Organization [working] . . . for the bosses of the U.S.A.," were accused of trying to murder Soviet military and civilian officials.[14] Meanwhile, as the persecution of Soviet Jewry escalated, ties between Israel and the USSR worsened and were finally broken off in February 1953, one month before Stalin's death.[15]

The Khrushchev Era

While diplomatic relations between Moscow and Jerusalem were restored soon after the death of Stalin—and the Doctor's Plot was declared to be a hoax thereby saving Soviet Jews from a possible massive pogrom—the USSR slowly began to shift to the Arab side of the Arab-Israeli conflict, for considerations not unlike those which motivated Stalin's decision to aid Israel almost a decade earlier. By the mid-1950s Soviet interest had shifted to Egypt, whose leader, Gamal Abdel Nasser, had adopted an anti-British posture much as the Israelis had done in the late 1940s. Once again the British were seeking to establish an anti-Soviet military alliance in the Middle East, this time with U.S. support. This alliance, known as the Baghdad Pact, came into being in early 1955 and soon became a target of both Soviet and Egyptian attack. The Soviets, as might be expected, were unhappy with the Baghdad Pact, since it sought to link the anti-Soviet NATO and SEATO alliances. For his part Nasser opposed the Baghdad Pact because he saw it as bringing the British back into the Arab world—a region Nasser sought for Egyptian influence—after they had agreed to leave Egypt following the signing of the Anglo-Egyptian Treaty of July 1954. As in the case of Soviet aid to Israel in the 1947–49 period, there was a commonality of interest, and once again the Soviet Union responded to a regional power's requests for diplomatic support and military aid. Nasser's acquisition of Soviet arms, however, posed a strategic threat to the Israelis, and one of the goals of the Israeli attack on Egypt on October 29, 1956 (which was joined by Britain and France for their own reasons), was to prevent Nasser, in his championing of the Arab cause, from using his newly acquired Soviet arsenal against Israel. The Soviet leaders, burdened at the time with a serious problem of their own (the revolt in Hungary), played a relatively small role in the crisis, as their threats against Britain, France, and Israel and their offer of Soviet "volunteers" came at a time when the crisis had already subsided. In the aftermath of the fighting, however, Moscow sought to take credit for forcing the withdrawal of Britain, France, and Israel from Egypt (in reality it was primarily U.S. pressure that accomplished this objective), and the Soviet Union later sought to capitalize on the Eisenhower Doctrine and the growing conflict between Egyptian and U.S. policy in the Arab world to enhance Soviet influence. The Soviets, however, were soon to find themselves on the horns of a dilemma as they sought to extend their influence in the region following the overthrow of the pro-British Nuri Said government in Iraq in July 1958. The contest for leadership in the Arab world that soon erupted between the new Iraqi leader, General Qasim, and Nasser posed a difficult problem of choice for the Soviets, one that was to be a recurrent problem for them in their Middle East policies, and their decision to side with the new Iraqi leader led to a temporary reconciliation between Egypt and the United States. In any case for the remainder of Khrushchev's rule (until October 1964) the Middle East was not a center point of Soviet diplomacy, as the Soviets sought gains elsewhere in the Third World while at the same time facing difficult problems in areas more central to Soviet interest (that is, the Berlin crises of 1958 and 1961, the Cuban missile crisis of 1962, and the escalation of the Sino-Soviet conflict from 1960 through 1964). Essentially, Soviet policy in the Middle East remained defensive during this period, and the Arab-Israeli conflict, which had flared into war in 1956, remained relatively dormant.

Meanwhile, as Moscow was siding with the Arabs, the status of Soviet Jewry remained tenuous. When Nikita Khrushchev consolidated his power in the Soviet Union in 1955, he was not burdened with Stalin's general paranoia or his paranoia about the Jews. However, Khrushchev did suffer from what might be termed a "native" anti-Semitism, as his occasional anti-Semitic remarks indicated. In addition, unlike Stalin, who had eased Soviet antireligious efforts during World War II and its aftermath, Khrushchev revived the Soviet antireligious campaign and closed a large number of Soviet churches and synagogues.

Nonetheless, it was not too far into Khrushchev's period of rule that international considerations began to affect the Soviet leader's treatment of Soviet Jews. In the first place China changed from an ally to an enemy, thereby precipitating a competition in the international Communist movement between China and the Soviet Union where Moscow, to a certain degree, had to court West European Communist parties. Second, Khrushchev's grandiose economic plans ran into difficulty, and the USSR began to seek American grain. These factors were to lead to a small amelioration of the condition of Soviet Jewry. Thus, in 1961, for the first time since Stalin had obliterated Jewish cultural institutions in the USSR in the late 1940s, a national Yiddish periodical, *Sovietische Heimland*, was introduced. As the Soviet minister of culture, Yekatarina Furtseva, reportedly stated several months earlier to the vice-chairman of the Franco-Soviet Cultural Society, "If the USSR did anything at all for Yiddish culture, it would not be for domestic reasons, but to please our friends abroad."[16]

Another indication during the Khrushchev years of a certain amount of Soviet sensitivity to Western pressure was the Soviet government's relaxation of a ban on the baking of matzoth in state bakeries in 1963 in response to protests from the West.[17] Yet another case of Soviet sensitivity can be seen from the consequences of the publication of Trofim Kichko's virulently anti-Semitic book, *Judaism Without Embellishment*, in 1963.[18] Coming at a time when the Soviet Union was beset by a very poor harvest and a serious slowdown in economic growth, the book slandered Judaism as a religion that fostered "speculation" and other illegal economic activities, many of which allegedly took place in synagogues. The publication of this book precipitated a wave of protest in the West, not only from Jewish groups, public officials, and clergy of all faiths, but also from the leaders of Western Communist parties whose allegiance the Soviet Union was then actively seeking because of the Chinese challenge to the USSR for leadership in the international Communist movement. The end result of the protests was a decision by the Soviet leadership, which had been forced to seek grain from the United States because of its poor harvest in 1963, to mildly condemn Kichko's book because "it might be interpreted in the spirit of anti-Semitism."

The Brezhnev Era

When Brezhnev became ruler of the USSR in 1964, Soviet-Israeli relations continued cool, but only in part because of Israel's continued pressure on behalf of Soviet Jewry. To be sure, the Soviet ambassador to Israel, Dmitri S. Chuvakhin, told the Israeli Foreign Ministry in April 1965: "You know well what stands in the way of an improvement of our relations with you. It is the problem of Soviet Jews and of your activities on the subject, especially in international forums. If you change your policy on this point and if you stop provoking us, an improvement in relations will follow."[19] Nonetheless, the main cause of Soviet-Israeli friction was Moscow's continuing support of the Arab cause in the Arab-Israeli conflict, not the Soviet Jewry issue.

Interestingly enough, however, while a part of the strain in Soviet-Israeli relations might have been explained by Israel's efforts on behalf of Soviet Jewry, these efforts, when coupled with the slowly rising tide of American Jewish pressure on behalf of Soviet Jewry, seemed to have had the desired effect. Thus on December 3, 1966, Soviet Prime Minister Aleksei Kosygin, speaking in Paris, indicated that no official Soviet policy prevented the "reunification of families." The reprinting of that statement by *Izvestia* spurred hundreds of Soviet Jews to apply to emigrate, albeit without immediate success. The turning point in the Soviet Jewry movement—and in Israel's relationship to it—came as a result of two major international events in the 1967–68 period: the June 1967 Arab-Israeli war and the liberalization movement in Communist Czechoslovakia that was aborted by the Soviet invasion of August 1968. Paradoxically, while the Soviet propaganda media were to blame an "alliance of Zionism and imperialism" for both the 1967 war and the liberalization movement in Czechoslovakia, the two developments were to activate a hitherto dormant Soviet Jewry that earlier had been characterized as "the Jews of silence."[20]

Yet to blame the issue of Soviet Jewry for the worsening of Soviet-Israeli relations in the 1967–68 period would be incorrect. While Moscow was to break diplomatic relations with Israel during the June 1967 war, the central issue between the two states was not Soviet Jewry but rather Soviet policy in the Middle East.

The Soviet Union's defensive stance in the Middle East had changed with the advent to power of the Brezhnev-Kosygin regime in October 1964. Having suffered serious reverses elsewhere in the Third World in countries such as Indonesia and Ghana, and perceiving new opportunities for extending Soviet influence into the Middle East, the new Soviet leadership soon decided to make the region the primary focus of Soviet efforts in the Third World. At the same time the Middle East looked particularly promising for the Soviet Union. In the first place Egyptian-U.S. relations had hit a new low and the once proud Nasser was bogged down in a war in Yemen. Second, England had announced in February 1966 that it was going to pull out of Aden, and there was increasing talk of the British pulling out of all of their holdings on the oil-rich Arabian peninsula. Third, a left-wing government had come to power in Syria in February 1966, which openly advocated improved relations with the Soviet Union and which invited Khalid Bakdash, an exiled Communist leader, to return to Syria in an apparent gesture of goodwill to the Soviet Union. In addition, the world political situation seemed propitious for a more active Soviet role in the Middle East. The United States was bogged down in the Vietnamese War, and its growing troop commitment in Southeast Asia was helping the Soviet Union to contain China—now a central Soviet goal. For their part the Chinese Communists had become bogged down in their so-called cultural revolution and could be expected to provide little opposition to Soviet policy in the Middle East.

The end result of this situation was that in May 1966, with Kosygin's visit to Cairo, Moscow embarked on a new policy in the Middle East, this time an offensive one.[21] Apparently seeing that the time was ripe to begin to push Western influence out of the Middle East, Moscow made its move. During his visit Kosygin urged the unity of the "progressive forces" of the Arab world and, in particular, an alignment between Egypt and Syria. In coming out explicitly for this strategy the Soviet leaders sought to solve a number of problems that had hitherto plagued them in their efforts to secure influence in the Middle East. These obstacles included the intra-Arab competition for leadership where, as in the case of the Nasser-Qasim feud, if the Soviets backed one side, they risked alienating the other; intrastate conflicts such as the ones between Syria and Egypt and between Egypt and Iraq; and the dilemma of the Arab Communist parties, which were perceived as potential or actual competitors for power by the one-party Arab regimes in the region. The Soviet leaders evidently hoped that these differences and conflicts could be subsumed in a larger Arab alignment against "imperialism" and what the Soviet leaders termed "imperialism's linchpin" in the Middle East—Israel. Interestingly enough, however, for the Soviet strategy to be successful Israel had to exist, and Soviet strategy required the continuation of Israel's existence, both for this reason and because Moscow did not wish to unduly alienate either the United States, or U.S. Jewry, by calling for Israel's destruction. Yet, by focusing Arab efforts against Israel, by supplying both Egypt and Syria with advanced Soviet weapons, and by actively supporting Arab diplomatic efforts against Israel, the Soviet leaders may have given such Arab leaders as Egypt's Nasser and Syria's Salah Jedid the impression that the Soviet Union would give them support should a conflict with Israel result from the growing Arab-Israeli tension.[22]

In any case the Syrian government, emboldened by both Soviet military aid and by an alliance with Egypt in August 1966, stepped up its guerrilla attacks against Israel, only to be met by increasingly severe Israeli retaliation. Fearing that Syria's pro-Soviet, albeit weakly based, regime might fall, both as a result of its internal problems and Israeli attacks, Moscow supplied false information to Egypt that Israel was preparing to attack Syria. Nasser, acting on this information, moved his troops into the Sinai in mid-May 1967, then ousted the United Nations forces there, and announced a blockade of the Straits of Tiran to Israeli shipping. These moves, together with the adhesion of Jordan to the Syrian-Egyptian alliance at the end of May, helped precipitate the Six-Day War. While the Soviet leaders seemed to have grasped the potential consequences of their actions in late May, they were ineffectual in arresting the trend of events as Israel decided to attack Egypt on June 5 and quickly defeated all three of its Arab opponents, capturing in the process the Sinai Peninsula, the West Bank and Gaza regions, and the Golan Heights.

The major Israeli victory seemed at first to be a significant defeat for the Soviet drive for influence in the Middle East. Soviet military equipment and training had proved of little value, and the Soviet leaders' failure to aid their client states while they were being soundly defeated also served to lower Soviet prestige in the Arab world. Indeed, the only substantive action taken by Moscow and its Eastern European allies, except Romania, during the war was to break diplomatic relations with Israel. Yet paradoxically, the aftermath of the war was to see Soviet gains in the region, although they were to prove temporary. One of the major results of the war was further radicalization of the Arab world and a concomitant weakening of the U.S. position in the area. Egypt, Syria, Algeria, and Iraq all broke diplomatic relations with the United States because of alleged U.S. aid to Israel during the war, and in 1969 there was a further deterioration of the U.S. position, as a left-wing regime came to power in the Sudan and the pro-Western regime of Libya's King Idris was overthrown.

Meanwhile, by quickly resupplying Egypt and Syria with the weaponry that restored their military credibility and championing Arab demands at the United Nations, the Soviet Union was able to restore its position in the Arab world. Nonetheless, the Soviet position was not without its problems, since the Arab-Israeli conflict, which had been relatively subdued in the 1957–66 period, now became a central issue not only in the Middle East, but also in world politics. In selecting its policy for this now highly salient issue, the Soviet leadership was faced with a dilemma. On the one hand, they wanted to continue to weaken Western influence in the Arab world while enhancing Soviet influence. On the other hand, however, with the main Arab interest now in regaining the lands lost to Israel in the 1967 war, the Soviet Union risked the possibility of direct confrontation with the United States, which by now was sending Israel advanced weaponry (hitherto France had been Israel's main supplier) and had taken a more overtly pro-Israeli position. The dilemma may have appeared particularly serious for the Soviets after the March 1969 border clashes with China signaled a further escalation of the Sino-Soviet conflict.

Meanwhile as Moscow was seeking to rebuild its position in the Middle East, for the first time Soviet Jews began to take independent action themselves, a development that was to discomfit both the Soviet leadership and, to a lesser degree, the government of Israel itself, long the champion of Soviet Jewry, which was initially unsure how to handle this new phenomenon of Soviet Jewish activism.

Heartened by Israel's victory in the June 1967 war, an event that restored their Jewish national pride and proved that Israel was a viable state, and convinced that liberalization in the USSR was no longer possible after the invasion of Czechoslovakia, activists among Soviet Jews began to apply to emigrate to Israel. The Brezhnev regime, perhaps spurred by its two bloody border skirmishes with China in March 1969 (and possibly hoping that once bereft of leaders the Jewish emigration movement would die down), permitted more than 2,000 Soviet Jews to leave in 1969. This may have been a calculated effort to gain Western support, or at least neutrality, in case the Sino-Soviet border battles were to escalate into a more serious confrontation.

As more Soviet Jews applied to emigrate in 1970, however, the Soviet leadership changed its policy, holding a series of "show trials" that appeared aimed both at stemming the flow of valuable scientists and engineers, which the regime could not afford to lose, and also at deterring other Soviet Jews from emigrating. By the spring of 1970 the Sino-Soviet border confrontation had diminished, and Soviet fears of a Sino-American alliance directed against the USSR may have been reduced by the American invasion of Cambodia. These developments may have encouraged the Russians both to stage the show trials and to cut Soviet Jewish emigration in half during 1970. Nevertheless, the show trials were ultimately to prove counterproductive to the Soviet leaders, and emigration was soon to rise again.

The first show trial opened in Leningrad in December 1970.[23] The defendants were a group of Soviet Jews who, having been refused exit visas to Israel, had allegedly conspired to hijack a plane (the hijacking never took place). The Jews were quickly found guilty and the two alleged leaders were given the death penalty. The international outcry that greeted the death sentences and the trial itself forced the Soviet leaders to commute the sentences to long prison terms. It also had the effect of bringing the Soviet Jewish emigration question to the forefront of public attention in the United States and Western Europe, and this in turn resulted in an international conference on Soviet Jewry in Brussels in February 1971.

The Brussels Conference, which could only further tarnish the Soviet image in the West (the USSR had not yet overcome the stigma of invading Czechoslovakia), was not the only problem facing the Soviet leadership in early 1971. Riots had broken out in Communist Poland in December 1970 as Polish workers had demonstrated in the streets in reaction to the Gomulka regime's decision to raise the prices of consumer goods. The disorders led to the fall of Gomulka and his replacement by Edward Gierek, and the Soviet Union was compelled to give Poland a large loan to help the country overcome the economic difficulties that had precipitated the crisis.[24]

It seems clear that the Soviet leaders, observing the riots in Poland, were concerned that a similar development might occur in the USSR where consumer goods were also of poor quality and in limited supply. Soviet leaders may have believed that popular unrest could be averted by Soviet imports of Western goods and technology, preferably on a long-term, low-interest, credit basis. It also may have seemed advisable to set some limits on the strategic arms race between the United States and the USSR so as to conserve scarce Soviet resources.

Given the fact that the Soviet economy was only one-half the size of the American economy and that, unlike the United States, all of the

Soviet Union's resources are committed every year, it appeared that a strategic arms agreement would be considerably more valuable to the USSR than to the United States. Reportedly, President Nixon tried to exploit this situation by indicating, in a series of messages to Brezhnev beginning in early 1971, that the United States might be willing to help assist the Soviet economy if the USSR would make concessions in a number of political areas, such as Vietnam and the strategic arms negotiations.[25] It was, therefore, perhaps not coincidental that in a major speech to the 24th Party Congress in April 1971 Brezhnev pledged a significant increase in consumer goods production[26] and that one month later the USSR made a major concession to stimulate strategic arms negotiations.[27]

In the interim however, the Soviet-Jewish activists had not been idle. Undeterred by the Leningrad hijack trial, a number of Soviet Jews staged a sit-in at the Soviet Parliament in March 1971—just before the opening of the 24th Party Congress when a large number of foreign newsmen were in Moscow.[28] As a result of their action, the activists obtained a conference with a general from the Soviet Ministry of the Interior (which handles emigration visas), and many were later permitted to leave the Soviet Union. Interestingly, while many of the sit-in activists were allowed to leave, the Brezhnev leadership, perhaps still unsure as to the proper way to deal with the emigration problem, staged another set of show trials in May and June. Nonetheless, this form of intimidation came to an end in July, and a major reappraisal of Soviet foreign policy was made necessary when Henry Kissinger made a surprise visit to Peking—the first official visit of a representative of an American administration since the Communist takeover of China in 1949. Kissinger's visit may well have aroused the concern of the Soviet leadership that the long-feared Sino-American alliance was now a real possibility. This concern, coupled with the large demonstrations on behalf of Soviet Jewry that greeted Kosygin on his trip to the West in the early fall of 1971, may have been the impetus that prompted Soviet leaders to allow a massive increase in the emigration of Soviet Jews in the last three months of 1971—from about two hundred per month in the first three quarters of 1971 to three thousand per month by December.

The Soviet-Jewish exodus continued through the first seven months of 1972 as Nixon visited both Peking and Moscow. During his visit to the Soviet capital, Nixon signed a strategic arms limitation agreement (SALT I) and made a commitment to increase Soviet-American trade.

Meanwhile, Soviet leaders encountered a number of severe problems. In addition to the specter of a Sino-American alliance, they were confronted with the worst harvest since 1963. Thus, they were forced to begin negotiations for a major grain purchase from the United States.[29] In addition, two months after the Nixon-Brezhnev Moscow summit of May 1972 in which the Middle East received little mention, the Russians were ejected from their air and naval bases in Egypt by Egypt's new President Anwar Sadat (Nasser had died in September 1970), an action that weakened their strategic position in the eastern Mediterranean. While the flow of Soviet Jews to Israel was not the cause of Sadat's decision to expel the Russians (Sadat had been unhappy with the lack of Soviet military support for his confrontation with Israel),[30] it is clear that the increasing exodus of Soviet Jews to Israel, many of whom were of military age and possessing technical skills useful to the Israeli economy, was very unpopular with the Arabs.

Soon after the Soviet departure from Egypt, the Brezhnev regime imposed a prohibitively expensive head tax on educated Soviet Jews seeking to emigrate to Israel.[31] This move may have been aimed both at soothing Arab feelings at a time when the Soviet position in the Middle East was deteriorating and at increasing the likelihood of securing Western funding for the expensive Western technology the USSR needed. It also may have been another attempt to deter Soviet-Jewish scientists and technicians from emigrating. Or, as Brezhnev himself reportedly stated, it may have been a "bureaucratic bungle."[32] Whatever the cause, the head tax precipitated a very strong American reaction, spearheaded by Senator Henry Jackson who sought to tie the exodus of Soviet Jews to the trade benefits (most favored nation treatment on Soviet exports and United States credits) sought by Soviet leadership in an agreement that was to be signed by the Nixon administration in October 1972 but that needed congressional ratification to become law. The Soviet Union's change of its position on the head tax was to be the most important example yet of Soviet sensitivity to Western concern on the emigration issue.[33] As congressional support for what became known as the Jackson Amendment to the trade bill began to rise, the Soviet leaders made a series of concessions. They exempted émigrés over the age of fifty-five from paying the head tax and reduced the required payment for others by the number of years a prospective emigrant had worked for the state. In addition, a number of Jews were allowed to leave without paying the tax. As the chief of the Soviet Ministry of the Interior's visa department told a group of Soviet-Jewish activists, "the waiver of the exit tax in certain cases was not a change in the authorities' approach to the emigration problem, but a gesture toward a certain foreign power with which the USSR is seeking to develop commercial and economic relations."[34]

Gestures alone, however, did not suffice to quell the rising tide of congressional support for the Jackson Amendment, particularly since the head tax had been adopted as a Soviet law in December 1972. During a trip to the United States the following February, the top Soviet expert on the United States, Georgi Arbatov, and Soviet Deputy Foreign Trade Minister V. S. Akhimov learned firsthand of congressional support for the Jackson Amendment. One month later U.S. Treasury Secretary George Shultz met with Soviet leaders in Moscow and conveyed the same message. Presumably by this time Brezhnev understood the situation, because four days after the Shultz visit the Soviet leadership permitted forty-four university-educated Soviet Jews to depart the Soviet Union without paying the head tax. This action was explained several days later by Viktor Louis, a Soviet "journalist" with close ties to the KGB, who stated in an article in the Israeli newspaper *Yediot Ahronot* that due to congressional pressure the head tax would "no longer be operative, although it would not be cancelled or changed."[35]

This concession, subject to reversal at any time, did not stop the momentum of the Jackson Amendment. Nor did calls for "quiet diplomacy" by the Nixon administration, which, on a number of occasions, demonstrated a greater interest in détente than in human rights. However, Brezhnev went on to make a number of highly optimistic statements about the development of Soviet-American trade at the April 1973 meeting of the Communist party's Central Committee, so it appeared that the Soviet leadership was willing to make concessions on the emigration of Soviet Jewry to obtain the benefits of American trade and technology.[36]

Unfortunately for the Russians, Soviet-American détente received a number of blows in the latter part of 1973. In September of that year the noted Soviet physicist and dissident Andrei Sakharov spoke out against détente unless it was accompanied by democratization in the Soviet Union. One month later came the Yom Kippur war in which the Soviet leadership acted to enhance its own position in the Middle East and undermine the United States position.[37] It did so by organizing an air and sea lift of weaponry to Syria and Egypt, by urging all the other Arab states to aid the Syrians and Egyptians in the conflict with Israel, by supporting the Arab oil embargo against the United States, and by opposing American initiatives for a cease-fire until the Arabs began to lose. These Soviet actions caused many Americans to begin to doubt the wisdom of détente and to question a number of the Nixon administration's policies toward the USSR, including its offers of massive credits. This concern was transformed in 1974 into what became known as the Stevenson Amendment to the trade bill.

The Stevenson Amendment limited American credits to the USSR to a total of $300 million and also prohibited credits for the production of Soviet gas and oil.[38] This was a major blow to the Soviet leadership, which had hoped for multibillion dollar credits from the United States, including up to $40 billion in credits to develop Soviet oil and natural gas reserves in Siberia.[39] While the Stevenson Amendment stipulated that the credit ceiling could be lifted by the president if he determined it to be in the "national interest," congressional approval was required for such an action, and Stevenson himself stated that this approval would be dependent on Soviet concessions, not only concerning Soviet-Jewish emigration, but also concerning the Middle East, arms control, and other areas of Soviet-American relations.[40] Having been shown by Soviet behavior in the Yom Kippur war that the Soviet leaders would not hesitate to violate either the spirit or the substance of détente if such action would benefit the Soviet Union's world position, Stevenson and the majority of other senators were determined to oppose the subsidization of the Soviet Union's economy without clear political concessions in return. It is important to note that while the Soviet leaders appeared willing to live with the Jackson Amendment, and even apparently worked out a formula for Jewish emigration via Kissinger's mediation, which both they and Jackson seemed to agree to, these concessions were predicated on the USSR's receipt of sizable American economic credits. When faced by the rigid credit limitations of the Stevenson Amendment in January 1975, the Soviet leaders repudiated the trade agreement they had reached with the Nixon Administration in 1972.[41]

The Soviet leadership did not terminate Jewish emigration after repudiating the trade agreement. However, the 1975 emigration total of 13,000 was only about one-third the record level of 1973. Moscow's willingness to continue emigration, albeit at a reduced rate (the 1973 war and its aftermath also may have made Israel appear less desirable in the eyes of Soviet Jews), may have been due to three factors. First, there was a new American president, Gerald Ford, who had committed himself personally on the issue of Soviet Jewry. Indeed, according to Senator

Jacob Javits, who together with Senator Jackson and Senator Abraham Ribicoff had visited Ford soon after Nixon's resignation, the new president had given his assurances that he would personally hold the Soviet Union to account for more humane emigration policies.[42] Second, another strategic arms limitation agreement was being negotiated (a preliminary arrangement had been worked out by Ford and Brezhnev at their November 1974 summit meeting at Vladivostok), and the Soviet leadership continued to put high priority on getting the agreement formally accepted. Third, the Soviet leaders wanted to hold a European security conference to ratify the postwar division of Europe, and they were compelled to give at least lip service to the principle of emigration for purposes of family reunification in order to get the Western powers to sign what has become known as the Helsinki Agreement. Soviet leaders also appeared not to have given up hope of getting credits from the United States, which in 1975 was beset by a severe recession. The Soviets may have felt that domestic economic pressure in the United States might encourage the Ford administration to grant credits to the Soviet Union in order to put unemployed American workers back to work. Indeed, despite the Soviet repudiation of the trade agreement, Soviet-American trade increased sharply in 1975 and 1976.[43] Given this overall situation, elimination of the Jewish emigration would have been counterproductive to the larger Soviet interest.

Thus, Soviet-Jewish emigration continued at a reduced rate throughout the Ford administration, although it was to rise somewhat at the end of 1976 as a possible signal to Jimmy Carter who had been elected president in November.

Meanwhile, as Soviet Jewish emigration was having its ups and downs while Soviet-Israeli relations remained highly strained, the Israeli government was demonstrating a certain amount of uncertainty as to how to handle the Soviet-Jewry problem. The so-called Israeli office without a name, originally headed by Shaul Avigur, who was succeeded by the controversial Nehemiah Levanon in January 1970, sought to aid Jews attempting to emigrate from Communist states. While American advocates of the cause of Soviet Jewry were calling for the publication of Soviet Jewish "open letters" and appeals for support, Levanon's office preferred to work via "quiet diplomacy"—ironically, calling for the same tactic that both Kissinger and Nixon urged during the discussions over the Jackson Amendment.[44] By November 1969, however, Israel switched policy as Prime Minister Golda Meir released an appeal that had been addressed to her and to the u.n. Human Rights Commission by eighteen Georgian Jewish families seeking to emigrate.[45] Israel's representative to the u.n., Yosef Tekoah, followed this up by transmitting the appeal to the u.n. secretary general and requesting that it be circulated as a u.n. document. Not unexpectedly, Moscow denounced the Israeli move.

Nonetheless, although it was now taking a more public role in supporting the cause of Soviet Jewry, the Israeli government, or at least Levanon's office, remained uncomfortable with American Jewry taking a more activist role on behalf of Soviet Jewry than Levanon thought wise. Differences of opinion became exacerbated when the nonestablishment Union of Councils for Soviet Jews (ucsj) was formed. While the establishment Jewish community at that time was willing to follow the lead of the Israeli government on matters pertaining to Soviet Jewry (as with other matters relating to Zionism), the ucsj was not, with the result that Dr. Louis Rosenblum, of the Cleveland Committee on Soviet Anti-Semitism, felt constrained to send a stiff letter to the then Israeli ambassador to the United States, Yitzhak Rabin:

On the assumption that you are not fully apprised of this matter, we wish to convey to you our concern with the behavior of a member of the Israeli Diplomatic Service, Dr. Yoram Dinstein, in what appears to be an overzealous discharge of his instructions.

During the past seven years, I, and others, have had occasional substantive differences with Meir Rosenne and Nechemiah Levanon. These differences, however, have not engendered the tiresome bullying tactics employed by Dr. Dinstein. For example, in a telephone call to me on March 29, 1968 (my reference is a transcript of the conversation taken by my secretary on an extension line), Dr. Dinstein summarily accused me of encouraging a rabbinical student, Hillel Levine, to disrupt the AJCSJ Biennial Conference. He threatened "I shall see to it that my government destroys you." On March 1 1970, during a discussion concerning the formation of the Union of Councils for Soviet Jews, and in the presence of Abe Bayer, Zev Yaroslavsky, and Harold Miller, Dr. Dinstein advised me, "I shall see that you are destroyed."

In addition to his intemperate speech, Dr. Dinstein has acted in a manner to suggest interference by your government in American Jewish affairs. For instance, during the Midwest Conference on Soviet Jewry held in Cleveland on February 28 and March 1 of this

year, Dr. Dinstein's public coaching and manipulation . . . was so
flagrant as to become a topic of conversation among the attendees.
And, more recently, it has come to our attention that Dr. Dinstein
has fomented the discharge of Zev Yaroslavsky from his position
with the Jewish Federation Council of Greater Los Angeles. Dr.
Dinstein's behavior is calculated to exacerbate the issue of Israeli
control of American Jewish organizations raised on the pages of
the *New York Times* last month by Mr. Phelps. Certainly, in view
of the above, there will be interest in observing the role played by
the Israeli government representative at the forthcoming West Coast
Conference on Soviet Jewry.[46]

The sharp upsurge in Soviet Jewish emigration after 1971 temporarily put an end to the clash between Israel and elements of the
American Jewish community over policy on the Soviet Jewish question,
but it was to reappear in 1976. By this time there was a marked change
in the pattern of Soviet Jewish emigration. While in the initial years of
the mass emigration (1971–73) the vast majority of emigrating Jews
went to Israel, by 1976 almost half were going elsewhere or "dropping
out" in the Israeli parlance. Israeli officials, calling these "drop outs" by
the derogatory name *noshrim,* warned that if this pattern continued Moscow would cut off emigration. At the same time the Israeli officials
asserted that the reason why the Soviet Jews were choosing to go to the
United States instead of Israel was not because of any deficiencies in
Israeli society or because of the threat of war in the Middle East or
because of Israel's bureaucratic ineptitude in resettling the emigrants,
but because the American-Jewish Joint Distribution Committee (JDC)
(ironically, the same organization tied by Stalin to the "Doctor's Plot")
and the Hebrew Immigrant Aid Society (HIAS) were offering them greater
economic incentives to go to the United States. A debate ensued, and
many American Jewish leaders, including those in the establishment,
opposed the policy urged by the Israeli government to compel Soviet
Jews to go to Israel. When a joint U.S.-Israeli committee recommended
terminating American Jewish aid to the *noshrim,* the boards of the JDC
and HIAS rejected the suggestions,[47] thus for the first time demonstrating
the American Jewish establishment's opposition to an Israeli policy
preference on Soviet Jewry.

The issue of the *noshrim* faded somewhat into the background during the period of the Carter presidency as emigration shot up from

14,261 in 1976 to 51,320 in 1979 (despite the U.S.-sponsored Camp David agreements) as Moscow sought a new strategic arms agreement, along with U.S. trade and grain benefits, and sought to prevent the formation of a Sino-American alignment.[48] Emigration dropped off sharply, however, following the Soviet invasion of Afghanistan, and the subsequent rapid deterioration of Soviet-American relations, and continued into the Reagan administration whose first year (1981) saw only 9,447 Jews permitted to emigrate. Under these circumstances the Israeli government, led by Jewish Agency Chairman Aryeh Dulzin and Prime Minister Menachem Begin, asserted that the reason for the decline in the emigration of Soviet Jews was the fact that a high proportion were "dropping out"—not going to Israel—and that the Soviet government was angered by the dropout phenomenon because the visas that it issued were for Israel. Many others strongly disputed the assertion of the Israeli leaders, pointing out that the decline in the Jewish exodus from the USSR reflected the deterioration in Soviet-American relations and noting that the emigration of Soviet Germans and Soviet Armenians had been equally severely restricted, though in neither of these cases was "dropping out" a factor.

Nonetheless, the Israeli government succeeded in persuading HIAS to withhold assistance to émigrés choosing not to go to Israel unless they had a first degree relative (spouse, parent, child) elsewhere. While HIAS went along with the plan in mid-December 1981, there were clearly mixed feelings in the organization, and, as a result, HIAS agreed only to withhold support for a three-month trial basis, beginning in 1982, to see whether the decline in emigration would be reversed, as the Israeli government had asserted. In fact, the monthly total of emigrants continued to drop, from 434 in December 1981 to only 288 in April 1982. The end result was that HIAS, in early May 1982, seeing that the Israeli officials were incorrect, returned to its traditional policy of aiding all Soviet Jews who, upon arriving in Vienna, opted to go to countries other than Israel.

Another Soviet-Jewish issue that proved divisive in the world Jewish community during this period was the postponement of the Third International Conference on Soviet Jewry, originally scheduled for Paris in October 1982. The lingering impact of the Israeli invasion of Lebanon and diplomatic difficulties between Israel and France (particularly between Prime Minister Begin and French President Mitterrand) led the Israeli government to urge a rescheduling and relocating of the conference to Jerusalem in March 1983. While Jewish leaders from other countries acquiesced, they were clearly unhappy both because a number of prominent world leaders had already agreed to address the Paris meeting and because they perceived that the scheduling of the conference in a European capital would have given the appearance of more universal support for the cause of Soviet Jewry.[49]

The dispute over the *noshrim* continued during the Jerusalem conference as Aryeh Dulzin, despite an explicit promise to the executive director of the National Conference on Soviet Jewry that no mention would be made of the *noshrim* issue in order to preserve unity, again loudly condemned the *noshrim*. A spirited debate ensued with many American Jewish leaders once again pitted against their Israeli counterparts on the *noshrim* issue.[50] Meanwhile, as might be expected, Moscow reacted negatively to the Jerusalem conference and set up an "anti-Zionist" committee which seemed to sound the death knell for the Soviet Jewish exodus. Emigration plummeted to only 1,315 in 1983 and continued to decline throughout 1984, dropping to only twenty-nine in October, the lowest monthly total in fifteen years.[51] The drop in emigration once again caused a questioning of Israel's tactics vis-à-vis the USSR, this time within Israel itself. In a parliamentary debate in October 1984, one month after Israel's National Unity government took office, Geulah Cohen, who represents the opposition Tehiyah party, and Rabbi Menachem Hacohen, of the government's Labour Alignment party, raised serious questions about Israeli policy on the Soviet Jewry issue. Hacohen went so far as to criticize Israel's "office without a name" for presuming "that only it and no one else, not even the former (Soviet) aliyah activists know how the struggle should be conducted." For her part Geulah Cohen charged that the "hush hush" policy of the Israeli government was not helping the Soviet Jewish activists trying to leave the USSR.[52]

The Gorbachev Era—a New Beginning?

The domestic debate in Israel was at least temporarily stilled, however, by the advent of Mikhail Gorbachev to the leadership of the Soviet Union in March 1985. Soon after taking power, Gorbachev sent a number of signals to Israel indicating that not only might a resumption in diplomatic relations between the USSR and Israel be possible, but that Moscow might also consider increasing the number of Soviet Jews being allowed to leave the USSR. Thus for the first time since 1967 *Izvestia* published a message from an Israeli president as Chaim Herzog congratulated the USSR for its role in defeating Nazism and declared that the Jewish people would never forget "the huge contribution made by the Red Army to the final rout of the Nazi scum in Europe and its assistance in liberating Jews still remaining alive from the concentration camps."[53] Given the fact that the Soviet propaganda media had long equated Israeli and Nazi activities, and had even accused Zionists of actively aiding the Nazis, the publication of this message seemed to be a major reversal of Soviet policy. Then, at the end of July the Israeli and Soviet ambassadors to France discussed the reestablishment of diplomatic relations and the renewal of large-scale emigration of Soviet Jews. According to the version of the talks broadcast over Israeli radio, the Soviet ambassador, Yuly Vorontsov, told his Israeli counterpart, Ovadia Sofer, that diplomatic relations could be restored if there was at least a partial Israeli withdrawal on the Golan Heights and if Moscow was invited to participate in an international peace conference on the Middle East and that large-scale emigration of Soviet Jews could take place if they emigrated to Israel and not the United States and if Israel ended the anti-Soviet propaganda it was undertaking in the United States and Europe.[54]

In looking for an explanation for this change in Soviet policy, it would appear that it was caused more than merely by a change in Soviet leadership. Not only was Moscow looking to improve its relations with the United States (hence the call for a stop to anti-Soviet propaganda by Israel in the United States), but the on-again, off-again Arab-Israeli peace process in which the United States played a leading role, seemed again on track. Thus, following the coming to power of moderate Israeli leader Shimon Peres in mid-September 1984, Jordan reestablished diplomatic relations with Egypt two weeks later (thus, in part legitimizing the Camp David agreements), and in February 1985 King Hussein and PLO leader Yasser Arafat agreed to a joint negotiating strategy vis-à-vis Israel. Throughout the spring and early summer of 1985 the United States was working to bring about negotiations between Israel and a joint Palestinian-Jordanian negotiating team, while at the same time Hussein and Arafat were seeking to get the August Arab summit at Casablanca to raitfy their agreement. Moscow was clearly concerned that the United States might succeed in making arrangements for a Palestinian-Jordanian delegation, which, openly supported by Egypt and tacitly backed by Iraq, might move quickly toward a peace agreement with Israel as all sides understood that Labor party leader Shimon Peres, who was willing to make compromises on the West Bank, had little more than a year left as prime minister before he had to turn power over to the hard-line Likud leader, Yitzhak Shamir, as part of the National Unity government agreement.[55] Under the circumstances Moscow, which clearly wanted to play a major role in Middle Eastern politics, felt it had to make some approach to Israel in the hope that it could gain Jerusalem's permission to participate in a Middle East peace conference, particularly since the United States in a statement at the end of May 1985 noted that if the USSR wanted to play a role in the Middle East peace process, it had to display "constructive behavior," such as the resumption of full diplomatic relations with Israel and improving the treatment of Soviet Jews, including their right to emigrate.[56]

Yet the Soviet hint of renewed relations, while welcome in Israel, was received in a highly negative way by Moscow's Arab allies, especially Syria. Syria, the USSR's main bastion in the Arab world, was incensed that the USSR would consider renewing ties with Israel while even part of the Golan Heights seized during the 1967 war remained in Israeli hands. As a result, the USSR in both official visits and radio broadcasts to the Arab world repeated the old Soviet position that diplomatic relations would not be restored until Israel gave up all the land conquered in 1967.[57] At the same time, however, while it was pleased that the Casablanca Arab summit had not formally endorsed the Hussein-Arafat agreement, Moscow continued to hint to Israel that relations could be restored if Israel agreed to Moscow's inclusion in a Middle East peace conference.[58]

For his part Peres also seemed to fluctuate in his comments about the USSR, one day demanding restored diplomatic relations as the price for Moscow's entry into the Middle East peace process, but on the next stating that it would be enough if Moscow allowed large numbers of Soviet Jews to emigrate to Israel. Meanwhile, Edgar Bronfman, head of the World Jewish Congress, traveled to Moscow in September, a visit that further spurred rumors about a breakthrough in Soviet-Israeli relations, including the possibility of 20,000 Jews leaving the USSR and flying directly to Israel.[59] The end result of this diplomatic dance was a Soviet gesture to Israel in the form of an agreement between its close Eastern European ally, Poland, and Israel, whereby the two countries agreed to establish "interest sections" in foreign embassies in each other's capitals—the first stage in the process of reestablishing diplomatic relations.[60] While Moscow was not yet resuming diplomatic ties itself, this was a clear gesture that it was prepared to so do, and Gorbachev, during his visit to Paris in early October, noted "as far as re-establishing relations (with Israel) is concerned, I think the faster the situation is normalized in the Middle East, the faster it will be possible to look at this question."[61]

So matters stood until the Israeli attack on PLO headquarters in Tunis (following a terrorist attack which killed three Israelis in Cyprus) and in particular the hijacking of the cruise ship Achille Lauro in mid-October seemed to upset the Middle East peace process. With the PLO and its leader, Yasser Arafat, at least indirectly involved (the master-mind of the hijacking, Mohammed Abbas, was a close ally of Arafat), Israeli leader Shimon Peres sought to capitalize on the hijacking to ex-clude the PLO from the peace process. Negotiations between Israel and Jordan had stalemated by early fall because of Israel's unwillingness to allow known PLO supporters to participate in the joint Palestinian-Jordanian negotiating committee, and with Jordan seen as too weak to enter into the peace talks by itself, Peres, in a speech to the U.N., agreed to "international auspices" for the peace talks—the type of international cover which Peres may well have thought Jordan needed to allow it to participate in direct negotiations with Israel.

Yet this move by Peres was not to prove successful. On the one hand it aroused a storm of protest from the Likud party, one of whose leaders, Arik Sharon, almost brought down the Israeli government with his charge that Israel was making a secret deal with Jordan. On the other hand Jordan did not move to embrace the Peres offer; instead, it moved toward its erstwhile enemy Syria and publicly eschewed a partial settle-ment. Under these circumstances the chances for peace appeared to recede and on the eve of the Reagan-Gorbachev summit in November Moscow was able to take a harder line on reestablishing ties with Israel, this time demanding that Israel first agree not only to allow the USSR to partici-pate in the international peace conference but also to allow the PLO to participate as well.[62] Perhaps because of this condition Peres again shifted his position and now stated that the resumption of the Soviet Jewish emigration from the USSR (aliyah) was more important than the restoration of diplomatic ties. "If they agreed to renew aliya," he stated, "we shall waive our objections to their taking part in an international conference on the Middle East."[63]

Peres thus presented Moscow with an interesting choice. As far as its position in the Arab world is concerned, it is far less costly for Mos-cow to release Soviet Jews than it is for it to reestablish ties with Israel, and Moscow has long wanted to participate in an international conference on the Arab-Israeli crisis. Yet it was doubtful whether the USSR would settle for just a symbolic role in an international conference—the most Israel seemed to be ready to concede in return for Moscow sharply increasing the number of Jews allowed to leave the Soviet Union. Indeed, Moscow took an increasingly hard line toward Israel after the summit.

Yet Moscow's harder-line policy toward Israel may have had additional causes. Arab leaders, perhaps remembering the 1972 Nixon-Brezhnev summit, seemed concerned that a superpower deal might be worked out at their expense,[64] and Reagan's presummit demand for linkage between an arms control agreement and Soviet behavior in the Third World may have heightened Soviet determination to prove that no such deal had taken place.[65] Indeed, in a spate of articles appearing in the Soviet media at the time of the summit, including Arabic language radio broadcasts and Novosti statements distributed in Beirut, the USSR dismissed as "fabrications and lies" claims that Arab interests would be compromised at Geneva.[66]

Nonetheless, despite Moscow's hardening rhetoric and the slow pace of the negotiations between Israel and Poland on the setting up of interest sections, Peres did not give up hope. Indeed the attendance of Israel's President Chaim Herzog at the National Convention of Israel's Communist party in early December, the first time an Israeli president had ever attended such a function, was a clear gesture to Moscow that Jerusalem was interested in continuing a dialogue with the USSR.[67] The head of the Soviet delegation to the party conference, Mikhail Menashev, stated, however, that Herzog's attendance at the convention would not influence Russia's policy on the exit of Soviet Jews or hasten the renewal of diplomatic ties.[68] Then, in mid-February 1986 when King Hussein denounced the PLO leadership for failing to move ahead in the peace process, the split between Arafat and Hussein intensified, and Soviet fears of an American-orchestrated Arab-Israeli peace agreement receded further, at least for the short term. Under the circumstances it appeared unlikely that Moscow would have to satisfy either of Israel's demands since the possibility of a Middle East peace conference greatly diminished.

Meanwhile, notwithstanding Moscow's flirtation with Israel, the condition of Soviet Jewry worsened during Gorbachev's first year. Despite the release of such well-known Soviet refuseniks as Anatoly Sharansky, Grigory and Isai Goldstein, and Eliahu Essas, the number of Soviet Jews allowed to leave the USSR plummeted, reaching a low of 47 during March 1986—the anniversary of Gorbachev's coming to power. At the same time Soviet pressure on Jews seeking to emigrate was stepped up, and nine Jewish activists were arrested and imprisoned.

The drop in the Soviet Jewish exodus in March 1986 may have reflected the decline in Soviet interest in the Middle East, as did Gorbachev's speech to the 27th Party Congress of the CPSU in February. If one takes Gorbachev's speech as a programmatic listing of his priorities, the Third World was low on his list and the Arab-Israeli conflict barely mentioned. This was in clear contrast with Brezhnev's speeches at previous party congresses where the Middle East received a great deal of attention and certain Arab countries, such as Syria, were singled out for praise. Gorbachev did, however, refer to the Middle East as one of the world's "hotbeds of the danger of war."[69]

Nonetheless, if Gorbachev was seeking to downplay the importance of the Middle East, the region, and particularly the Arab-Israeli conflict, again soon demonstrated its importance for Moscow. In the first place Syrian-Israeli relations again heated up in 1986, and there were an increasing number of press reports that war would break out between the two countries. Contributing to the heightened tension were the Syrian decision to construct a series of artillery and tank emplacements near Israel's security zone in South Lebanon, Israel's forcing down of a Libyan plane which contained high-ranking Syrian Ba'ath party officials (instead of the PLO terrorists Israel was seeking) and perhaps most important of all the direct Syrian linkage to terrorist attempts to blow up Israeli civilian airplanes in London and Madrid.

But it was not only the Syrian linkage with terrorism that posed problems for Gorbachev. After a minicrisis in January 1986 when the United States blamed Libya for terrorist attacks in Rome and Vienna in late December 1985, two military confrontations between the United States and Libya took place (in March and April 1986). During the U.S.-Libyan crisis of January 1986, the then Soviet Foreign Ministry spokesman, Vladimir Lomeiko, in refusing to answer a press conference question on what the stand of the USSR would be if the United States attacked Libya, noted only that Soviet actions were aimed at "preventing conflicts," not at "constructing scenarios for their escalation."[70] The same Lomeiko, at a Moscow press briefing on March 25 after the first U.S. attack on Libya, noted only that the USSR had provided "moral and political support" to the Libyan people and would take "all measures appropriate within the framework of existing treaties."[71] The absence of any promised *military* support in Lomeiko's statement and the fact that the USSR still had no formal treaty pledging Moscow to come to Qaddafi's aid demonstrated, however, that the USSR was not willing to back up Qaddafi with more than words, and this was again shown during and after the more extensive American raid on April 15. Indeed, the most that Moscow would do at the time was postpone (and only temporarily) a scheduled Shultz-Shevardnadze meeting—a minimal action that could not have impressed many Arab states.

In the aftermath of the U.S. bombing of Libya for its alleged terrorist activities, Moscow could not be certain the United States would refrain from taking action against Syria, another sponsor of terrorism. An American—or an American-backed Israeli—punitive strike against Syria would again raise serious questions of Soviet credibility if Moscow did not aid its Middle Eastern ally in such a situation (especially after its failure to aid Libya). However, if Moscow went to Syria's aid, there would be a very real possibility of a superpower confrontation. Given these unpalatable alternatives, Gorbachev seems to have decided to move diplomatically to avert the possibility of such a clash by both publicly cautioning Libya and Syria against terrorism in order not to give "the imperialists" any pretexts for attacks and also by negotiating seriously with Israel to arrange consular-level talks in Helsinki, and also acceding to Israel's demand to make the talks public.[72] The latter diplomatic ploy, Moscow may well have felt, would deter an Israeli attack on Syria, lest it harm a possible improvement of Soviet-Israeli relations which in turn held out the possibility of an increase in the number of Soviet Jews being allowed to leave the USSR.

A second Middle East development that may have contributed to Moscow's decision to initiate public contacts with Israel was the USSR's efforts to play a role in the Middle East peace process. Following Jordanian King Hussein's split with Arafat in February 1986, Moscow sought to exploit the new diplomatic situation by calling for a preparatory committee made up of the u.n. Security Council's five permanent members to prepare for an international conference on the Middle East.[73] When in late July, however, Israeli Prime Minister Shimon Peres and Moroccan King Hassan had a surprise meeting in Morocco, Moscow may have become concerned that it would once again be left on the diplomatic sidelines as a major peace initiative unfolded. (The last surprise summit, it will be recalled, was Sadat's visit to Jerusalem in November 1977 which led to the Camp David agreements less than a year later.) To avert this possibility, therefore, Moscow may also have agreed to public diplomatic talks with Israel.

A third contributing factor behind Moscow's request for consular talks may have been the Soviet desire to improve ties with the United States. It would not appear accidental that the Soviet announcement of consular talks with Israel on August 4 coincided with the announcement of the scheduling of the September 19 and 20 meeting between U.S. Secretary of State George Shultz and Soviet Foreign Minister Edward Shevardnadze to prepare for a U.S.-Soviet summit. (The earlier meeting had been postponed by Moscow, it will be remembered, because of the American bombing of Libya in April.) The nuclear disaster in Chernobyl, the precipitous drop in world oil prices (more than 60 percent of Soviet hard currency earnings come from oil and natural gas sales), Gorbachev's efforts to restructure the Soviet economy, and the major economic difficulties facing the USSR were all factors moving the Soviet leadership toward an arms control agreement that would prevent another expensive spiraling of the arms race. For this reason Gorbachev sought a second summit with the United States, and, given Moscow's tendency to overestimate Jewish influence in the United States, the new Soviet leader may well have felt that the gesture to Israel would help pave the way for the summit.

Nonetheless, the Soviet-Israeli talks in Helsinki, the first such official diplomatic negotiations between the two countries since the 1967 war, did not immediately produce the results either side said it wanted, although the symbolic significance of the talks was probably much more important than their content. While the Soviets wished to send a team of officials to inventory Soviet property (primarily owned by the Russian Orthodox church) in Israel, the Israeli delegation, under heavy domestic pressure from such individuals as Moshe Arens and Anatoly Sharansky, raised the issue of Soviet Jewry at the talks, and the meeting ended after ninety minutes.[74] Nonetheless, the very fact that the talks were held, and the fact that one month later Israeli Prime Minister Peres and Soviet Foreign Minister Shevardnadze held detailed (and apparently cordial) negotiations at the United Nations,[75] as well as subsequent meetings between the Soviet and Israeli ambassadors to the United States, all indicated that the Soviet Union was keeping alive its contacts with Israel.

Following the Shevardnadze-Peres meeting came the Reykjavik summit between Reagan and Gorbachev, the second summit between the

Soviet and American leaders in less than two years. No arms control agreement was reached at the summit, primarily because Gorbachev linked such an agreement to the termination of the American Strategic Defense initiative; nonetheless, the issue of Soviet Jewry was emphasized by Reagan at the summit,[76] thus reminding the Soviet leader that one of the ways Moscow could demonstrate its desire for an improved relationship with the United States was to permit an increase in the number of Soviet Jews allowed to leave the USSR. Secretary of State Shultz's participation in a Passover seder with refuseniks during his Moscow visit in mid-April 1987 made the same point.

Soon after the Reykjavik summit, for which Reagan was severely criticized both in the United States and Western Europe for inept planning and insufficient consultation, came another blow to the Reagan administration—the Iran-Contra scandal. This scandal, among other things, put the United States on the diplomatic defensive in the Middle East as many of the Arab states which had looked to it for protection against Iran became bewildered at the "arms for hostages" diplomacy carried on by the United States with Iran. This created somewhat of a vacuum in Middle East diplomacy, and Moscow sought to exploit this situation by stepping up its efforts to achieve an international conference on the Middle East, to be arranged by a preparatory conference of the five permanent members of the U.N. Security Council. By early 1987 the USSR had received support for its position from such diverse groups as the nonaligned movement and the U.N. General Assembly; and at the end of January 1987 Moscow also received the endorsement of the Islamic Conference.

The idea of an international conference was also increasingly welcome to Shimon Peres who, after stepping down as prime minister from the National Unity government in October, had now become foreign minister and vice prime minister. In addition, the United States, with an Irangate-weakened administration, came under increased pressure from Arab states such as Egypt and Jordan to agree to an international conference. It was in part to deflect such pressure that Prime Minister Shamir traveled to the United States in mid-February where he branded the idea of an international conference "a Soviet-inspired notion supported by radical Arabs."[77] During his visit Shamir also sought to get the U.S. government to deny refugee status to Soviet Jews so as to deter them from coming to the United States, but his effort failed as he met strong opposition from the American Jewish community.[78] Meanwhile, Peres went off to Cairo where he and Egyptian President Hosni Mubarak called for an international conference in which Israel would have the right to approve the participants. Their call for an international conference was reinforced by the EEC who also called for such a conference.[79]

For his part Shamir stepped up his criticism of the international conference further as his office, on March 11, published a formal statement repudiating the idea of such a conference. In this document he was particularly critical of Soviet efforts to achieve an international conference, claiming that rumors of Soviet efforts to improve Soviet-Israeli relations were essentially "disinformation" and noting that Moscow's goal all along had been a total Israeli withdrawal from territories captured in the 1967 war.[80]

As the internal Israeli debate on an international conference heated up, Moscow began to step up its signals to Israel to demonstrate its desire for improved ties. Thus although a more restrictive emigration decree went into effect on January 1 that limited emigration to first degree relatives (mother, father, sister, brother, child) of people abroad, statements by a number of Soviet officials indicated that emigration would rise, and indeed after averaging less than 100 per month in 1986, emigration shot up to 470 in March 1987 and 717 in April, with a Novosti official, Sergei Ivanko, predicting an exodus of 10–12,000 by the end of the year.[81] It was in this context that two major non-Israeli Jewish leaders, Morris Abram, president of both the National Conference on Soviet Jewry and the Conference of Presidents of Major Jewish Organizations, and Edgar Bronfman, president of the World Jewish Congress, journeyed to Moscow in late March and met with a number of Soviet officials including Anatoly Dobrynin, the former Soviet ambassador to the United States, who was now the director of the International Department of the CPSU Central Committee. According to Abram, they received "assurances" from the USSR in a number of areas pertaining to Soviet Jewry, in return for their willingness to consider changes to the Jackson-Vanik and Stevenson amendments. Given the importance of this meeting, the text of the "assurances" in the Abram report is listed below:[82]

1. Soviet Jews with exit visas for Israel will travel via Rumania on flights to be established.
2. All refuseniks and their families will be allowed to emigrate to Israel within a one-year period, except for legitimate national security cases. A procedure will be established, however, to re-

view previous visa denials on national security grounds. This procedure may involve officials on a level as high as the Supreme Soviet.

3. First degree relatives may emigrate for family reunification within an established time frame. There may be flexibility within the framework of the current narrow interpretation of "first degree relative."

4. Cases of those refuseniks recently placed in a "never allowed to emigrate" category will be reviewed.

5. All Jewish religious books may be imported into the USSR, and a recommended list of books will be submitted.

6. Synagogues will be opened in all sites where there is a demonstrated need.

7. Soviet Jews will be allowed greater access to rabbinical training. Some may even be allowed to study in the United States.

8. The teaching of Hebrew in school or synagogue settings will be considered together with similar restrictions applied to other religious groups.

9. A kosher restaurant will be opened in Moscow, and liberal provisions will be made for ritual slaughter.

The Bronfman-Abram mission got a mixed reaction in Israel. While Peres warmly endorsed it, Shamir deprecated its value, and Soviet Jewry activists such as Anatoly Sharansky, Lev Elbert, and Yuri Shtern, fearing that once the 10,000 refuseniks were allowed to leave the gates would close permanently, denounced it, with Elbert claiming it was a "trade of 3,500 families for 2 million people waiting to leave."[83]

In arranging the meeting with Abram and Bronfman (although subsequently denying that any "deal" had been made),[84] Moscow apparently had two goals. In the first place, with a new summit on the horizon because Gorbachev had "decoupled" SDI from other arms agreements and with the Soviet leader now energetically pushing his plan for an intermediate-range nuclear arms agreement, the sharp increase in the number of Soviet Jews allowed to leave the USSR, the promise of a still greater exodus inherent in the Bronfman-Abram visit, and the Soviet decision to free almost all the jailed prisoners of Zion (those imprisoned for wanting to go to Israel) all clearly had major public relations value in the United States. In addition, however, it also gave political ammunition to Peres who saw in the increased emigration the price which Moscow was paying to qualify for attendance at an international conference, a price which Peres had cited back at the time of the first Reagan-Gorbachev summit in 1985. For his part Shamir at first sought to counter this development by trying to formally separate the issue of Soviet-Israeli relations from the Soviet Jewry issue, a development that angered Soviet Jewish activists in Israel.[85]

Meanwhile, however, Peres pursued his efforts for an international conference. Meeting for the first time publicly with pro-PLO Palestinians, Peres claimed that the Palestinians expressed the desire for Palestinian representatives acceptable to Israel.[86] At the same time China, also evidently interested in an international conference, began formal diplomatic talks with Israel at the United Nations.[87] As the momentum for the conference built, the Soviets announced they again wanted to send a consular delegation to Israel (albeit without any reciprocal visit by an Israeli delegation),[88] and Peres stated that Moscow had already requested visas for the delegation.[89]

Thus, in early April, as Peres set out for visits to Spain and to the Socialist International meeting in Rome, he was actively pushing for an international conference, and Shamir, who was just as actively opposing the conference, publicly stated that he hoped Peres's efforts to arrange an international peace conference would fail.[90] It was thus in an atmosphere of the beginning of a domestic political crisis in Israel that Peres met with two high-ranking Soviet officials in Rome, Karen Brutents, deputy director of the International Department of the CPSU, and his Middle East adviser Alexander Zotov, in what Peres was later to describe as "the first serious direct dialogue between the two nations."[91] The meeting created a major political stir in Israel with Peres, although agreeing to keep the details of the six hours of discussions secret,[92] giving the impression of major progress in the negotiations both in terms of the exodus of Soviet Jews and in the improvement of Soviet-Israeli relations and going so far as to assert that "if there is no international peace conference within the next few months, the chance for peace could slip away."[93] He also leaked the information that the USSR had spoken against any "coercion" by the superpowers in the context of an international peace conference or by the conference itself, that Moscow had agreed to the idea of bilateral talks as part of the international conference, and that they had spoken of Palestinian representation at the conference in more general terms than just the PLO.[94]

The Likud political counterattack was not long in coming. Even as

Peres was meeting with the Soviet officials in Rome, the Likud chair-
person of the Knesset subcommittee on immigration, Uzi Landau, accused Peres of creating the impression that moves toward an international
conference were a condition for Jewish emigration from the USSR.[95] Shamir was even sharper in his criticism on April 10, denouncing the idea of
an international conference as "national suicide."[96] The Labor party, in
a formal meeting several days later, responded by stating that it would
not accept any reduction in the pursuit of the peace process and the resumption of emigration from the USSR and asserted that Shamir's statement that the idea of an international conference was conceived by Peres
during a nightmare might deal a blow to Israel's vital interests and the
government's performance. The Labor party also stated that Peres would
submit a "practical proposal" for convening an international conference
to the government within a few weeks.[97] For its part the Likud party
through a spokesman, Yosi Ahimeir, issued a statement that Israel's
stated willingness to take part in the Geneva talks (the international conference planned for 1977) became null and void with the signing of
Camp David. The statement also noted that Likud was the first to start
the struggle for the sake of Soviet Jewry and that the (Labor) Alignment's
claim that Likud was curbing the emigration of Soviet Jewry "is aston-
ishing and ridiculous." Ahimeir also stated that "there is no connection
whatsoever and there should be no connection between emigration and
the concession of Judea and Samaria."[98] Shamir himself, seeking to rally
the Soviet Jewish activists in Israel in his political battle to torpedo
Peres's plan for an international conference, deprecated Peres's efforts to
show there had been a real change in Soviet policy, asserting "there are
only rumors and piecemeal reports about a few hundred Jews who have
been allowed out, but this does not represent a change. If the Soviet
Union wants to improve its image and attain a different attitude from the
West by changing its policy on Jewish emigration, it must open its gates
and allow hundreds of thousands of Jews out without imposing any restrictions and qualifications. We must not sell the Jewish cause cheaply."[99]

   While the internal Israeli debate raged in April, Moscow was not
idle. On the one hand it was active in helping the PLO achieve a sem-
blance of unity as both PFLP (Popular Front for the Liberation of Palestine) leader George Habash and DFLP (Democratic Front for the Liberation of Palestine) leader Naef Hawatmeh agreed once again to cooperate
with Arafat at the Algiers meeting of the Palestine National Council, albeit on condition that the PLO break with Jordan and Egypt (Moscow

was apparently rewarded for its efforts with a seat on the PLO executive committee for the pro-Soviet Palestine Communist party). While the return of the extremist Habash to the PLO would appear to have lessened the chances for the PLO participating in the peace talks, Gorbachev sought to reemphasize Moscow's interest in improved ties with Israel and to reinforce the idea of a Middle East conference during his talks with visiting Syrian leader Hafiz Assad in late April when the Soviet leader implicitly warned Assad against going to war because of the danger of nuclear escalation and asserted that the absence of relations between the USSR and Israel "cannot be considered normal." He went on to say, however, that the reason Soviet-Israeli relations were broken was Israel's "aggression against the Arabs." After repeating Moscow's recognition of Israel's right to a "secure and peaceful existence," Gorbachev also noted that changes in Soviet relations with Israel were possible only if there were a Middle East settlement.[100] Moscow also invited a group of blind Israeli athletes to the USSR as yet another signal of its desire to improve ties.[101]

By now a full-fledged political crisis had erupted in Israel with Peres using the issue of an international conference to try to bring down the National Unity government. Indeed, Peres went so far as to claim that Israel had "an opportunity that we have not had since the creation of the State of Israel."[102] In using such hyperbole, however, he left open some very basic questions about the international conference, such as (1) who would represent the Palestinians (Peres claimed Jordan had agreed to abandon the PLO which had broken with it at the PNC [Palestine National Council] conference in Algiers, but Jordan denied this);[103] (2) the role of the USSR at the conference (in none of its public statements had Moscow agreed to the basically ceremonial role Peres had stated for it); and (3) whether or not the conference as a whole would have to confirm the decision of the bilateral committees (the USSR had continued to indicate it wanted the conference as a whole to approve all bilateral agreements). In any case the debate, at least in the short run, became academic as Peres found he did not have sufficient Knesset votes to bring down the government on the issue of an international conference, and by mid-May he announced he was not going to submit the plan for the international conference to the Israeli cabinet.[104] Nonetheless, the internal Israeli debate about the international conference and its relationship to the exodus of Soviet Jews is a useful point of departure for examining the issue of Soviet Jewry as a factor in Israeli foreign policy since the creation of the State of Israel in 1948.

Conclusions

In examining the issue of Soviet Jewry as a factor in Israeli foreign policy in the 1948–87 period, several conclusions can be drawn. In the first place, despite protestations as to the significance of the issue by Israeli officials, or criticism of Israel by the USSR for "interfering in its internal affairs" by advocating the exodus of Soviet Jewry, it really has not been a major factor in Soviet-Israeli relations. To be sure, the persecution of Soviet Jewry was a cause of the rupture of diplomatic relations in 1953, but neither Moscow's original decision to recognize Israel in 1948 and aid it in its war against the Arabs, nor its decision to reestablish relations with Israel later in 1953, nor its decision to break diplomatic relations again with Israel in 1967, nor its raising the possibility of renewing relations in the 1985–87 period seemed to have much to do with the issue of Soviet Jewry. The geopolitical needs of the USSR were the dominant factor in each of these cases, as they were in Moscow's decision to allow more than 250,000 Jews to leave the USSR from 1970 to 1987—at a time when diplomatic relations between the USSR and Israel were severed. In the first four cases the Soviet need to strengthen its Middle East position lay behind its policy of establishing and then breaking and then hinting about renewing relations with Israel, while the decision to permit large-scale Jewish emigration, and the decision to lift the head tax on prospective emigrants, seemed based on Moscow's desire to obtain strategic arms agreements and trade benefits from the West. When the possibility of such benefits evaporated following the Soviet invasion of Afghanistan, Soviet Jewish emigration plummeted but began to rise again in 1987 when another Soviet-U.S. strategic arms agreement seemed in reach and Moscow hoped that an international conference on the Middle East would soon take place.

Interestingly enough, while the issue of Soviet Jewry may have played a relatively minor role in Israel's foreign policy vis-à-vis the USSR, it played a considerably more important role in Israel's relations with Diaspora Jewry, particularly American Jewry. While in the late 1960s it was the nonestablishment Union of Councils for Soviet Jews that was challenging Israel's leadership on the Soviet Jewry issue by calling for a more activist policy, by the mid-1970s the American Jewish establishment itself was challenging Israel's policy on the *noshrim* (dropout) issue. While Prime Minister Begin was able to get a temporary cessation of HIAS aid to emigrants choosing to settle in countries other than Israel in 1981, the reversal of this decision in 1982, and the fact that Israeli leaders have been proven wrong on the dropout issue, has led to a serious challenge of Israeli leadership on the issue of Soviet Jewry by Diaspora Jewish leaders. Indeed the failure of Shamir, during his visit to the United States in February 1987, to get U.S. support to deny refugee status for Soviet Jews coming to America demonstrated this clearly.

Finally it may also be concluded that the issue of Soviet Jewry has, albeit belatedly and possibly only temporarily, become an important one in Israeli domestic politics. Prior to the advent of Gorbachev, it had been a peripheral issue, with only such fringe politicians as Geula Cohen actively embracing it. By 1986, however, a key Likud leader, Moshe Arens, was involved in the issue, and he and ex-refusenik Anatoly Sharansky, along with other former Soviet Jews, effectively pressured the Israeli government at the time of the Helsinki talks in August 1986 to take a harder line on Soviet Jewry than it might otherwise have done. Then, in March 1987 the issue became even more salient in Israeli politics as Peres sought to link the issue of the Soviet Jewish exodus to an international peace conference with Moscow obligingly increasing the exodus as Peres spoke out more and more forcefully for the conference and even sought to bring down the National Unity government on this issue, while Shamir sought to exploit the rising tide of discontent among Soviet Jewish activists living in Israel over Peres's actions by claiming that Peres (and Bronfman and Abram) had "sold out" to Moscow for too few Jews.

In sum, so long as there are hundreds of thousands of Soviet Jews who wish to leave the USSR, the issue of Soviet Jewry will continue to play a role in Israeli foreign policy, because Israel, which sees itself as the homeland of world Jewry and the haven for oppressed Jews, considers it a Zionist obligation to aid Soviet Jews to come to Israel. Nonetheless, Israel by itself appears to have had little influence over the Soviet decision to allow Jews to emigrate or in the ultimate destination chosen by recent emigrants. While this may be a blow to Zionist theorists, it reflects the geopolitical realities of the contemporary world.

5. The West European Approach to the Soviet Jewry Problem

Howard Spier

The West European Perspective

Since World War II Europe's decline in terms of global power and influence has been swift. Some of the parliamentary democracies which constitute the political entity known as Western Europe were until comparatively recently world powers in their own right. A number of them, Great Britain in particular, have found it a very difficult matter to come to terms with their new status in international affairs. In addition, many of the countries of Western Europe face long-standing internal problems. France, for example, has had considerable difficulty in absorbing large numbers of North African immigrants from its former colonies; Belgium continues to struggle with divisive linguistic problems; Great Britain is beset with intractable economic and industrial problems. Some of the West European countries also face significant internal security problems. In the case of Great Britain, for instance, there is the Protestant-Catholic conflict in Northern Ireland; in Spain there is the Basque separatist movement. In addition to these problems there is, of course, the European dimension of the relatively new problem of international terrorism, usually emanating from Middle Eastern sources.

In foreign policy matters the nations of Western Europe are confronted with one major and overriding challenge—Soviet power. Without doubt, by virtue solely of its military power, the USSR presents the most formidable external threat to the cohesiveness and well-being of the nations of Western Europe. It cannot be stressed sufficiently that West Europeans are constantly mindful that they lack individually and, for that matter, collectively, the kind of "clout" which the United States is seen to be able to wield in its relations with the USSR. This is not to say, of course, that West Europeans necessarily impute all, or even most, of the world's problems to Soviet hegemonic pretensions.

Relations of the West European countries with the USSR at the present time may be said to fall essentially into three major categories:

security, economic and technological cooperation, and human rights. These categories are reflected in the three "Baskets" of the Helsinki Final Act, as discussed below. There are few illusions among the governments of Western Europe regarding the fundamental ideological and political hostility of the Soviet leaders toward the West. There are even fewer illusions, least of all in the government circles of those West European countries which share common borders with the USSR (most notably, West Germany), about Moscow's capacity to inflict massive destruction—nuclear and conventional—on Western Europe. It is for this reason that the governments of a number of states in Western Europe turned to the United States, their NATO ally, for military and political support. At the end of the 1970s these governments requested the United States to install Cruise and Pershing II nuclear missiles on their territories as a counterweight to equivalent Soviet missiles stationed in East European countries and targeted on Western Europe. In addition, France and Great Britain continued to develop independent nuclear deterrents.

The post-détente period—that is, the period which has elapsed since the end of the 1970s and continues to this day—has coincided with the decision of individual West European states to install U.S. nuclear missiles, the USSR's intervention in Afghanistan, and the accession of the hard-line anti-Soviet administration of Ronald Reagan. These factors, combined with the evident lack of self-confidence among the publics of some of the West European nations, have led to the growth of peace movements of varying degrees of resilience, especially in Holland, West Germany, and Great Britain. Proximity to the Soviet borders, anti-Americanism, neutralist sentiment, apprehension that Europe may become the battleground of superpower rivalry—all these elements, fanned by skillful Soviet propaganda, coalesced into resistance to the installation of U.S. nuclear missiles. However, the determination of the West European governments to proceed with the installation, coupled with a relative thaw in Soviet-U.S. relations and a return to the arms talks negotiating table, has drawn a certain amount of the sting out of the peace movements.

It is worthwhile mentioning that the issue of the Strategic Defense Initiative (Star Wars) seems likely to remain a focus of profound concern in Western Europe. Indeed, there were signs immediately following the 27th CPSU Congress of a renewed Soviet drive to capitalize on West European differences with the United States over security matters and on the key issue of Star Wars in particular, a development exacerbated by the clash on this issue at the Iceland summit of October 1986. This "European offensive" was understood to be one of the centerpieces of Soviet foreign policy for 1986.[1]

It should be stressed that in Western Europe economic relations with the USSR are by no means the contentious issue that they are in the United States. This is notwithstanding the fact that the offering of advantageous trade deals by Moscow to one or another West European country is a standard Soviet technique for attempting to split Western solidarity. One particular instance which the USSR was able to exploit successfully in the early 1980s was the difference of views between the West German government and the Reagan administration over the installation of a gas pipeline in the USSR. The fact is, however, that West European nations trade with Moscow on a country-by-country basis. The USSR clearly sets great store by the high quality of technological equipment—machinery, computers, etc.—obtainable from Western Europe; West Europeans, for their part, are clearly very anxious to trade with Moscow. However, even if the political will for a lengthy and sustained trade boycott of the USSR over human rights in general or Soviet Jewry in particular existed in Western Europe—which it clearly does not—it seems most unlikely that the West European countries, acting individually or in concert, could achieve what the United States, with its denial to the USSR of most-favored-nation status, has signally failed to achieve.

It is, of course, the second "battleground" of East-West relations—the ideological warfare on human rights—that concerns us most. The signing by the USSR, the United States, Canada, and thirty-two European states of the Final Act of the Conference on Security and Co-operation in Europe (CSCE) in Helsinki in August 1975 was a unique feature of the détente that characterized East-West relations in the 1970s. The Final Act (not a legal instrument but an expression of political intent) comprises three so-called Baskets. Basket One deals with security matters and Basket Two with economic cooperation. However, by its acceptance of Basket Three—humanitarian matters—the USSR agreed to the principle of implementing an entire spectrum of human rights, including the principle of reunification of families, the very framework in which the Jewish emigration of the last decade and a half has proceeded. A larger number of the provisions contained in the Third Basket had, moreover, a direct or indirect relevance to the Jewish minority in the USSR.[2]

In the years immediately following the signing of the Helsinki Final

Act, there were indications that the USSR, sensitive to world opinion, was carrying out with some degree of seriousness the human rights obligations it had undertaken. However, Soviet compliance with these provisions of the Final Act deteriorated with the demise of détente at the end of the 1970s as well as with the increasing incapacitation of Soviet President Leonid Brezhnev who, as one of the architects of the Final Act, had a large personal stake in its progress. Jewish emigration from the USSR declined from its peak of over 50,000 in 1979 to around one thousand annually in the mid-1980s. Simultaneously, Jewish activists and refuseniks began to be subject to stepped-up persecution and harassment as the Soviet authorities put into effect an increasingly hard-line policy.

Follow-up meetings in the so-called Helsinki process produced ever fewer results. Conferences called to review implementation of the Helsinki accords at Belgrade (October 4, 1977, to March 9, 1978)[3] and Madrid (November 11, 1980, to September 9, 1983)[4] revealed increasingly less common ground on human rights as relations between East and West deteriorated. This was the case also with specialist meetings held in the context of Basket Three—the Meeting of Experts on Human Rights and Fundamental Freedoms in Ottawa (May 7 to June 17, 1985) and the Cultural Forum in Budapest (October 15 to November 25, 1985). The CSCE meeting on human contacts and reunification of families held in Berne in May 1986 also ended in disagreement. It took place in hardly auspicious circumstances—the sharpening of superpower tensions following the initial euphoria induced by the 1985 Geneva summit.

The tensions that have been evident in the countries of Western Europe over security matters and, to a much lesser degree, economic matters, vis-à-vis the USSR have been for the most part lacking in the human rights area. With very few exceptions, including among the parties of the left, there has generally been consensus on this issue, with criticism of the USSR's human rights performance remaining constant. West European goverments and media alike have paid considerable attention to Soviet human rights abuses and especially the fate of the Jewish community in the USSR. The names of Andrei Sakharov and Anatoly Sharansky have become household names in Western Europe just as in the United States. Access by human rights and Jewish campaigners in the West European countries to government officials and the media has invariably been available and even encouraged. Jewish communities in the countries of Western Europe, while lacking the numbers and influence of the American Jewish community, have shown themselves no less adept at using the considerable official and media channels open to them to advocate what is perceived as a humanitarian cause which enjoys widespread public sympathy.

Collective Action on Behalf of
Soviet Jewry in Western Europe

Activities on behalf of Soviet Jews, by governments and Jewish populations, in the countries of Western Europe are conducted on a collective West European basis as well as on a national basis. However, it should be stressed that, in the conditions of Western Europe, collective action on behalf of Soviet Jews, like most collective West European activities, notwithstanding the framework of the Helsinki process, tends to be far less common, and seemingly considerably less effective, than action undertaken by individual countries. Actions on behalf of Soviet Jewry in Western Europe are generally the sum total of actions occurring in individual countries. We will therefore look first at collective efforts on behalf of Soviet Jewry before describing in detail the activities and institutions prevailing in one country, Great Britain, which relate to Soviet Jews. Although the Jewish population of Great Britain is the second largest Jewish population in Western Europe, after that of France (see table 5.1), there exists in Britain a particular concentration of activities and specialized publications dealing with the struggle for Soviet Jewry; moreover, these data are most easily accessible to us. The situation with respect to the movement for the rights of Soviet Jewry in other West European countries mirrors to a greater or lesser extent the situation in Great Britain.

Collective action on behalf of Soviet Jewry in Western Europe was conducted through a number of European institutions. By far the most significant of these were the follow-up conferences and specialized human rights meetings held in the context of the Helsinki process. The Helsinki Monitoring Committee of the International Council of the World Conference on Soviet Jewry prepared (under its chairman, Stephen Roth, director of the London-based Institute of Jewish Affairs) a series of detailed reports on Soviet compliance with the Helsinki accords in the Jewish sphere. These were submitted by the Jewish communities of the West European states, the United States, and Canada to their respective governments. Jewish communal figures backed up the conclusions of the reports by intensive personal lobbying at the conferences in question.

Table 5.1. Jewish Populations of the Countries of Western Europe*

Country	Total Population**	Jewish Population**
Austria	7,548,500	12,000
Belgium	9,853,023	40,000
Cyprus	648,600	25
Denmark	5,112,130	9,000
Federal German Republic	61,420,700	28,000
France	54,273,200	535,000
Greece	9,740,417	44,875
Ireland	3,508,000	2,000
Italy	56,742,374	34,500
Luxembourg	365,800	1,200
Malta	329,189	50
Netherlands	14,362,381	30,000
Norway	4,134,353	950
Portugal	10,099,000	300
Spain	37,746,260	12,000
Sweden	8,330,573	16,000
Switzerland	6,423,106	18,300
Turkey	47,279,000	23,000
United Kingdom	56,376,800	330,000

* Includes West European countries which are members of the Council of Europe and on the Jewish community of which up-to-date numerical data are available.
** Data taken from *Jewish Communities of the World,* vol. 1: *Europe,* published by the Institute of Jewish Affairs on the occasion of the 8th Plenary Assembly of the World Jewish Congress, Jerusalem, January 1986.

Perhaps the most active and influential long-standing institution in Western Europe from the viewpoint of the Soviet Jewish cause is the Council of Europe, based in Strasbourg. The assembly of this institution comprises parliamentarians on an all-party basis, including Communists, from (currently) twenty-one West European democracies. Indeed, the Council of Europe, whose work on behalf of Soviet Jewry began as early as 1965, seems to have been the first international organization to champion the cause of unrestricted Jewish emigration from the USSR.[5] Making good use of materials prepared by Jewish sources, council representatives submitted to the Parliamentary Assembly detailed reports on the Jewish condition in the USSR at regular intervals.[6]

A second important vehicle for the expression of pan-European sentiment on the situation of Soviet Jews is the Parliament of the European Economic Community (EEC, also known as the European Common Market and also based in Strasbourg). As of January 1, 1986, the EEC was composed of twelve states—Belgium, Denmark, the Federal German Republic, France, Greece, Ireland, Italy, Luxembourg, the Netherlands, Portugal, Spain, and the United Kingdom. The original long-term goal of the founders of the EEC—the political and economic unity of Western Europe—presently seems a forlorn hope.[7] During the period with which we are concerned, the European Parliament adopted a number of resolutions calling on the foreign ministers of the twelve member states to express to the Soviet government their concern about the harassment of Soviet Jews and the sharp reduction in the number of emigration permits allowed.[8] On one occasion, in May 1982, Piet Dankert, president of the European Parliament, met with a delegation of West European Jews who had collected one million signatures for a petition on the situation of Soviet Jewry.[9]

A number of detailed memoranda on the position of the Jewish minority in the Slavic republics of the USSR were prepared by the Institute of Jewish Affairs in London for meetings of the Geneva-based Human Rights Committee established under the International Covenant on Civil and Political Rights. The memoranda were submitted by the European Branch of the World Jewish Congress.[10] At a meeting held on the initiative of the French Socialist party in Paris in June 1980, the European Inter-Parliamentary Conference for Soviet Jewry was formed. The meeting was attended by thirty-eight parliamentarians from fourteen West European countries.[11] A meeting of the organization in July 1984 attracted seventy-five parliamentarians.[12]

The International Parliamentary Group for Human Rights in the Soviet Union, a joint U.S.-West European endeavor, held its first meeting in Paris in May 1980. The group was concerned with general Soviet human rights abuse but appeared to have a particular interest in family reunion, clearly an important Jewish concern.[13] Many other collective activities on behalf of Soviet Jewry were held in Western Europe in recent years. One such was a three-day seminar held in mid-1985 by wives of parliamentarians from at least fourteen West European countries. The

seminar met in London and was hosted by both Houses of the British
Parliament jointly with the European Parliament.[14]

The Movement for Soviet Jewry in Great Britain

Institutions. The movement for Soviet Jewry in Great Britain has not
lacked organization—in fact, some would say that the British Jewish
community tends to be over-organized. As in many other spheres of Jewish communal activity in Great Britain, an impetus to the campaign for
the rights of Soviet Jews was given by the youth. In May 1966 the Universities Committee for Soviet Jewry held the first demonstration on behalf of Soviet Jews in London.[15] The committee subsequently acquired
premises from which to operate and, until the beginning of the 1970s,
was the principal organization in its field in Great Britain. One of the earliest British student leaders active on behalf of Soviet Jews was Colin
Shindler. Currently, the Student and Academic Campaign for Soviet Jewry
is very active in this field.

In 1971, following the first Leningrad trial of Jewish activists, a trial
which evoked unprecedented coverage in the mass media of the West,
and the first Brussels Conference, which was convened by the Western
Jewish communities together with Israeli organizations, the so-called
Thirty-Fives Committee was formed. The Thirty-Fives, or Women's Campaign for Soviet Jewry, was established as the brain child of Barbara
Oberman.[16] The group received its name due to the fact that it sprang
into being to fight for the right to emigrate from the USSR of the thirty-
five-year-old Raisa Palatnik; it also seems that thirty-five women attended
the group's first meeting. Branches of the Thirty-Fives were later set up
in British provincial towns as well as in a number of other countries, including Canada.[17]

The Thirty-Fives pride themselves on their spontaneity and swift reaction to events. They are also distinguished by an outstanding flair for
public relations. The organization continues to maintain independent premises in London. The Thirty-Fives are affiliated with the Washington-
based Union of Councils for Soviet Jews. Also in 1971 the Board of
Deputies of British Jews, the representative body of the British Jewish
community, whose members are elected on the basis of synagogue affiliation, formed a Soviet Jewry Action Committee. This was chaired by Michael Fidler, a Conservative member of Parliament. However, following
the expression of a certain degree of dissatisfaction with the allegedly

slow reaction of the board to events,[18] about one hundred activists for Soviet Jewry from around the country met in December 1975 to form a National Council for Soviet Jewry of Great Britain and Ireland, a body which, however, retained some links to the Board of Deputies. Marcus Einfeld was elected the first chairman of the National Council.[19] This body is an approximate parallel to the U.S. National Conference on Soviet Jewry.

Prominent among specialized groups working in Britain on behalf of Soviet Jewry over the last decade have been the All-Party Parliamentary Committee for the Release of Soviet Jewry, which, as its name implies, is active among members of Parliament, and the Medical Scientific Committee for Soviet Jewry. These groups, with all their numerous affiliated organizations, continue to represent the main structure of activism for Soviet Jewry in the country.

Publications. Many of the large number of British groups active in the cause of Soviet Jewry have their own publications, bulletins, newsletters, etc. Particular attention should, however, be paid to three specialist publications in the field which have appeared regularly during at least the last decade and a half and have acquired thereby a certain authoritativeness among campaigners for Soviet Jewry. These are *Insight: Soviet Jews, Jews in the USSR,* and *Soviet Jewish Affairs.*

Insight: Soviet Jews,[20] a monthly publication comprising on average eight pages, has appeared since 1975 and is edited by Emmanuel Litvinoff, a noted Anglo-Jewish writer and novelist. It is attractively produced and is a lively journalistic and analytical account, based in great part on material from the Soviet media, of topical matters affecting Soviet Jews. It is published by the Contemporary Jewish Library in London. *Insight* is in effect the successor of *Jews in Eastern Europe,*[21] a highly informative and analytical magazine founded as early as March 1958 and also edited by Emmanuel Litvinoff. *Jews in Eastern Europe* is possibly the first publication of its kind to have appeared anywhere in the world.

Jews in the USSR[22] is a weekly compilation of "raw material" on Soviet Jews which is invaluable for researchers on Soviet Jewry. While it provides comparatively little analysis, it does contain up-to-date personal information, culled from many sources, on Soviet Jewish activists and refuseniks. *Jews in the USSR* was founded in 1971 and was first edited by Colin Shindler, one of the early British student activists for Soviet Jewry. It has been edited by Nan Greifer since 1975. *Jews in the USSR* is read in countries as far apart as Zambia and Japan.[23] Like *Insight,* it is published by the Contemporary Jewish Library in London.

Soviet Jewish Affairs[24] is a scholarly journal which appears three times a year. It was founded in January 1968 under the title *Bulletin on Soviet Jewish Affairs.* Its first editor was Jacob Miller, and it is currently edited by Lukasz Hirszowicz. *Soviet Jewish Affairs* has an editorial board comprising some of the leading scholars in the field of Soviet studies in Britain. From the journal's foundation the chairman of the editorial board was Leonard Schapiro. Following his death in November 1983, Schapiro was succeeded by Chimen Abramsky, professor emeritus, London University. In early 1986 an International Advisory Board, with members in the United States, Israel, Holland, and West Germany, was formed. *Soviet Jewish Affairs,* the only scholarly journal of its type in the English language, is published by the Institute of Jewish Affairs, the London-based research arm of the World Jewish Congress.

The Institute of Jewish Affairs also publishes research papers devoted to Jews in the USSR and Eastern Europe among its regular *Research Reports,*[25] as well as a number of books in this field.[26] The institute has published, in addition, a series of brochures monitoring Soviet compliance with the humanitarian provisions of the Helsinki Final Act in the Jewish sphere.[27]

At the time of writing, a fourth publication, the *Journal of the Academic Proceedings of Soviet Jewry,* is scheduled to be launched in London in mid-1986. The new journal is to appear twice yearly and publish, inter alia, papers by refusenik scientists. Martin Gilbert, the well-known biographer of Churchill and author of a number of popular works in the field of Soviet Jewry, is deeply involved in this project.[28]

The question of Soviet Jewry has also been discussed in Britain at a number of conferences, seminars, and other intellectual forums in the period under discussion. The Institute of Jewish Affairs was particularly well equipped to contribute to serious analysis of the problem by virtue of its specialized library and archives on matters pertaining to the Jews of the USSR and Eastern Europe. One event of particular importance was the Experts' Conference on Soviet Jewry Today, which was held in London in January 1983 under the auspices of the Institute of Jewish Affairs and the Israel-Diaspora Institute of the University of Tel Aviv. The conference was attended by over forty scholars and specialists from around the world.[29]

Activities. As we have said, the campaign in Western Europe for the rights of Soviet Jews has invariably met with a sympathetic response on the part of governments and media. This was certainly the case in Great Britain. British government officials, not least Mrs. Margaret Thatcher, the prime minister (whose north London constituency incidentally contains a large number of Jews), met frequently with activists for Soviet Jewry, giving constant reassurances of support for what was perceived as a humanitarian concern. Government officials, in particular officials at the Foreign and Commonwealth Office, repeatedly met with delegations and individuals, Jewish and non-Jewish, who expressed concern for the fate of Soviet Jews.

Particular attention was given by British government officials to meetings with, and briefings of, Jewish delegations in connection with the various follow-up meetings of the Helsinki process. In a lecture to the Institute of Jewish Affairs in March 1981, Peter Blaker, minister of state at the Foreign and Commonwealth Office, provided one of many reassurances to Jewish activists, claiming the United Kingdom gave "special prominence" to the problem of Soviet Jews at the then current Madrid CSCE meeting.[30]

Perhaps one of the most significant roles played by British government officials in regard to the plight of Soviet Jews was that of Peter Blaker's successor at the Foreign and Commonwealth Office, Malcolm Rifkind. Rifkind, an observant Jew, was one of the youngest ministers in Mrs. Thatcher's government and, by many accounts, one of the most able. Rifkind was diligent in meeting human rights campaigners and sympathetic to them in the frustration they frequently displayed. In mid-1985 he became the first British minister to visit the Moscow Choral Synagogue.[31]

In November 1984, in one of many addresses he gave to the House of Commons on the issue of human rights in the USSR, Rifkind showed a particularly fine grasp both of the interconnectedness of the security and human rights "Baskets" of the Helsinki Final Act and of the specific limitations of Britain's (and, for that matter, Western Europe's) capacity to affect Soviet decisionmaking in this area. His address is worth quoting almost in its entirety:

What can we do realistically to show our concern and to encourage more humane practices in the Soviet Union? First, the Government will ensure that the issue of human rights and the Soviet Union's Helsinki and Madrid commitments are kept firmly on the agenda of our ministerial contacts with the Russians. These matters must figure but that will not be to the exclusion of the many other important matters that we have to discuss with them. We must show that these questions have not been, and will not be, forgotten. Secondly, as well as mentioning the wider issues, we should on occasion mention individual names of those we are trying to help. At times—and recent years have been such times—this may be without apparent result, but that does not make it worthless. Anatoly Sharansky may be lying in an inhospitable camp in the Urals, but a telegram has just got through to his wife to let her know where he is and that he is still alive. Would this have happened 40 years ago? Certainly it did not happen in the case of Osip Mandelstam, the great Russian Jewish poet of the 1920s and 1930s. Would it have happened if it had not been for the efforts of Mrs. Sharansky, which have made the name of her husband a household name in the West? To mention someone who is not Jewish, would we have seen the strangely concocted films of Dr. Sakharov and his wife in Gorky if it had not been for the constant mention of his name by Western representatives. . . . A question that is often raised is whether these approaches should be publicized or remain confidential? My experience leads me to believe that what is required is a carefully judged mixture of both. If these matters remain confidential, there will be little public pressure on the Russians for visible improvements. If everything is done in a blaze of publicity, the Soviet reaction will tend to be not to respond, out of pride and stubborness. . . . The power we have in our hands is the potent one of example and of persuasion but it does not go much beyond that. Occasionally, those who are impatient for results and anxious for early progress suggest that some way should be found to force the Russians to behave better—that we should not speak to them until there is a major improvement in their observance of human rights, or that we should not trade with them. Experience, however, shows that rigid linkage of any kind is an ineffective and unrealistic way of proceeding either in terms of our own interests or in the interests of those we are trying to help. . . . We are now experiencing the lowest level of permitted Jewish emigration since the early 1970s. When the Soviet Union feels itself isolated, it has tended to treat its own citizens worse, not better. We should, therefore, welcome recent signs of greater willingness on the part of the Russians at least to talk, because it is only through the process of increasing contacts and a fuller mutual understanding that we can achieve the sort of East-West confidence that is likely to lead to better relationships and reduced tension. . . . Meanwhile, the Government will continue to plug away at this issue, to press for improvements in Soviet treatment of its Jewish community, and the other minority communities that suffer discrimination of one kind or another. We will do this not only because it is a most important part of the CSCE process that we should do so, and not only because common humanity compels us to do it. We shall continue to explain that the way that the Soviet authorities treat their citizens creates in itself a wider and real problem of trust and understanding in this country. If they wish us to accept the genuineness of their desire for peace and security, there would be no better earnest of their intentions than to show in the way that they treat their own citizens and especially those who wish to travel or to emigrate that their motives vis-a-vis their neighbors and the West are indeed peaceful and friendly.[32]

Opposition members of parliament were equally sympathetic in relation to the cause of Soviet Jewry. Neil Kinnock, leader of the Labour party, said, following a visit to the USSR in late 1984, that he had received written undertakings on five cases, four of them involving Jews, which he had brought to the attention of the Soviet authorities. Although he was not prepared to give names, Kinnock said the Soviets had agreed to grant exit visas for three Jews and commute the sentence of a fourth from prison to exile.[33] Members of the alliance parties—the Liberal party and the Social Democratic party—were equally outspoken on behalf of Soviet Jewry. On one occasion, an all-party group of members of parliament, on returning to London from a four-day visit to Moscow, where they had met a large number of refuseniks, called for a total freeze on scientific contacts between Great Britain and the USSR.[34] Such an appeal seemed, however, mainly rhetorical since there was little likelihood it would be followed up.

There were, however, a number of isolated instances of nonconformism with the general human rights perspective of mainstream British opinion. Among such incidents was a mid-1984 decision by the far left Labour-controlled Liverpool City Council to "twin" with the Black Sea port of

Odessa. This decision went ahead despite protests from more moderate city councillors and Jewish activists that Odessa was at that time experiencing a wave of harassment of Jews.[35] A somewhat discordant note was also struck at a meeting on "Disarmament and Human Rights," which was organized in November 1983 by the British Jewish peace group JONAH (Jews Organized for a Nuclear Arms Halt). The principal speaker, E. P. Thompson, a prominent left-wing historian and a leading member of the British and West European peace movements, stated that while he approved of emigration from the USSR in principle, as well as of Jewish emigration, he preferred to see Jews remain in the USSR and contribute to the "democratization" of that society.[36]

Despite these isolated cases, the numerous rallies, demonstrations, marches, and other public manifestations of support on behalf of Soviet Jewry were invariably reported sympathetically in the British media, especially the press. From the "upmarket" end of Fleet Street—for example, *The Times, Guardian, Daily Telegraph, Sunday Times, Observer*— to the "downmarket" (more popular) end of Fleet Street—the *Daily Mirror, Sun, Star* and others—editors were pleased to give wide coverage to such events. The tone of editorial columns was invariably warm and sympathetic with a firmly anti-Soviet stance. There were, of course, occasions when media coverage was not readily forthcoming owing to "saturation," but there were also periods when newspaper editors seemed unable to obtain enough material for their requirements. It appeared that the campaigners for Soviet Jewry were well able to provide the frequently sensationalist British press with the sort of "copy" it most appreciates— a simple human story with good visual action.

Among the numerous manifestations on behalf of Soviet Jewry in the period discussed, two may be regarded as being of special interest. On one occasion many prominent British citizens from all walks of life, Jews and non-Jews, artists, writers, scholars, religious leaders, politicians, etc., signed a petition, published in the *Jewish Chronicle,* specifically directed against granting any kind of legitimacy to the Soviet Anti-Zionist Committee.[37] A second activity, which was held under the aegis of the National Council for Soviet Jewry, evoked particular resonance across the entire spectrum of the British media. In February 1986, in an event timed to coincide with the 27th CPSU Congress, the well-known playwright Tom Stoppard organized a "dawn-to-dusk" ceremony in bitterly cold weather outside the National Theatre in London at which 9,000 names of Soviet refuseniks were read slowly and in a dignified manner by a host of prominent British personalities from all walks of life—stage, film, media, politics, etc.

There were rare occasions when an activity on behalf of Soviet Jews struck a discordant note in the British media. One action, in which militant youths were ejected from a London concert of the Moscow Philharmonic Orchestra for demonstrating too noisily on behalf of Anatoly Sharansky, was condemned by a writer in the quality newspaper *Guardian Weekly* as "cultural hijacking." "Taking it out on some of the most warmly responsive Russian musicians we have heard at the Festival Hall for years seemed a shabby way to promote any cause, good or bad," it said.[38] This verdict was shared by the editorial writer of Britain's prestigious weekly Jewish newspaper, *The Jewish Chronicle,* who, while encouraging the involvement of youth in the campaign on behalf of Soviet Jewry, questioned what had been achieved by this activity in particular. The disruption of the concert, the editorial concluded, had been "bad tactics."[39]

In early 1983 Jewish activists on behalf of Soviet Jews were thrown into confusion by an extraordinary statement by Soviet President Yuri Andropov which appeared in the French Communist party newspaper *l'Humanité.* Andropov stated, in effect, that the situation of Jewish prisoners in the USSR, and of Anatoly Sharansky in particular, was jeopardized rather than assisted by demonstrations and rallies in the West on their behalf. The less noisily the Western demonstrators conducted themselves, Andropov implied, the sooner Sharansky would be released. Following stormy discussions, the National Council for Soviet Jewry decided to call off a planned rally through London.[40] As the subsequent months coincided largely with Andropov's increasing incapacitation— with neither the release of Sharansky nor an improvement of the condition of Soviet Jewish prisoners taking place—it will never be known if Andropov's plea was ever anything more than a public relations exercise. In off-the-record contacts with Western Jewish figures, and indeed in many of their "anti-Zionist" writings, Soviet representatives have not made a secret of the fact that, like some of their counterparts in other East European countries, they tend to have an exaggerated view of the power of the Jewish lobby, in particular over the U.S. government and media.

An important development in British-Soviet relations was the visit to Great Britain in December 1984 of Mikhail Gorbachev, at that time a Politburo member whom many Western observers of the USSR regarded as the most likely successor to the then ailing Konstantin Chernenko.

Gorbachev's robust style, so much at variance with that of the conventional Soviet politician and diplomat, considerably impressed many who came into contact with him, including Prime Minister Thatcher. The "Iron Lady" was impressed sufficiently to exclaim that she liked Gorbachev and found him a man with whom Britain could "do business."[41]

The style had changed but the message clearly had not. The primary purpose of Gorbachev's visit, it became evident, was the long-standing one of seeking to promote divergences between West European and U.S. policies, in this case over the Star Wars project. Subjected to some zealous questioning by British members of parliament on human rights issues, Gorbachev revealed a more abrasive side to his personality. On Jewish matters he displayed a mastery of the official data and statistics on the subject; however, no concrete results are known to have emerged from this encounter in the human rights sphere. During a visit to Paris in October 1985, on this occasion as the Soviet Communist party leader, Gorbachev displayed a similar mastery of the official data on Soviet Jewish matters. Of greater interest than what Gorbachev actually said on this occasion was the fact that, in an unprecedented development, the text of his comments, including a press conference with President Mitterrand in which he had responded directly to questions on human rights, including the subject of Soviet Jewry, was fully published in the Soviet media. Again, a change in style, if not in substance.

Soviet media coverage of the Western movement on behalf of Soviet Jews in the period under discussion remained highly critical. Soviet Jewry activists were attacked frequently, often in terms of personal abuse, as is the custom of Soviet propaganda. From the formation in April 1983 of the Anti-Zionist Committee of the Soviet Public, much of the criticism of the Western efforts to aid Soviet Jews was carried on by that organization. One member in particular of the Anti-Zionist Committee, the elderly Ukrainian Jewish playwright and publicist Tsezar Solodar, continued to specialize in writings of this type. Solodar had made several journeys through West European capitals and had met with a number of activists in the field of Soviet Jewry; many more had refused his invitation to a meeting. In long and detailed articles, predominantly in the glossy Soviet magazine *Ogonyok,* Solodar portrayed what he described as the workings of a host of Soviet Jewry groups active in carrying out "provocations" against the USSR and socialist countries, invariably financed by Western intelligence agencies and functioning on behalf of "international Zionism."[42] This Soviet propaganda concept is reminiscent in some respects of such classic anti-Semitic images as the octopus and the snake. No Soviet anti-Zionist volume in recent years has been complete without reference to the "self-styled protectors of Soviet Jewry in the West."

At the time of writing it is difficult to be optimistic that considerable progress will be made regarding the USSR's implementation of the human rights obligations it has undertaken. Furthermore, the date of the Soviet leader's visit to the United States, in line with the agreement reached at the 1985 Geneva summit, has still not been decided. Also, the Chernobyl disaster may have weakened Gorbachev's position both at home and abroad. Thus, without real progress in both the arms limitation and human rights fields, there seems a distinct possibility, despite the less vitriolic superpower relationship in recent months, that the "Helsinki process" itself will effectively grind to a halt. After the Berne conference the Vienna review meeting is due to begin deliberations in October 1986. Given the possibility of a U.S.-Soviet stalemate on human rights generally and the issue of Soviet Jews specifically, it is difficult to see what leverage is available to West Europeans to influence matters concretely.

Conclusion

In the period discussed West European activists for the rights of Soviet Jews were generally no less diligent than their coactivists in the United States. But their possibilities of influencing Soviet decisionmaking in Jewish matters—both in regard to emigration and the possible continuity of Jewish life in the USSR—were considerably less. The countries of Western Europe, whether individually or in concerted action, wield the power only of nations whose influence on world affairs is declining at a comparatively fast rate. The extract given above from the parliamentary address by the British government minister Malcolm Rifkind shows a clear appreciation of this reality. The countries of Western Europe are not seeking confrontation with their powerful Eastern neighbor; on the contrary, they desire a return to the détente of the 1970s. There is no political will for "linkage" in Western Europe. Apart from all other considerations, the fact remains that West Germany has its own special interest, in the emigration from the USSR of Soviet ethnic Germans and in the maintenance of ties with East Germany.

As the Gorbachev era develops, it is difficult to be optimistic about a renewal of the large-scale Jewish emigration of the 1970s. The new Soviet leadership, wrestling with deeply ingrained economic and social problems, appears intent on extracting the maximum possible gain out of each minor "concession" in regard to Jewish emigration. There is despondency among West Europeans, as among world Jewry in general, about the nature of future action to be taken in regard to the problem of Soviet Jewry. Nonetheless, given the fact that the issue of Soviet Jewry has steadily risen over the last decade and a half to be perhaps the second most pressing problem for world Jewry after the continued existence and security of the State of Israel, there seems no reason to doubt that this state of affairs will continue into the second half of the 1980s and that activists in Western Europe will be among those continually seeking new means of influencing the Soviet leadership.

6. Jewish, German, and Armenian Emigration from the USSR: Parallels and Differences

Sidney Heitman

Since the end of World War II more than 450,000 citizens of the USSR have emigrated to the West in a unique and unprecedented movement today called the "Third Soviet Emigration." In contrast to two earlier flights of refugees from revolution and war, the Third Emigration is a voluntary, legally sanctioned process involving three national minorities— 294,000 Jews, 110,000 Germans, and 53,000 Armenians until now. Jews have resettled chiefly in Israel and the United States, Germans in West Germany, and Armenians in the United States.

The origins of this exodus go back to the early postwar years, but the vast majority of emigrants left during the decade of the 1970s, when the Soviet government relaxed its historic antipathy to the free movement of its citizens for a time. After 1980 emigration was restricted again to a mere trickle of individuals annually, compared to the more than 67,000 persons who left in the peak year of 1979, stranding thousands of others who also wanted to leave and raising questions as to whether the movement had ended or might yet be revived in the foreseeable future, under what circumstances it might be revived, and what, if anything, could be done in the West to encourage it. Since the beginning of 1987 there has been a notable increase in the monthly quotas of emigrants, but the reasons for it, its significance, and its portents for the future are not yet clear.

Of the total number of emigrants who have left the USSR, Jews comprise by far the largest number. For this reason and others, they are of special interest today, and there is a large body of literature dealing with various aspects of their emigration, resettlement, and assimilation— or absorption, the term preferred in Israel. Until now, however, most of what has been written about Jewish emigration has dealt with it in isolation from the parallel and related experiences of the Germans and Armenians, resulting in one-sided and limited understanding. This chapter[1] is intended to provide a more balanced perspective of Jewish emigration by viewing it within the broader context of Soviet postwar emigration generally, comparing it to the exodus of Germans and Armenians, and eliciting the insights that the parallels and contrasts afford. This will be done by examining four of the many questions raised by the Third Emigration—namely, the evolution of the movement from its inception to the present, its causes and precipitants, Soviet emigration policy toward the three groups, and the current status and future prospects of the movement under the present leaders of the USSR. Each of these points will be dealt with in turn.

Evolution of the Third Emigration

For all that has been written about the Third Emigration, there is still no general or comprehensive account of the movement in any language today, and many aspects of it are shrouded in obscurity. The research on which this paper is based has uncovered hitherto unknown or unused data and information that are summarized in the following five tables and three figures that provide a succinct picture of the movement from its inception in 1948 through the end of 1985, the last year for which complete annual statistics were available at the time of writing in the fall of 1986.

Table 6.1 lists the number of emigrants who have left the Soviet Union annually since 1948 according to nationality. The 14,000 Jews who were repatriated to Poland (and later emigrated to Israel), the 11,000 Germans who resettled in East Germany, and the 12,000 Armenians who emigrated to France and the 22,500 to the United States (the latter group without identification as Soviet Armenians—hence the designation "undocumented")[2] cannot be broken down by specific years, for only the totals are known. In order to make comparisons for the period since 1970 possible, however, annual figures were adjusted as shown in table 6.2. This was done by adding to the known yearly numbers in table 6.1 proportionate numbers of the unspecified Germans and Armenians according to the percentage each known annual figure comprised of the total for the period since 1970.

This calculation was based on two presumptions. One was that approximately the same proportionate number of Germans were permitted to emigrate to the German Democratic Republic as were allowed to go to West Germany each year between 1971 and 1985. The same presumption was made concerning the approximate proportionate number of Arme-

Table 6.1. Jewish, German, and Armenian Emigration from the USSR, 1948–85

Year	Jews	Germans To FRG	To GDR	Armenians To USA	To France
1948					
1949	—				
1950	—				
1951	—	1,803			
1952	—	107			
1953	18	0			
1954	53	18			
1955	105	152			
1956	753	1,003			—
1957	149	898			—
1958	12	4,052			—
1959	7	5,557			c. 12,000
1960	102	3,261			
1961	128	334			
1962	182	889			
1963	388	200			
1964	539	231			
1965	1,444	365			
1966	1,892	1,243			
1967	1,162	1,079			
1968	379	594			
1969	2,902	310			
1970	1,046	342			
1971	14,300	1,145			
1972	31,478	3,420		75	
1973	34,922	4,493		185	
1974	20,181	6,541	—	291	
1975	13,139	5,985	—	455	
1976	14,138	9,704	—	1,779	
1977	17,159	9,274	—	1,390	
1978	30,594	8,455	—	1,123	
1979	51,547	7,226	—	3,581	
1980	21,471	6,954	1,000	6,109	
1981	9,860	3,773	—	1,905	
1982	2,700	2,071	—	338	
1983	1,320	1,447	—	193	
1984	908	910	—	88	
1985	1,140	406	10,000	109	
Totals	c.290,000[1]	c. 105,000		c. 52,000[2]	

Sources: Israeli Embassy, Washington, D.C.; Israeli Ministry of Immigrant Absorption; Hebrew Immigrant Aid Society (HIAS); West German Foreign Office, Ministry of Interior, emigrant reception center at Friedland, the Landsmannschaft der Deutschen aus Russland, and the Internationale Gesellschaft für Manschenrechten: Armenian informants; and the U.S. State Department. 1. Plus c. 14,000 Jews repatriated to Poland, 1957–59. 2. Includes 22,500 undocumented emigrants to the United States, 1972–85.

Table 6.2. Adjusted Annual Jewish, German and Armenian Emigration, 1970–85

Year	Jews	Germans	Armenians	Totals
1970	1,046	342	—	1,388
1971	14,300	1,145	—	15,445
1972	31,478	3,420	170	35,068
1973	34,922	4,635	421	39,534
1974	20,181	6,683	662	27,526
1975	13,138	6,127	1,036	20,302
1976	14,138	9,846	4,050	28,034
1977	17,159	9,416	3,165	29,740
1978	30,594	8,597	2,557	41,748
1979	51,547	7,368	8,153	67,068
1980	21,471	7,096	13,909	42,476
1981	9,860	8,153	4,337	22,350
1982	2,700	4,461	769	7,930
1983	1,320	3,127	439	4,885
1984	903	1,960	200	3,068
1985	1,140	870	248	2,258

Source: Data in table 6.1.

nians who left the USSR and ultimately resettled in the United States unidentified as Soviet Armenians ("undocumented") and those Armenian immigrants from the USSR who were registered as such. Though these assumptions cannot be proven, they are reasonable given what is known about Soviet emigration, and they are supported by other knowledgeable persons. They thus make cross-national comparisons possible here.

Table 6.3. Emigration by Periods, 1948–85

Nationality	1948–70	%	1971–80	
Jews	25,200	42.3	248,000	
Germans	22,400	37.6	64,200	
Armenians	12,000	20.1	34,000	
Totals	59,600	100.0	347,000	1

Source: Tables 6.1 and 6.2.

The tables and figures reveal several important characteristics of the Third Emigration and the roles of the three emigrant groups in it. First, it may be seen that the movement has evolved through three distinct stages marked by changes in the numbers, composition, and destinations of the emigrants (see tables 6.3, 6.4, and 6.5), as well as changes in the motives of the emigrants for leaving and the policies of the Soviet government toward them. These stages consist of an initial period extending from 1948 to 1970, a second stage lasting from 1971 to 1980, and a third stage that began in 1981. A notable increase in monthly emigrant quotas of all three groups since the beginning of 1987 may be the start of a new stage in the movement, but it is too early to know whether this is a temporary aberration or a trend. During the first stage only 59,600 emigrants, or 13.3 percent of the total number, left the USSR over a twenty-two year period under circumstances that are discussed below and which established the precedents for the second stage of emigration. During the second period more than three-fourths of the total number of Soviet emigrants left the USSR, or an average of 34,700 annually, compared to the 2,700 emigrants each year in the preceding stage. Between 1981 and 1985 the flow declined greatly, with only 40,300 having left, or 9 percent of the total emigrants since the inception of the movement (see figure 6.1).

The tables and figures also show that of the total number of emigrants since 1948, Jews constitute nearly two-thirds (64.9 percent), Germans just under one-fourth (23.5 percent), and Armenians the remaining 11.6 percent, raising questions concerning the reasons for these disparities, considering that the overall number of Jews and Germans in the USSR was approximately equal in the 1970s and the number of Armenians was the total of the other two nationalities combined. It is also noteworthy that while the respective numbers of Jews, Germans, and Armenians who were permitted to emigrate during the first and third stage

:–85	%	Totals	%
◖00	39.5	290,000	64.9
◖00	45.6	105,000	23.5
)00	14.9	52,000	11.6
◖00	100.0	447,000	100.0

Table 6.4. Emigration by Nationalities, 1948–85

| Period | Jews | | Germans |
	Number	%	Number
1948–70	25,200	8.7	22,400
1971–80	248,900	85.8	64,200
1981–85	15,900	5.5	18,400
Totals	290,000	100.0	105,000

Source: Tables 6.1 and 6.2.

did not differ widely, far more Jews than Germans and Armenians left during the second stage of the movement (see table 6.3 and figure 6.2), raising other questions concerning the reasons for these shifts in ratios among the three groups.

Figure 6.3 depicts the trends of emigration by nationality between 1971 and 1985 on a logarithmic scale that telescopes the quantitative differences among them to make comparison easier. The patterns of annual increases and decreases in emigration for each group over time show wide differences and divergencies from one another, disproving a common belief that Soviet emigration policy was monolithically and uniformly applied to all three nationalities and raising questions as to what in fact motivated Soviet policy and how and why it was applied as it was. To answer all of these questions—insofar as the available information relating to them permits—it is necessary to turn to the issue of the causes

Table 6.5. Destinations of Emigrants, 1948–85

| Period | Jews | | | | |
	Israel	%	U.S.	%	Other
1948–70	11,200	44.4	—	—	14,000
1971–80	156,300	62.8	83,400	33.5	9,200
1981–85	8,000	50.3	7,100	44.6	800
Subtotals	175,500	60.5	90,500	31.2	24,000
Totals	290,000				

Source: Tables 6.1 and 6.2 and information provided by the Israeli Embass Washington, D.C., the Hebrew Immigrant Aid Society (HIAS), and Armenia formants.

Armenians		Totals	%	Annual Average
nber	%			
)00	23.0	59,600	13.3	2,700
)00	65.5	347,100	77.7	34,700
)00	11.5	40,300	9.0	8,000
)00	100.0	447,000	100.0	—

and precipitants of the Third Emigration, or respective emigrant motives for leaving and the events that set their exodus in motion and sustained it.

Causes and Precipitants of Emigration

Each of the three emigrant nationalities will be considered in turn and comparisons among them made in appropriate places. Because the causes of Jewish emigration are generally well known, however, they will be discussed in less detail than the causes of German and Armenian emigration, which are not as well understood in the West today.

Jewish Emigration.[3] On the eve of the dramatic rise in Soviet emigration in the 1970s, there were approximately two million Jews in the USSR living as a dispersed, unassimilated minority without a territorial base[4] or

Germans				Armenians			
G	%	GDR	%	France	%	U.S.	%
)00	100.0	—	—	12,000	100.0	—	—
200	98.4	1,000	1.6	—	—	34,000	100.0
400	45.7	10,000	54.3	—	—	6,000	100.0
)00	89.5	11,000	10.5	12,000	23.0	40,000	77.0
	105,000				52,000		

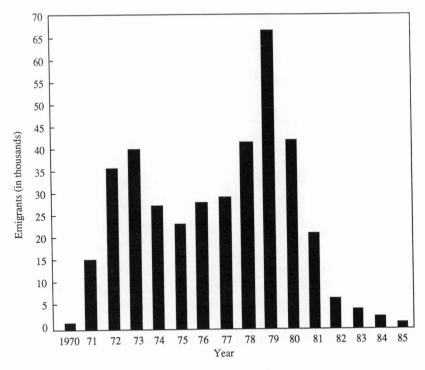

Figure 6.1. Total Annual Emigration from the USSR, 1970–85

an institutional structure for their historic religion and traditional culture that constituted the basis of their national identity and consciousness. They were comprised of two main groups—the so-called Asiatic Jews and the Ashkenazi. Each of these was further divided into subcultures based on history, geography, and customs. Asian Jews were comprised of Georgian, Bukharan, and Mountain (or Tat) Jews, who lived in the Caucasus region and Central Asiatic Russia, were religiously observant, and were devoted to their traditional culture and folkways, forming unassimilated islands in the surrounding non-Jewish sea. They were predominantly craftsmen, workers, traders, and white collar employees.

The Ashkenazi consisted of "western" Jews and "core" (or "heartland") Jews. The western Jews lived in areas that had been annexed by the Soviet Union during World War II—the Baltic states, eastern Poland, Carpatho-Ukraine, and Moldavia. They were traditional and observant,

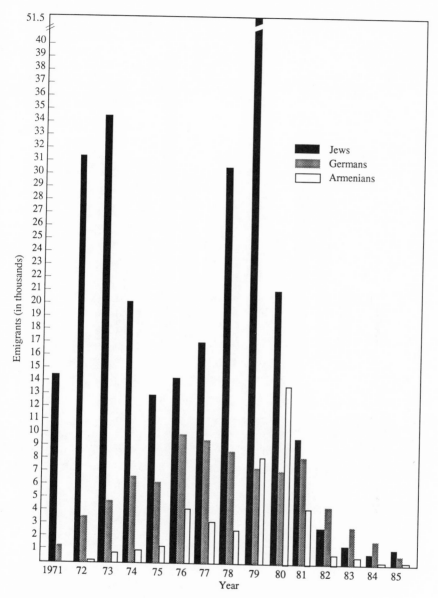

Figure 6.2. Emigration by Nationality, 1971–85

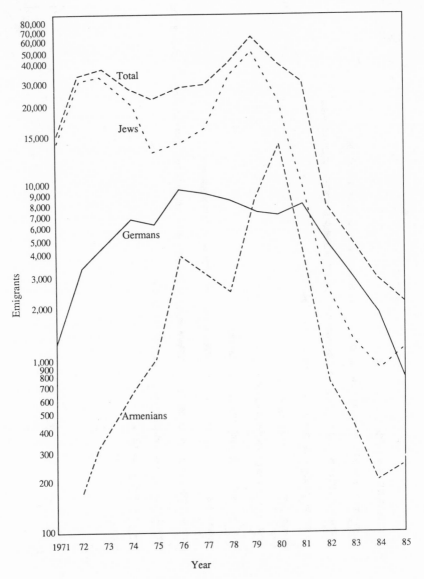

Figure 6.3. Comparative Emigration Trends, 1971–85

spoke Yiddish, and were strongly Zionist. The core Jews lived in the RSFSR, Ukraine, Byelorussia, and Kazakhstan since the founding of the Soviet Union in 1917 and were Russified, secular, and largely assimilated. Both groups were predominantly urban, and many were well-educated and disproportionately represented in scientific, academic, artistic, and other professions. There was little interaction among the different groups of Jews, but the Second World War and the Holocaust had made them conscious of a common bond and heritage.

All Soviet Jews shared one other common experience—endemic anti-Semitism and periodic persecution in the USSR, but this was a fact of Soviet life they had learned to cope with. Escape by means of emigration abroad was simply unthinkable, for Soviet law and policy did not permit voluntary emigration. To be sure, between 1948 and 1970, several thousand elderly or infirm Jews had been permitted to emigrate to Israel to rejoin families as a result of the intervention of Israeli officials (see tables 6.1, 6.2, 6.3, and 6.4). But their departure was not considered to have either broken or set any precedents or violated the long-standing Soviet antipathy to emigration from the USSR at will.

Three developments in the late 1960s and early 1970s changed this state of affairs, however. One was the rise of a particularly virulent wave of anti-Semitism, which touched off a vociferous reaction in the West that forced the Soviet government to rescind it, but not before it had convinced many Soviet Jews that they had to leave the USSR. The second was the stunning Israeli victory in the 1967 Six-Day War, which stirred Jewish pride throughout the world, including the Soviet Union. The third was the advent of détente.[5] Fear of renewed anti-Semitism, the relaxation of internal Soviet political controls that accompanied détente, and the mobilization of world Jewry on behalf of the Soviet Jews encouraged growing numbers of them to apply to emigrate to Israel. Surprisingly, the Soviet government relented and permitted increasingly large quotas of Jews to leave (see tables 6.1, 6.2, 6.3, and 6.4) on the official grounds of family reunification established before 1970, which was now more liberally interpreted and applied.

During the first half of the 1970s the emigrants were primarily Asiatic and western Jews, who were the least integrated and most strongly Zionist elements among the Soviet Jews. In the second half of the 1970s Jewish emigration changed in character, motives, composition, and direction, as increasing numbers of core Jews joined the exodus, not only to escape discrimination, but also to seek improved personal, professional, and economic opportunities in the West. These emigrants increasingly "dropped out" at the Vienna way station to Israel, where all emigrants had to stop, and resettled mainly in the United States (see table 6.5). By the end of 1985 nearly 40 percent of the total Jewish emigrants since 1948 had resettled in countries other than Israel,[6] creating the problem of the so-called *noshrim* for both the state of Israel and other Jews in the USSR who hoped to follow them.

For Israel the diversion of increasing numbers of emigrants away from there to other countries had important internal demographic, social, economic, and political implications. For the Jews in the USSR who still hoped to leave, it helped to close the spigot of emigration because the Soviet government used the drop-out phenomenon to justify cutbacks in Jewish quotas on the grounds that the *noshrim* had emigrated under false pretenses and violated Soviet policy and law. By the time emigration had dwindled to a mere trickle of individuals in 1985, a total of 290,000 Jews, or more than 15 percent of the total number of Soviet Jews in 1970, had left the country, but another estimated 300,000 to half million more who also wanted to leave were no longer able to do so. In 1985 only 1,140 Jews were permitted to emigrate, compared to the more than 51,000 who had left in the peak year of 1979. In 1986 the annual figure declined to 943, and in the first six months of 1987, 3,095 Jews were permitted to emigrate, but the significance of these shifts is not as yet clear.

German Emigration.[7] The causes and precipitants of German emigration have both parallels and contrasts with those of Jewish emigration. Two million ethnic Germans in the USSR in the postwar years were, like the Jews, an unassimilated, dispersed, and alienated national minority with strong cultural traditions and ethnic consciousness. They also shared with the Jews a history of persecution and discrimination under both the Russian monarchy and the Soviet regime. These people were descendants of German colonists invited to Russia in the late eighteenth and early nineteenth centuries by Catherine the Great and Alexander I to develop new lands. They consisted of two main groups—the Volga Germans, who had settled along the lower Volga River Valley, and the Black Sea Germans, who had colonized the northern littoral of the Black Sea. Smaller numbers of other Germans settled in other parts of Russia, but the two largest groups were the most important elements. Each had different origins in Germany, followed distinctive customs, and lived apart from the other, as they did from various groups of Germans who had come into the Russian Empire at other times, such as urban Germans who had been invited by Ivan IV or Baltic Germans who lived in areas annexed by Peter the Great.

For a century after their arrival the German colonists flourished as a result of their legendary diligence and skill as farmers and craftsmen, which had commended them to their patrons, and of special favors they had been granted, including economic privileges, cultural autonomy, religious freedom, and exemption from compulsory military service. In the late nineteenth century their fortunes turned, however, when they lost their privileged status as a result of the reforms of Alexander II and experienced economic setbacks, increasing population pressure on the land, and growing prejudice and persecution, driving many thousands to emigrate to the New World. Those who remained suffered successive tragedies in the First World War, the Revolutions of 1917 and the civil war and famine that followed, and the forced collectivization of agriculture and the Stalinist terror of the 1930s.

There was a brief respite during the New Economic Policy period in the 1920s, when a showcase Volga German autonomous republic and several autonomous districts were formed by the Soviet government to advertise its new nationality policy and attract support in Germany. Until Stalin began to persecute non-Russians in the 1930s, a vigorous German cultural life flourished in the USSR, including hundreds of German-language schools, five institutions of higher learning, a German theater and publishing house, and several German-language newspapers. Ethnic Germans participated actively in political life, governed and administered themselves in their autonomous units, and filled important posts in the Soviet government and the Communist party of the USSR.

World War II ended all organized German life in Russia that had survived the Stalinist terror. When the Nazis invaded the Soviet Union in 1941, Stalin unjustly suspected the Germans of being disloyal and ordered them to be moved en masse to the east. Some 650,000 Volga Germans were uprooted and brutally deported to Siberia and Central Asia, where they were interned in MVD (Ministry for Internal Affairs) special labor camps under exceedingly harsh conditions. Their autonomous units were dissolved, their cultural and religious institutions were closed, and their property was confiscated. The German clergy who had survived Stalin's purges accompanied their parishioners into exile, where most of them perished, ending organized German religion in Russia thereafter.

The Black Sea Germans were overrun by the Nazis before they too could be deported, and 350,000 of them were evacuated to the west, resettled in Poland, and incorporated into the Third Reich. After the war all but 100,000 of them were forcibly returned to the USSR by the allied armies in accordance with the Yalta agreement, and they too were deported to the east and confined to the MVD camps.

By the end of the war the Germans in the USSR had been totally uprooted from their historic homes; their social, religious, and cultural institutions had been destroyed; and nearly half a million of them had perished from the inhuman conditions and brutal treatment in the forced labor camps, a calamity reminiscent of the Jewish Holocaust that is not generally known in the West. Though the end of the war in 1945 ended the pretext for their deportation, the Germans were confined in the special labor camps for a full decade before they were released in 1955, when the Soviet government granted them an amnesty upon the intercession of Chancellor Konrad Adenauer of the new West German Republic.

The Germans were permitted to leave the camps and resettle in southwestern Siberia and Central Asiatic Russia, but they were prohibited from returning to their former homes, restoring their autonomous status, or seeking restitution for lost property and lives. In 1964 they were officially rehabilitated—that is, cleared of wartime charges of treason—but all the restrictions remained. Gradually, their conditions improved, particularly their economic status, for their diligent and productive labor in agriculture and industry were highly valued and well rewarded by the Soviet government. However, they continued to chafe under their disabilities and restrictions, the subtle to overt discrimination, and what many Germans believed to be inadequate opportunities to sustain an authentic German culture and religious life. As a result of these growing dissatisfactions, the Soviet Germans began to move in three directions. One group increasingly surrendered to the pressures to Russify and assimilate, abandoned their German identity, and merged into Soviet society. Another group chose to resist and joined the national and religious dissident movements. A third group, inspired by the success of the Soviet Jews in emigrating from the USSR, sought to join them in the exodus.

The first attempt to leave occurred in 1965, when most of the recently amnestied Black Sea Germans applied to emigrate to West Germany to be reunited with families from which they had been separated by the war and its aftermath. There were precedents for such family reunification, since the Soviet government had permitted small numbers of Jews and Germans to leave for that purpose as far back as the 1950s as a result of the intervention of the Israeli and West German governments. These had all been special hardship cases, and the Soviet government had permitted only elderly or infirm persons of no value to the state to emigrate. There had also been a special dispensation for some 12,000 Armenians to return to France, from where they had recently immigrated, as it will be seen further on.

The initial request of the Black Sea Germans was rejected, but under pressure from the West German government, representatives of the German and Soviet Red Cross organizations met in Vienna in 1965 to draw up lists of special cases eligible for emigration. Anxious to normalize conditions within the USSR and to improve relations with the Federal Republic, a few thousand emigrants were permitted to leave—again mainly elderly and infirm individuals—until 1968, when the deterioration of East-West relations over the Soviet invasion of Czechoslovakia brought this exodus to an end (see table 6.1). Rebuffed a second time, the Black Sea Germans gave up hope of further emigration and gradually began to assimilate into Soviet society.

Two new developments in 1970 raised the issue of German emigration again, however. One was the adoption of a new *Ostopolitik* by the government of Chancellor Willy Brandt, who used the easing of tensions between the Federal Republic and the Soviet Union to press for the release of Germans who still wanted to emigrate from the USSR. The other was the aftermath of an unsuccessful effort by the Volga Germans following their rehabilitation to have their prewar status and property restored. Having failed in this, some of them began to look to emigrating in emulation of the Black Sea Germans and the Jews.

The decision of the Volga Germans to emigrate to West Germany created a new problem, however, for unlike the Black Sea Germans, they could not claim divided families in the West since they had been deported en masse to the east early in the war. Events played into their hands, however, for the Soviet government, anxious to improve relations with the Federal Republic and with the West in the spirit of détente, eased emigration requirements by permitting increasing numbers of Volga Germans with arranged *vyzovs* from nonexistent relatives to emigrate to West Germany. Now, however, the exodus was not restricted only to the elderly and infirm but opened to entire families. Between 1971 and 1979 some 56,000 Germans emigrated from the USSR to the Federal Republic, a tenfold increase over the total of 5,600 for the preceding decade (see tables 6.1 and 6.2), and during the same period an additional 1,000 emigrants were permitted to go to East Germany as well.

After 1980 German emigration, like that of Jews and Armenians, was sharply reduced, but by the end of 1985 a total of 105,000 Soviet Germans had left the USSR since the end of the war, the vast majority (94,000) for West Germany, the rest for East Germany (11,000). It is believed that those who chose to resettle in the German Democratic Republic did so either because they had relatives or friends there or else thought it would be easier to reemigrate to West Germany from there than directly from the USSR, which an undetermined number in fact did. Today, it is estimated that from 100,000 to one million other Germans would still emigrate to the West, if permitted to.

Armenian Emigration.[8] In contrast to Jewish and German emigration, which have some parallels and similarities, Armenian emigration is unique. Both the status of the Armenians in the USSR since World War II and their reasons for leaving are different from those of the Jews and Germans, and it requires some background information to clarify them.

Since 1920, when a short-lived independent Armenian state was annexed by the Soviet Union and established as a union republic of the USSR, there has been a nominally sovereign Armenia in part of what is considered today by Armenian nationalists as greater—or historic—Armenia. In 1979, 4.14 million of the world's estimated 5 million Armenians lived in the USSR, 70 percent of them in the Armenian SSR, the remainder in other Soviet republics. Within the Armenian SSR, Armenians comprised 90 percent of the population, largely spoke Armenian,[9] and freely observed traditional customs, religion, and cultural practices. They also governed themselves, albeit under the guidance of the Communist party, in which they held high offices, and the Armenian SSR was and still is one of the most prosperous republics in the Soviet Union with a high average standard of living by Soviet measure. The Armenians are well educated, take pride in a rich cultural and intellectual legacy, and rank high in scientific, technical, and other intellectual achievements today. In recognition of their accomplishments, a branch of the Academy of Sciences of the USSR has been established in the Armenian republic, and by the testimony of both visitors to Armenia and natives themselves, life is uncommonly bountiful and free by Soviet standards.

Why then have more than 50,000 Armenians emigrated from there, and why do many thousands more want to do so today? The answer is that the impetus for emigration has come not from the native Armenians, but from a unique group of recent immigrants to the Armenian SSR who arrived during the years following the Second World War and then tried to return to the West again. Shortly after the end of the war the Soviet government issued a call to former nationals (and others) to help rebuild the country by returning to their former homeland, where they would be granted citizenship and provided with assistance to establish new lives. Among those who responded between 1946 and 1970 were an estimated 200,000 to 250,000 Armenians living in Europe, the Middle East, North Africa, North America, and elsewhere where they and their forebears had taken refuge after the Turkish massacres of the early years of this century. Though they were not former Soviet citizens, they considered the Armenian SSR their national "homeland" and religious center, and they were also attracted by exaggerated promises of Soviet agents sent abroad to recruit them concerning the conditions that awaited them.

Instead of the reception they had been told they would receive, the urbane, Westernized newcomers found a backward, undeveloped land with an uneducated, impoverished peasantry that spoke a different dialect than theirs, had little in common with them, and viewed them with suspicion and resentment. This resentment turned to hostility when the authorities forcibly billeted the newcomers in the homes of the natives because the housing they had been promised did not exist. The money and property they had brought with them were confiscated, and when several thousands of them protested publicly, they were arrested and deported to Siberia. Though the immigrants had advanced Western skills and knowledge, they were kept from the best positions in the administration and economy and barred from rising to the highest levels by jealous local officials.

As a result of this rejection and hostility, they concentrated in ghettos apart from the local inhabitants, nursed their grievances, passed on their alienation to their children, and awaited an opportunity to return to the West. Though they applied their skills and knowledge to the postwar economic revolution that transformed the sleepy Caucasian republic into a productive and modern region and themselves prospered in the process, they knew they could fare even better in the West, which they were repeatedly reminded of by visitors from the Armenian diaspora abroad.

Such an opportunity arose in the middle 1950s for approximately

12,000 Armenians who had immigrated to the USSR from France when the French government intervened on their behalf and obtained permission for them to return. Anxious at the time to please the French, the Soviet government assented on the technical grounds of "repatriating" former citizens of another country so as to avoid a conflict with the legal obstacles to voluntary emigration and to prevent setting a precedent for others to follow.[10]

By 1960 the first exodus of Armenians had ended, but the remainder awaited an opportunity to follow them to the West. This came unexpectedly when the Soviet government eased the requirements for emigrating for Jews and Germans on the grounds of family reunification, as it has been seen. Disaffected Armenians could also claim relatives in the West, owing to their large extended families in various parts of the world. Applying to leave on the same grounds as Jews and Germans, at first a few and then increasing numbers of Armenians sought successfully to leave the country. Surprisingly, the Soviet authorities—actually, Armenian officials who tended to be lenient toward their compatriots—permitted the exodus to grow between 1972 and 1980, when it peaked with nearly 14,000 emigrants in the latter year (see tables 6.1 and 6.2).

No sooner had the movement reached a peak in 1980, than it rapidly declined, paralleling the cutback of Jewish and German emigration levels after that date. In 1985 fewer than 250 Armenians were permitted to leave, slightly more than the preceding year. Most of the emigrants (other than the 12,000 who returned to France) resettled in the United States, though they had not originally come from there, 90 percent choosing the Los Angeles area, the rest older Armenian communities around Boston and New York. Knowledgeable informants report that 200,000 additional Armenians would leave today if permitted to, or, in other words, the entire original immigrant community. No native Armenians have sought to leave and none have been permitted to do so until now.

Soviet Emigration Policy

If these factors explain emigrant motives for leaving the USSR, what accounts for Soviet policy toward the exodus? Why did the government of the USSR relax its historic antipathy toward voluntary emigration by Jews, Germans, and Armenians for a time and then restrict it again? The most honest and direct answer to these questions is that no one really knows. There are clues, indications, and suggestions but no concrete evidence. What is presented here is a distillation of informed opinion on the subject of Soviet politics and emigration and the results of original research.

As regards Jewish and German emigration, Soviet policy appears to correlate with three sets of factors—namely, internal developments within the USSR, American and West German diplomacy vis-à-vis the Soviet Union, and international public opinion.[11] Internal Soviet developments include the general relaxation of political controls in the 1970s under Brezhnev that accompanied détente with the West and heightened pressure by Soviet Jews and Germans for the right to leave. Members of both nationalities circulated petitions, staged public demonstrations, sent appeals to Soviet and foreign officials, stormed Western embassies in Moscow, held unauthorized press conferences with foreign correspondents, and engaged in other forms of protest, civil disobedience, and resistance calculated to attract international attention. Though the efforts of both nationalities were conducted independently of one another, there is evidence that the Germans were inspired by and consciously emulated the Jews.

Surprisingly, the Soviet authorities dealt leniently with this unaccustomed behavior and permitted increasing numbers of emigrants of both nationalities to leave. There is no doubt that had the government chosen to do so, it could have repressed these movements with ease—as it has done since 1981—but why it yielded instead is not positively known.

Dealings with the West also were an apparent factor in the easing of emigration for Soviet Jews and Germans. Détente and *Ostpolitik* promised the USSR improved relations and security, increased trade and technology exchanges, and other benefits. Both sides openly used emigration as a bargaining chip in their negotiations, the United States and West Germany pressing for more liberal emigration policies for Jews and Germans, while the Soviet government traded callously in humans for concessions from the West. The signing of the Helsinki accords in 1975, viewed by some observers as a turning point in East-West relations, was, in fact, a confirmation of ongoing processes epitomized by the trade-off between Western carrot-and-stick tactics with respect to the USSR and the ups and downs in emigration quotas.[12]

The influence of international public opinion on Soviet emigration policy is difficult to gauge, but there is reason to believe that the wide press coverage given to the issue of emigration, the activities of human rights organizations and special interest groups concerned with the emigrants, demonstrations before Soviet embassies in Western capitals, parliamentary declarations and denunciations, and confrontations with Soviet diplomats in the West by activists supporting the emigrants all helped to ease Soviet emigration policy for a time. At least in the 1970s the government of the USSR appeared to be sensitive to Western public opinion in order to improve its image and influence foreign governments through their constituencies. When tougher leaders succeeded Brezhnev, they became increasingly insensitive to outside criticism, however, even from Western Communist parties.

If these factors suggest reasons why the Soviet government eased emigration restrictions for Jews and Germans during the 1970s, its parallel policy toward the Armenians is more difficult to explain.[13] In contrast to the Jews and Germans, the Armenians had no Western government championing their interests, for although the United States provided the Armenian emigrants with a haven, the American government did not represent them. Indeed, the leaders of the international Armenian diaspora strongly deplored and discouraged emigration from the Armenian SSR, for they believed it weakened and discredited the only national "homeland" they had and which they hoped would one day become the core of a restored "Greater Armenia." Therefore, there was no Armenian lobby in Washington or other Western capitals and no pressure groups working on the Armenian emigrants' behalf, as was the case with the Jews and Germans.

Thus, it is difficult to account for Soviet leniency toward Armenian emigration. Several explanations have been suggested, including the benign neglect of the Armenian republic under the Brezhnev regime; the desire of Armenian officials to be rid of troublesome malcontents who might attract unwanted attention from Moscow; efforts by the central Soviet authorities to dispel the impression that they had caved in to Western pressure on behalf of the Jews and Germans by permitting another "eligible" nationality to emigrate; and the Soviet government's policy of courting Armenian goodwill both within the USSR and in the international diaspora against a time when possible difficulties with Turkey or in the Middle East might make the Armenian SSR a strategic buffer or base.

Whatever the reasons, policy toward all three groups changed after 1980. Exit quotas were sharply reduced thereafter (see tables 6.1 and 6.2), visa procedures were made more difficult and costly, persistent applicants (refuseniks) were dealt with increasingly harshly, and the government intensified its propaganda campaign against leaving.[14] The reasons for this change of policy are as unclear as those that account for the original liberalization of emigration, but two sets of factors have been suggested. These are the presumed adverse effects of the Third Emigration on the USSR and certain internal and foreign developments.

With respect to the consequences of the Third Emigration for the Soviet Union, the conventional wisdom holds that there have been four main negative results. These are the loss of skilled and productive labor at a time of economic stagnation and a declining work force; the destabilizing effect of allowing some but not other disaffected groups to emigrate from the USSR; the pressure the exodus exerted on the regime to improve conditions within the Soviet Union so as to stanch the flight abroad; and the embarrassment the exodus caused the Soviet leaders who boasted that they had created a socialist utopia in the USSR and resolved the nationality problem there "for all time."[15]

On analysis, however, these alleged negative consequences do not suffice to explain the reversal of Soviet emigration policy at the end of the 1970s. The total number of workers lost to the Soviet economy over the years of the movement is relatively small, compared to the total work force. Moreover, the loss of Jewish scientific and technical specialists in particular was offset by their gradual supplanting by non-Jewish specialists as early as the 1960s, and the Germans who left in the 1970s were important but hardly critical to the agricultural, industrial, and service sectors of the Soviet economy when weighed in the larger balance.

As for pressure on the Soviet leaders exerted by the exodus or the claimed threat to the political stability of the USSR, it is simply unarguable that the Soviet regime has more than adequate means to mold public opinion in the USSR, maintain domestic order and control, and compel conformity with official norms. With respect to the alleged embarrassment the exodus caused the Soviet leaders, this may have been true in Brezhnev's time, but since his passing his successors have proven to be increasingly indifferent to Western criticism, even from fellow West European communists. Thus, the presumed negative consequences of the Third Emigration do not suffice to explain the change of Soviet emigration policy after 1980.

Rather, shifts in the internal and international factors that originally led to the liberalization of emigration policy appear to have been more consequential. These include a general tightening of political controls in the USSR beginning in Brezhnev's last years, which was directed at all forms of dissidence and nonconformity, including emigration, which had always run against the grain of Soviet political authoritarianism; the erosion of détente and Soviet disillusionment with the failure of its promised material benefits to materialize by the late 1970s; and the growing confrontation between the USSR and the United States over such issues as nuclear arms control, regional conflicts, and East-West trade and technology transfer. At the same time relations between the USSR and West Germany also cooled during the second half of the 1970s under Chancellor Schmidt and his successor Helmut Kohl.[16]

Finally, pressure from international public opinion declined in the late 1970s as new problems diverted the attention of human rights groups and fatigue or discouragement drained the vitality of organizations that continued to champion emigration. Why the Soviet government also restricted Armenian emigration, considering its unrelatedness to Jewish and German emigration, is as difficult to explain as are Soviet motives for originally permitting it. In any case by the middle 1980s détente was dead, emigration by all three groups was at a virtual standstill, and the future of the movement was in great doubt.

Future Prospects

What do the coming years hold in store for those who still want to leave the Soviet Union, estimated to total as many as two million Jews, Germans, and Armenians—not to speak of other disaffected groups in the USSR? What are the prospects of a revival of the Third Emigration; under what circumstances might this occur; and what, if anything, can be done in the West to encourage it? These are complex questions that cut across the entire spectrum of Soviet internal and foreign relations and require predicting Soviet behavior, which is even more difficult than explaining past conduct. Answers here can be only brief and speculative, for a fuller treatment of them would exceed the scope and available space of this paper.

Judging by recent events affecting Soviet emigration, however, the future prospects of the movement do not appear to be promising. Notwithstanding Secretary Gorbachev's vaunted policy of glasnost, there has been no relaxation—indeed a reinforcement—of political controls, social regimentation, and pressures for conformity in the USSR. These have been directed toward all forms of dissidence in the Soviet Union, including efforts to emigrate from the country. Though a number of prominent dissidents have been permitted to leave since Gorbachev has come to power and in recent months there have been modest increases in the number of emigrants, these concessions have been carefully orchestrated by the Soviet government to blunt criticism at the Vienna review conference of Helsinki Accord signatories and to soften Western attitudes concerning outstanding East-West issues. Moreover, most of the recent emigrants from the USSR have been longtime refuseniks whose cases have been activated in order to clear a backlog of appeals, not new applicants. Indeed, the new emigration regulations issued in 1986 and scheduled to take effect on January 1, 1987, will make emigration more difficult, not—contrary to Soviet claims—easier for prospective new applicants.[17]

Even if the best possible construction were to be put on Gorbachev's policies and intentions, there are questions among Western Soviet observers as to how firmly he is in control of power in the USSR and how long he will endure. In any case there is no reason to doubt, and much cause for confidence, that even if he remains head of the Soviet government he will continue to hold emigration hostage to East-West relations and yield only what and when he must. A return to the liberal emigration policies and comparatively large numbers of emigrants of the Brezhnev era is simply inconceivable in the foreseeable future. This prognosis contains a number of policy implications for Western governments concerned with the prospective emigrants who still want to leave the USSR, but this subject transcends the scope and purpose of this paper.[18]

Nevertheless, there are possible future developments that could alter this pessimistic prognosis—such as a breakthrough in East-West negotiations on nuclear arms control and other issues in dispute; a Mideast settlement that involves Soviet participation and a resumption of diplomatic relations between the USSR and Israel; or a decision of the Soviet leaders to resolve the issue of emigration once and for all by permitting those who want to leave to do so, providing this does not jeopardize any vital national interest. To fall back on an overused but still valid cliché—only the future will tell.

Epilogue

Since this essay was written in late 1986, fast-moving events in the USSR have overtaken its pessimistic forecast, which was justified by the state of affairs at the time of its writing. The revival of East-West détente, the

Table 6.6. Emigration by Nationality, 1971–85

Year	Jews	Germans	Armenians	Total
1986	914	931	247	2,092
1987	8,155	14,488	3,296	25,939
1988 (January–July)	7,886	20,913	7,882	36,681

adoption of the policies of glasnost and perestroika, and the rapprochement between the Soviet Union and Israel, among other developments since 1987, have radically affected the Third Emigration. By mid-year 1988, when this epilogue is being written, the emigration of Jews, Germans, and Armenians has revived, contrary to the discouraging signs at the end of 1986. The numbers of emigrants who have left since the end of 1985, the last year covered by the data above, may be seen from table 6.6, which covers the period since 1985 through July 1988.

Several aspects of these statistics are noteworthy. One is the fact that the total emigration from the USSR since the inception of the movement in 1948 now exceeds half a million persons. Second, the dramatic increase in emigration has reached the point where 1988 will probably become the second highest year since the exodus began, lagging behind only the peak year of 1979 when 67,000 persons left the USSR. Third, the statistics show that German emigration has far exceeded Jewish emigration for the first time during 1986–88, reversing the ratio between them until now. Finally, the number of Armenian emigrants has also increased since 1986, despite the disturbances in the Armenian and Azerbaijan SSRs, which did not involve prospective Armenian emigrants or apparently affect the rate of their exodus.

Reasons for the rise in numbers of emigrants and the shifts in proportions of Jews and Germans are not known. Presumably they are linked to the changes in East-West relations and the relaxation of internal Soviet political controls since 1987, as well as Soviet efforts to woo West Germany and seek a rapprochement with the State of Israel. But these are only presumptions and do not alone explain the changes in the movement. Soviet emigration policy remains as enigmatic today as during earlier stages of the Third Emigration and therefore precludes reliable predictions concerning possible future developments.

Part Three

Alternative Strategies for Promoting the Emigration and Resettlement of Soviet Jews

7. Soviet-American Trade and Soviet Jewish Emigration: Should a Policy Change Be Made by the American Jewish Community?

Marshall I. Goldman

When historians look back a century from now at American-Soviet relations, one of the biggest puzzles they will have to explain is how the "Jewish" question came to be such an important issue. On the one hand they will probably be astounded that the Soviet leaders "caved in" so often on the issue of emigration, something they had always been so inflexible about. On the other hand they will marvel at how the Jewish community overplayed its hand and found itself a victim of dogmatic policy. Ironically, they seem to have fallen victim to a form of hard-line conformity that traditionally was assumed to be a shortcoming of Soviet, not American leaders.

This chapter will attempt to provide some of the answers for those historians of the twenty-first century. We will examine how Jewish emigration came to play such a central role. We will also consider what if anything could have been done to achieve an even more successful result. Along the way we will make some strong assumptions and some painful assertions. This analysis may also suggest some of the pitfalls that face leaders of any large pressure group. It is frequently easier to develop a coalition and form a consensus than to reroute that consensus in a different direction once that initial agreement has been reached.

Soviet authorities traditionally insist, loudly and frequently, that the Soviet Union never bends to outside pressure. In their minds they are a proud and strong nation and thus will not be pushed around by outsiders as so many of the weaker nations of the world have been. (Of course much of that pushing comes not only from the United States, but from the Soviet Union itself.) There is no doubt that the Soviet Union does resist pressure and is well noted for its stubbornness as any secretary of state or minister of foreign affairs will testify.

Yet having heard the Soviet assert their independence for so long, one cannot help but feel they are protesting too much. Such protests are not only used as an offensive measure to ward off attempts at pressure, but also as a psychological palliative to mask feelings of inferiority. More confident individuals or nations normally need not be as strident. After all every nation, including the Soviet Union, sometime or another makes concessions to one foreign interest group or another when they consider it to be in their best interest to do so. The United States presidents do it all the time. That, after all, is politics. It may just be that the Soviets fear that a public acknowledgment of one concession will likely lead to demands for more concessions from the same as well as other pressure goups. Certainly that helps to explain Soviet refusal to yield the four islands that are referred to as the Northern Territories by the Japanese. They fear that if they were to return those islands to the Japanese, this act would be seen by the Japanese as a sign of weakness which would lead the Japanese to escalate their demands to include, for example, cash compensation for the years the islands have been in Soviet hands. Even more of a concern is the fear that the Chinese will regard any Soviet return of territory as a precedent that logically should lead to the return of Soviet territory that has long been claimed by Chinese irredentists. Since the territory in dispute involves thousands of square miles, there is a considerable amount at stake here. Yet even on the territory issue, the Soviets have occasionally found it expedient to cede territory. Thus they have returned parts of Karelia to Finland and withdrawn their troops from Austria, again because they judged that the benefits of such withdrawals outweighed the costs of insisting on the status quo.

The treatment of Jews in the Soviet Union is one of those issues where the Soviets have been most strident in their language but at the same time often remarkably flexible in their behavior. Nor is the "Jewish issue" a new phenomenon in that part of the world. In 1911, before the revolution, the treatment of the Jews by the czarist government became a major source of dispute between the American and Russian governments. Jewish groups and the U.S. government began to protest the pogroms against Russian Jews the czarist government seemed to tolerate if not encourage. This evoked public protest in the United States and led to calls for legislation that would limit the exports of Russian goods to the United States. As a consequence, in December 1911 the House of Representatives voted 300 to 1 to terminate the U.S. trade treaty with Russia. After some resistance President Taft finally agreed to go along in order to put pressure on the Russian government. He sought to pressure the Russian government into cracking down on the pogroms then underway.[1] Some improvement in conditions for the Jews in Russia did result. It's unclear to what extent, if any, this historical precedent did influence either American analysts in their decision to adopt similar pressures on the Soviets in the 1970s or Soviet leaders in their decision to yield to pressure. However, even though the two confrontations have involved quite different concerns, there are some intriguing similarities in the way policy eventually evolved.

Even though there was the President Taft precedent, the fact that Soviet Jews would ultimately take the lead in forcing the Soviets to change their rigid policy on emigration is not something that most analysts would have predicted. The Jews had been among the most quiescent of all the different Soviet ethnic groups. There seemed to be little overt concern about the destruction of all but a few synagogues throughout the country. Nor did the Jews evidence much protest over the decision to join with the Nazis in the Nazi-Soviet Pact in 1939.[2] Even more dispiriting, the Jews seemed to fall victim to Stalin's massive post-World War II crackdown on the Jews when he executed a large number of Jewish leaders and intelligentsia in the early 1950s and then again when he inaugurated the Doctors' Plot just before his death in 1953. We know that the Jews were aware of what was happening to them and what would probably happen as the Doctor's Plot began to reach its climax.[3] But there seemed to be little protest or organization for self-defense.

It was not only that the Jews were docile; by 1970 even the most militant groups in the Soviet Union seemed to have come to accept their fate. Stalin had crushed most of them, and although Khrushchev and Brezhnev after him had relaxed the pressure on nationality groups somewhat, only the most benign forms of cultural or nationalistic assertions seemed to continue.

This was demonstrated to me in an unusual experience I had in December 1970. I had been invited to the Soviet Union as a participant in a dialogue between Soviet and American peace groups. Our goal was to thrash out issues that divided us in an informal way in the hope that we could then reach an agreement in a more relaxed environment. These solutions then might be picked up at a more formal level by official bilateral negotiators. This meant that at our level we could and did discuss some of the most sensitive issues without having to worry about a record being kept. In that spirit I raised the issue of the trial of a group of Soviet Jews, mostly from the Leningrad region, who had been sentenced to death for plotting to hijack an airplane and fly it to Israel. They were stopped before they even boarded the plane. Nonetheless, why I asked, as if out of naïveté, was the Soviet Union being so insistent on the death penalty for those allegedly involved in the hijacking? Spain, which had originally sentenced a group to death, had just announced that it had commuted the sentences to a prison term. Finally I argued that the Soviet Union should take a more enlightened stand on the question of emigration. There were not many people involved so why was the Soviet Union making such a fuss, particularly when doing so set off a clamor in world public opinion.

One of my Soviet counterparts responded immediately. I should understand, he said, that all of this was not directed specifically at the Jews. Hijacking was something we all condemned, and as for emigration, no one is allowed to emigrate from the Soviet Union. So why should we make a special exception for them? If we did, we would have many different people and groups of people asking to go. So it is not just a policy against the Jews.

Then an unusual event occurred. The leader of the Soviet delegation asked for the floor. Apologizing to his colleague, he then proceeded to contradict him. That was a breach of Soviet protocol I had never seen before. Usually, right or wrong, the Soviets are monolithic. But, nonetheless, the leader of the Soviet group felt obliged to report that he had just flown to Vienna, and to his surprise the bulk of the plane had been filled with Jews who had just been authorized to emigrate from the Soviet Union. This came as a big surprise to him (and to most of the rest of us in the room), but he felt he should report it. He had just seen and we had just heard a policy change.

What accounted for this remarkable turn of events? As a look at Appendix I suggests, through 1970 the number of Jews allowed to leave the country averaged less than 2,000 a year. This increased to 13,000 in 1971 and tripled in 1972. It is hard to know precisely, but two factors were quite important in precipitating the change, and they included both internal and external pressures.

Internally many Jews in the Soviet Union developed a form of militance that was unprecedented for them. Most observers agree that, as much as anything, the chief catalyst was the Six-Day War in Israel.[4] The fact that the Jews of Israel had stood up for themselves and for their lives and won a stunning victory did more for Jewish nationalism around the world than almost anything since Moses at Sinai. If anything, the effect in the Soviet Union was even more electric because the Soviet Union had allied itself with the Arabs. Watching the Soviet Union work for the defeat, and thus the presumed destruction of Israel and the death of those Jews living there, was a breaking point for many. They had watched the Holocaust and Stalin's attacks, and no one did anything about any of it. But in this instance Israel had triumphed, and it was such an unexpected victory by what had been regarded as such a fragile state that it sparked sympathetic responses all over, including the Soviet Union. It was not only that the Jews had stood up for themselves and won, but that they now had a legitimate state that demonstrated that it was capable of defending its citizens. After many long and painful years of anti-Semitism, there was now a state that would speak for all Jews if they could only gain access to its borders.

This realization emboldened many to apply for permission to emigrate—a revolutionary initiative. Moreover, more and more began to teach themselves Hebrew and the religious observances. To the Soviet authorities, who at the time prohibited the formation of all private groups, this was subversive. For the most part the authorities were unyielding. Nonetheless, more and more joined the ranks of these unofficial groups despite police crackdowns which almost always meant the loss of jobs and sometimes even a prison sentence.

As impressive as these acts of defiance were, they might still have come to naught if it had not been for developments external to the Soviet Union. During the the late 1960s the Soviet Union began an effort to improve its relationship with Western Europe. Major commercial contracts were signed with European companies. The agreement in 1968 with Fiat in Italy to build a massive automobile assembly plant at Togliatti was just one instance. To encourage such interaction the Soviets decided it would help improve their image if they could show a more humane attitude. The increase in emigration was one consequence.

Accommodation had its limits however. Even in their "Mister Nice Guy" mode the Soviets never went so far as to let everyone out who asked to go. Moreover, visa permits were almost always accompanied by raids, beatings, arrests, and the publication of anti-Jewish tracts. These two-pronged policies are traditional in Russia. It is necessary to keep the population guessing. If there were no risks attached to seeking permission to emigrate, almost everyone eligible would apply. Moreover, those ineligible to apply because they were not Jewish would become difficult to deal with. As it is, there is considerable resentment that some groups, the Jews and growing numbers of Germans and Armenians, were being treated as a special exclusive category. Soviet officials evidently decided that there should be some risk and uncertainty for those who wanted to desert the Soviet Union.

The concern about outside public opinion increased as the Soviet desire for improved foreign relations was extended to encompass the United States. Any such opening had first to overcome the fact that the United States was fighting in Vietnam and the Soviet Union was backing North Vietnam. However, the Soviet Union was particularly eager to avail itself of American products and technology and to do this it needed to expand trade and qualify itself for credits from the Export-Import Bank and commercial banks in the United States. This the Soviet Union could not do, however, because it had defaulted on its World War II debt to the United States. But except for Finland, most of our allies had also not paid their debts. To circumscribe this awkwardness the United States government then passed the Johnson Act which barred access to credits unless those who had defaulted their Lend Lease obligations of World War II joined the World Bank and the International Monetary Fund, something the Soviet Union had refused to do. But in 1971, while it did not agree to join either the World Bank or the International Monetary Fund, the Soviet Union did agree as a show of good faith that it would begin the process of repaying its Lend Lease debt according to a predetermined schedule. This was an unprecedented concession by the Soviets who heretofore had insisted that they had no reason to pay back such debts (even if the specific debts were incurred after the end of hostilities) because the Soviet Union had already paid a high price in lost lives during the war. Indeed, in a discussion with the United States secretary of commerce before negotiations over this issue was to begin, most of the academic advisers the secretary asked had agreed the Soviet side would never budge on this issue.[5]

In exchange for such concessions the United States made some of its own. In the October 18, 1972, U.S.-Soviet trade agreement, the United States agreed to extend most favored nation status (MFN) to the Soviet Union. This meant that American businessmen could import Soviet goods at tariffs that were no higher than the tariffs applied to similar products from other producers of the world. Heretofore the buyers of Soviet goods had been forced to pay the considerably higher tariffs imposed during the Smoot-Hawley protectionist days of the 1930s. In principle this had put Soviet goods at an almost impossibly high disadvantage. In fact, however, the higher tariffs made relatively little difference because the Soviet Union was unable to manufacture much that was of interest to American buyers. For the most part the Soviet Union could only find buyers for its raw materials, particularly its oil and natural gas. The proof of this was indicated by the failure of the Soviet Union to sell any significant volume of manufactured goods to countries which did extend MFN to the Soviets. Even these countries concentrated most of their purchases from the Soviet Union on oil and natural gas.

It was generally agreed, therefore, that the main reason the Soviet Union wanted MFN status was first of all for reasons of national pride— it wanted to be treated just like everyone else. A second factor, however, was that with MFN the Soviet Union became eligible for both government and increased commercial credits, and for the most part this was considerably more important to the Soviet Union than MFN.

To make all these arrangements as palatable as possible to the American public, the Soviets decided to show their "Mister Nice Guy" side. It is certainly more than coincidence that the emigration doors which had been barely left open for long were opened wider and wider in the courtship and subsequent honeymoon days of détente. By 1972, as Appendix 1 indicates, the flow had expanded to 31,681 and 34,733 in 1973.

Sensing how eager the Soviets were to avail themselves of MFN and those credits, a unique alliance of various American groups was formed to see if it could obtain even more concessions, particularly in the way of emigration from the Soviet Union. At least this was the motivation of many of the Jewish organizations and liberal human rights groups involved in this coalition. However, there were others, conservatives, who joined in with the more liberal representatives for other reasons as well. Many of these conservative organizations were interested in joining any effort to restrain U.S.-Soviet relations and hoped to pressure the Soviets and hold down U.S.-Soviet trade.[6] Thus the AFL-CIO was particularly active in supporting the bills jointly sponsored by Senator Henry Jackson and Congressman Charles Vanik of Ohio. Largely the conception of Senator Jackson's assistant, Richard Perle, this bill, which penalized the USSR for imposing an exorbitant "head tax" on educated Jews seeking to emigrate from the USSR, hit right at the heart of what the Soviets wanted from the process of détente—credits and MFN status. Moreover, the Jackson-Vanik amendment turned out to be one of the few issues that conservatives could sponsor that would attract liberals as well. It was a brilliant strategy and by default, came to occupy the center of U.S.-Soviet relations for what remained of the period of détente. (For the text of the amendment, see Appendix 2.)

It took some time for the Soviets to comprehend exactly what had happened to them. Initially they had assumed that once they had signed the U.S.-Soviet trade agreement, all they had to do was draw down the credits. After all, even signing the agreement had been a strain because it looked for quite a while that the United States would never agree to sign any such documents. Official American policy has traditionally been that trade is multilateral, and therefore the United Startes has been opposed to signing bilateral agreements with the Soviet Union or anyone else for that matter. Thus the reluctant American agreement was considered by the Russians to be quite a triumph.

What the Soviets had taken for granted, and what no one else had bothered to make much fuss about, was that an agreement by the executive branch of the American government to support an international agreement does not necessarily mean that the agreement has been put into effect. Unlike the Soviet Union, in the United States the Congress often heads in a direction different from that of the executive branch. In fairness to the American watchers in the Soviet Union, however, it should be noted that disagreement between Congress and the executive branch was to become much more common after 1972 when the move toward détente began. In fact, disagreement over what our policy should be with the Soviet Union led to an abnormally high number of clashes between the two branches of government so that now almost everyone in the Soviet Union has come to realize that no agreement with the United States becomes effective until the Congress as well as the administration approves of it. But, unfortunately for American-Soviet relations, the experience with MFN proved to be an expensive and painful learning exercise. On top of everything else, the Soviets, having heard their own Marxist rhetoric, had assumed that the American business community determined all American policy.[7] The overwhelming bulk of the American business community had testified and worked actively for congressional passage of MFN status for the Soviets. Moreover, after each delay a new group of American businessmen would troop to Moscow and urge Soviet leaders to be patient; approval would be imminent.[8]

Whatever the doubts the Soviets ultimately came to have about what Marx said about the power of capitalist businessmen, it seemed clear that they began to have a new appreciation for Russian folklore which attributed even more power to the Jews. It was hard not to believe that the "Zionists" dominated Congress. Therefore, it seemed to make sense to be responsive to the demands of the Jewish community and increase the number of those allowed to emigrate.

For a time it actually looked like an informal agreement had been reached. The Soviets would allow as many as 45,000 Jews a year to emigrate (Jackson thought the number should be 60,000) in return for modification of the proposed Jackson-Vanik bill that would authorize MFN status for the Soviet Union if the American president was convinced that the Soviets were adhering "substantially to the achievement of the objectives" of Jackson-Vanik. This arrangement had apparently been put together by Andrei Gromyko and Henry Kissinger in a May 1974 meeting in Cyprus.[9] This semiofficial understanding was spelled out in an exchange of letters between Kissinger and Jackson and between Kissinger and Gromyko in October 1974 (see Appendix 5). After the Vladivostok summit meeting between President Gerald Ford and Leonid Brezhnev, everything seemed to be in order. However, on January 14, 1975, Kissinger unexpectedly reported that the Soviet Union had decided not to go through with the understanding.

What caused the reversal? It is hard to know exactly, and there are some who argue that there had never been an agreement in the first place. Gromyko's letter is ambiguous and does allow for such an interpretation, but it is also possible to read it as indicating that a careful understanding had indeed been reached. There were probably several contributing factors for the reversal. Apparently, some Soviet leaders did not like the idea of any such understanding.[10] In particular they were apparently offended by the way that Senators Jackson, Jacob Javits, and Abraham Ribicoff trumpeted what initially seemed to be their victory. It would perhaps have been smarter to have made no fuss at all.

Even more important, the Soviets seemed to be particularly distressed by the passage of two other amendments to the Jackson-Vanik amendment which had apparently been lost sight of in the fuss over

MFN. These two amendments, introduced by Senator Frank Church and Senator Adlai Stevenson III, focused not on MFN but credit limits and credit for energy development. The Stevenson amendment was approved by Congress on December 19, 1974. Since, as pointed out above, there would probably be little in the way of increased Soviet exports to the United States, even with MFN, the real Soviet hope was to use MFN only as a wedge to obtain more credits. Once it was decided to deny or strictly circumscribe those credits, there was nothing to be gained from the Soviet point of view, and so they denied that they had agreed to any such arrangement. Gromyko pointed to his October 26, 1974, letter which could be interpreted either way. That is why as late as December 18, 1974, Kissinger continued to insist that an understanding did exist and that Gromyko's October 26 letter indicated as much, provided no further public crowing took place.

The Soviets were quick to demonstrate their bitterness. As Appendix I indicates, emigration was curbed even more in 1975 to about two-thirds of what it had been in 1974. In fact emigration figures generally remained low throughout 1977. None of this is meant to argue that the Soviets attempted to "fine-tune" the flow of emigration to reflect the

Table 7.1. U.S.-Soviet Trade 1972–84

	1972	1973	1974	1975	1976	197
U.S. Exports (millions $)						
Food and live animals	370	842	292	1,113	1,359	876
Chemicals	21	17	28	44	37	40
Manufactured goods	10	35	27	52	116	89
Machinery and transportation equipment	62	204	225	547	605	374
Miscellaneous manufactured articles	9	9	13	36	7	44
Total	547	1,187	612	1,833	2,306	1,623
U.S. Imports (millions $)						
Mineral fuels	7	76	106	96	54	64
Chemicals	1	2	12	6	6	6
Manufactured goods	64	118	204	97	85	97
Machinery and tools	.5	.1	2	5	4	3
Total	95	215	349	254	220	234

prospects for MFN status. However, the increase and decrease in the numbers allowed to emigrate was not unrelated to the Soviet desire to win favor or demonstrate anger.

Progress, or lack of it, in achieving MFN status seemed to have played a more important role in setting emigration levels than the flow of U.S.-manufactured exports to the Soviet Union. Except for 1970 and 1971, the low point of Jewish emigration in the 1970s occurred in 1975 and 1976 which, as table 7.1 indicates, was when U.S. machinery exports to the Soviet Union reached record highs. A large percentage of the machinery exported in both years was intended for the Kama River Truck Plant. Thereafter, except for 1979, the dollar value of machinery exports in both current and real dollars declined. Total American exports, at least in current dollars, reached a high in 1979, but that was because the Soviet Union experienced a very bad grain harvest. Grain production fell 25 percent from 237 million tons in 1978 to 179 million tons in 1979, and the Soviets compensated by importing a substantial portion of that shortfall from the United States. It should be remembered that there is often a gap between the time when an order is placed and the time the product is actually exported, particularly for major construc-

78	1979	1980	1981	1982	1983	1984
42	2,283	972	1,600	1,642	1,195	2,585
30	134	31	180	288	239	208
57	48	25	32	26	30	17
83	363	269	301	225	149	110
98	110	99	46	59	76	66
49	3,604	1,510	2,339	2,589	2,002	3,283
44	16	17	112	11	59	203
37	68	149	94	131	161	235
03	160	139	88	63	91	108
3	4	3	2	2	4	3
40	550	453	347	248	367	602

tion projects like the Kama River Truck Plant. However, even with such an allowance, the Soviets do not appear to have used actual orders or shipments as a lever to win MFN status. They did, of course, hold out the temptation of very large contracts to American businessmen if the United States would grant MFN status, but these contracts were as much dependent on the willingness of the U.S. Department of Commerce authorities to grant licenses, as Congress's voting to extend MFN.

With the final signing of the Jackson-Vanik amendment in January 1975, the flow of immigrants from the Soviet Union for the next few years fell, and conditions generally were much bleaker than they had been in the more optimistic years of 1972 and 1973. It was not only a question of numbers but also of pressure in the form of arrests. Anatoly Sharansky was arrested in March 1977, not only because he had been a Jewish activist but because he was charged with being a CIA agent. Subsequently, President Carter expressly denied Sharansky had any connection with the CIA. In a direct affront to Carter, however, the Soviets held to their accusation and eventually sentenced Sharansky to jail.[11]

Yet as bleak as events were at this time, efforts were still being made to reach some understanding. Using American businessmen such as Donald Kendall and Armand Hammer, Jewish groups in the United States sought periodically to arrange for the release of various individuals or groups. The Jewish groups kept asking for a sign, promising that such gestures would be taken as an indication that the Soviets would be interested in working out some kind of compromise. The quid for such quo would then be that the American Jewish groups would dampen their rhetoric and seek a more accommodating trade posture with the Soviet Union.[12]

In what, at the time, often seemed to be a set of random gestures, the Soviets did release some of the more publicized refuseniks. Yet, the Jewish community never seemed to follow through on its part of the understanding. There was no let up in the pressure.

I can remember one particular instance in the 1970s when, in a discussion at the New York conference on Soviet Jewry, I urged that the Jewish community should adopt a more flexible stance. Stanley Lowell, then one of the leaders of the organization, urged instead that nothing be done publicly. Private negotiations were underway, he insisted, and any open change in policy would jeopardize what were then very sensitive negotiations. The end result was that the Soviets responded, but the Jewish community failed to reciprocate.[13]

In what appears to be an anomaly, the Soviets increased the emigration figures in 1978 and again in 1979 to an all-time record high of 51,320. Given that U.S.-Soviet relations had been subject to some particular strains at that time, such as the arrest of the American J. Crawford and the trial and sentencing of Anatoly Sharansky, this relaxation seemed out of character. There were arms control talks at the time; President Carter was busy kissing Secretary General Brezhnev on the cheek in Vienna; and the Soviets were buying substantial quantities of American grain in both 1978 and 1979, but a more likely explanation is that the Soviets were responding primarily to a reconsideration of Jackson-Vanik by the U.S. Congress.

A series of hearings were held in both 1978 and 1979 about revising or abandoning Jackson-Vanik. The 1979 hearings involved the consideration of extending MFN not only to the Soviet Union but to China as well.[14] As before, almost all segments of the organized Jewish community opposed any change, at least in the case of the Soviet Union. When representatives from the American Jewish Congress suggested that some flexibility might be warranted, they were subjected to a barrage of criticisms from other organizations and from within the American Jewish Congress itself. They were accused of breaking ranks, of being untrue to Soviet Jews, and of yielding to pressure from the business community. They responded by arguing for more flexibility.[15] The Soviet Union, after all, had increased the flow of emigrants significantly. At one time the informal understanding was that an outflow of 45,000 emigrants a year would qualify for MFN status. Even though Senator Jackson had argued for 60,000, a rate of 51,000 certainly warranted recognition of what the Soviets had done. As the American Jewish Congress representative saw it, it was important that American Jews and the American government at large show the Soviets that we not only have sticks, but carrots which we are prepared to offer. Such flexibility was particularly important if the Chinese were to be given MFN, which seemed very likely. In the end the Chinese did receive MFN, and the Soviets got nothing. Some of the more extreme groups like the Student Struggle for Soviet Jewry continued to insist on a unified front, and the middle of the road groups, like the National Conference on Soviet Jewry, whatever their internal discussions, held to an inflexible position.

This inflexibility turned out to be disastrous. In retrospect 1978 and 1979 offered a unique opening, and the Jewish community did not respond. Just as the Jewish organizations should be praised for acting so decisively in 1972, for rallying to the Jackson-Vanik bill, so too should they be criticized for refusing to back away from it in 1979. Unfortunately, the Jewish community apparently found itself wrapped up in its rhetoric and unable to consider new, more timely approaches. As a look at the 1979 emigration figures indicates, the Soviets had clearly altered their policies. While the possibility that Congress might grant them MFN status might not have been the only reason that the Soviets decided to raise their border gates, it certainly was a major factor. It must have been particularly disappointing for them to see that not only was their gesture unrequited, but that it was the Chinese who got the carrot of MFN, not the Soviet Union.

There is a danger in attributing everything that happened to a single factor, but what happened subsequently does seem linked to the Soviet failure to win MFN. American-Soviet relations deteriorated rapidly and hit a low with the Soviet invasion of Afghanistan in December 1979. There were many reasons for the invasion: Soviet concern that a new fundamentalist Muslim regime in Afghanistan might infect Soviet Muslims and that the Marxist government installed but a year earlier might be overthrown, and Soviet perception that the United States was so distracted by the U.S. hostage crisis in Iran that we would hardly notice any action the Soviets took in Afghanistan. But, at best, the situation in Afghanistan did not threaten the existence of the Soviet Union; the benefits of such an act were not all that evident. This naturally raises the question of whether or not the Soviets would have acted if they had felt that they had more to lose from such an invasion. In other words, if they had obtained MFN from the United States, would they have been so ready to jeopardize their newly won privileges by the invasion of Afghanistan? This is not to argue that MFN status was all that valuable to them. However, it would have raised the cost of such hostile action. As it was, by failing to obtain MFN the Soviets could only conclude that the United States, and by extension the Jewish community, was inflexible. They could punish, but they could not reward. It is easy to see how, from the Soviet point of view, Soviet leaders would be ill-advised to restrain themselves in hopes of better treatment from the United States.

What explains such inflexibility by the Jewish community? Basically, it is hard to show flexibility to the Soviets or appear to be too generous in dealing with them. It would serve no purpose to write a revisionist history of the period and argue that the full blame for the invasion of Afghanistan was due to an unthinking, bullying policy by the American Jewish community. The Soviets were not innocent in all of this. They always seem to have a knack for doing the wrong thing at the right time. In addition to the arrest of Sharansky and Crawford and the harassment of other refuseniks and dissidents, they also increased their involvement in Africa (Angola and Ethiopia) and Asia (Vietnam and Afghanistan). Under the circumstances, it would have been politically awkward for the American Jewish community to do an about face and embrace the Soviets. That did not rule out, however, a display of somewhat less hostility and an end to attacks on those who favored repeal of the Jackson-Vanik amendment.

There was another factor, however, that also served to temper those who might have come out for MFN for the Soviet Union. Senator Jackson opposed any tampering with his law. Interestingly enough, Congressman Vanik had concluded that the law had outlived its usefulness, but Jackson was as enthusiastic as ever.[16] This posed a real dilemma for the American Jewish community. Senator Jackson had always been a good friend. It was not that his Jewish constituency in the state of Washington was large—it was not. Apparently, his support for such issues stemmed in considerable part from the fact that he had been among some of the first Americans to enter German concentration camps during World War II. Thereafter, he had tried to do all he could to ensure that Jews were not discriminated against, whether it be in the Soviet Union as individuals or in how other countries of the world treated Israel. In the eyes of many it would have been ungrateful for the Jewish community to turn its back on Jackson and support the repeal of Jackson-Vanik.[17] What Vanik thought was of no consequence in this matter; Jackson was the one who counted.

There was also pressure within the Jewish community. As in so many other instances, those in the center found themselves under considerable stress from those who opposed any relaxation of policy. The Jewish Defense League was particularly outspoken, but the Student Struggle for Soviet Jewry was hardly more tolerant.[18] Adding to the pressure were the continuing protests inside the Soviet Union and of émigrés outside the Soviet Union, who kept insisting that the Soviet Union only responds to pressure. These protests were always combined with admonitions that only someone brought up in the Soviet Union could really know how the Soviet mind functioned. What they did not allow for, however, was how the American government might react and how the Soviet government might respond to American signals.

Whatever the explanation, the fact is that the American Jewish community found that it had become captive to its own hard-line policies. Change, and even adaptation, became impossible. After the invasion of Afghanistan, relations between the United States and the Soviet Union all but collapsed. The United States declared a partial grain embargo, decided to boycott the 1980 Olympics in Moscow, and suspended a multitude of exchanges and joint activities, including the suspension of contracts to construct some very large industrial enterprises. As one contract after another was suspended or canceled, the Soviets found that they had less and less reason to hope that they might be able to curry American public opinion. With little at stake Soviet leaders cracked down on dissidents and, as appendix 1 indicates, abruptly reduced the outflow of emigrants so that by 1980 the number of emigrants was reduced to less than half of what it had been in 1979; the numbers were reduced by more than one-half again in 1981, in 1982, and also in 1983. The number of emigrants is now down to about 1000 a year; the question, therefore, is what should our policy be now?

As the Soviets see it, they are the ones who proved the point. They demonstrated that they could survive without American technology and, if need be, without American grain. Turning to alternative sources may sometimes be more costly and less convenient, but the Soviets highlighted the fact that in technology at least the United States no longer could veto sales to the Soviet Union. In many fields there were other equally good, if not superior, suppliers. This was vividly demonstrated as the Soviets found it necessary to look elsewhere for compressors and turbine generators for the natural gas pipeline that they decided to build to Western Europe. The substitute equipment they were forced to use may not have functioned as well, but the pipeline was built, and it has been operating, even if below rated capacity.

At the same time the Soviets proved forcibly that they would not cave-in to too much foreign pressure. Their earlier release of emigrants shows that despite their protestations, they do respond to outside pressure, but only when the benefits outweigh the costs. When the benefits are too meager, they can be unbending. Once the chances for MFN were all but eliminated, the flow of emigrants was slashed to about a thousand a year, and the Soviet authorities all but destroyed the last vestiges of the dissident and peace movements.

The Jackson-Vanik strategy is also considered a failure in the eyes of many in the American foreign policy establishment. This may be a rationalization on their part. For some the human rights issue, wherever it may arise, is a needless obstacle standing in the way of more effective diplomacy. Undoubtedly, there are cases where that is true—after all, today almost every opponent of a government tries to wrap himself in the mantle of human rights. However, there does seem to be a case for arguing that the denial of MFN status to the Soviet Union, once it had been promised, was the main reason why Soviet-American relations never reached their full potential. Along with the desire for an arms-control agreement, most-favored-nation status and the credits which would have followed were the main factors behind the Soviet interest in détente. Once that seemed out of reach, the Soviets felt betrayed. This also raised some doubt about whether or not the United States could be counted upon to honor its commitments. Whatever the precise explanation, the fact remains that American-Soviet relations never reached their full potential. A major victim of this was arms control. The United States and the Soviet Union never fully resolved all their disagreements. It may well have been that given the major differences that separate the countries, arms-control disputes were unresolvable. Yet, there are enough American diplomats who feel that because of Jackson-Vanik, the two countries never accomplished as much as they might have. More importantly, these diplomats are resolved never to let what they regard as subsidiary issues interfere again. As important as emigration may be, in their minds, arms control is even more important.

Having reached the present impasse, we must now look to see what lessons we can learn from the last fifteen years and see if anything can be done to start the flow of émigrés again. The first lesson is to be wary of falling victim to policy consistency. When conditions change, lobbying groups must be able to adapt. When conditions change, those implementing policies must also change. Second, it seems safe to say that Jackson-

Vanik has outlived its usefulness and that, if the Soviets show any inclination that they are prepared to be more flexible, Jewish organizations should be equally, if not more, responsive.

There are several reasons why the situation today may be more promising than it was a few years ago. The climate between the United States and the Soviet Union has improved. While the relationship between Reagan and Gorbachev leaves much to be desired, neither country talks of war, as the Soviet Union, in particular, was doing in 1984. Secondly, there have been some other hopeful signs. Some Soviet diplomats have sought out Jewish leaders to see what could be done to improve relations. In 1985, before he retired, Vladimir Alkhimov, the former president of Gosbank, remarked that "if good relations were restored with the United States, 50,000 Jewish émigrés annually would be no problem."[19] Though the numbers remain low, there has also been the release not only of Sharansky, but of some other well known refuseniks, like Eliahu Essas and Mark Nashpitz.

On the American side there is some awareness that adhering to the status quo may have outlived its usefulness. Moreover, Senator Jackson is dead, so there is no longer a question of offending him. Although no one would argue that the Soviet Union has become a center of liberal enlightenment (the KGB is still beating up Hebrew teachers and other innocent refuseniks, and the Soviets are still in Afghanistan), there does seem to be considerably more interest in seeking improved American-Soviet relations and increased trade and MFN status for the Soviets.

Just as it was foolhardy to be stubborn about holding back MFN in an inflexible way, so it would also be a mistake to show too much eagerness and grant MFN without accompanying concessions by the Soviets. What we need is a carefully designed schedule of tits for tats. For example, we could begin by seeking to repeal legislation which bans the import of certain kinds of furs and crabmeat from the Soviet Union. Similarly, we should also seek the repeal of the Church and Stevenson amendments. This is not to deny that repealing such legislation will be easy. In some respects, it may be easier to grant MFN. The president, on his own, can issue a waiver and allow MFN—assuming, of course, that there is good cause for his assertion that the Soviets are beginning to meet the conditions specified in Jackson-Vanik.

The important thing, however, is to understand that we cannot expect the Soviets to keep making gestures without receiving something in return. Admittedly, it may sometimes seem like blackmail, but if that is what has to be done to convince the Soviets to respond, it may be worth the cost. For instance, very little, if anything, was done to acknowledge the Soviet release of Sharansky. We did participate in an exchange of spies, but since we insisted that Sharansky was not a part of that arrangement, we should have gone beyond that and subsequently offered up a hostage of our own, such as the Church or Stevenson amendments.

In looking back over Soviet behavior there does seem to be good reason to argue that the Soviets are on their best behavior whenever they are on the verge of obtaining something from the United States. Relations are better when there is more, rather than less, at stake. The Soviets always seem to be more forthcoming when we are about to decide on selling them grain, sending a delegation to the Olympics, authorizing an export license, or passing MFN. This might be called a policy of linkage interruptus.

Whatever it is for the Soviets, trade and other interchanges which accompany it are sometimes more important for the promise they hold, than for the benefits they ultimately bring. If we want the Soviets to be more forthcoming on emigration, we must be more forthcoming than we have been in the recent past. It requires little courage and equally little intelligence to persist with the status quo—but that does not necessarily mean that the status quo is always the soundest policy.

Part Four

Patterns of Soviet Jewish Resettlement in the United States and Israel

8. Soviet Immigrant Resettlement in Israel and the United States

Zvi Gitelman

In the 1970s Israel and the United States were the major host countries for over 250,000 Soviet Jewish immigrants, just as they have been the prime recipients of Jewish immigration for most of this century. For the first five years or so of the Soviet Jewish emigration, almost everyone who left the USSR went to Israel. But beginning in 1974 significant numbers of Soviet émigrés, almost all of whom had visas for Israel, began to drop out at the Viennese transit point and elect other countries of immigration, primarily the United States. By 1976, 49 percent of those leaving the USSR did not immigrate to Israel, and in the last years of the 1970s more than two-thirds of the émigrés went to the United States. This trend alarmed Israeli and Jewish Agency officials, leading to debates with U.S. Jewish leaders about the desirability and feasibility of reversing it. Some administrative and other measures were taken but to no avail. By the early 1980s Soviet Jewish emigration had slowed to a trickle—some attributing this to the drop-out phenomenon—thus rendering the debate largely moot.

I believe this trend resulted from the declining attractiveness of Israel after the 1973 war, the effects of chain migration, and the fact that the Israeli immigrants include a high proportion of Central Asian, Georgian, and Baltic Jews, all with relatively high Jewish consciousness, while over three-quarters of the U.S. immigrants come from the Slavic heartland and are much more acculturated to Russian culture. The former group is more pulled to Israel, whereas the latter migration stream is more pushed from the USSR.[1]

Israel and the United States, both countries of mass immigration, differ substantially in their ideological and administrative approaches to immigration. Israel exists as a nation to gather the Jews dispersed all over the world and restore their political independence, economic self-sufficiency, and self-respect. Israelis are taught from childhood that the existence of the Jewish state, its security and economic well-being, depend heavily on Jewish immigration. Indeed, to the Jewish population of some 660,000 in 1948, nearly 1.7 million immigrants were added by 1980.[2] Even compared with other countries of mass immigration—the United States, Canada, Argentina, and Brazil—Israel has counted an extraordinarily high number of immigrants as a proportion of its population.[3] One of the first acts of the government following the creation of the state in 1948 was to abolish the restrictions on immigration imposed by the British Mandatory authorities. Since that time the gates have remained wide open, and a liberal immigration policy has been followed, at least as far as Jews are concerned (non-Jews may also immigrate but go through a naturalization process rather than acquiring almost instant citizenship, as Jews do under the Law of Return).

By contrast the United States has been a more attractive country, even to Jews, but a more restrictive one. For nearly a hundred years the prevailing U.S. perception has been that, rather than the United States needing immigrants, the immigrants have needed the United States. Therefore, physical, ethnic, vocational, geographic, and political tests have been set up to ensure highly selective immigration and at times hardly any immigration at all. Despite the motto, "Give me your tired and your poor, your huddled masses," for most of the twentieth century the United States has not particularly welcomed immigrants, especially those who have been perceived as poor and wretched.

There are, of course, profound differences in the situations of Israel and the United States. While the size and wealth of the United States make it more able to absorb immigrants, because of its power and security it has less need for them. Resource-poor Israel, existing in a constant state of insecurity, is more dependent on immigration for labor, intellectual resources, technical skills, and the sheer numbers required to offset partially the far more numerous populations of hostile neighbors. Thus the ideological context of immigration, as well as the perceived place of immigrants in the national history and destiny, differ quite sharply in Israel and the United States. Not surprisingly, the organization of immigration and immigrant resettlement differs as well.

Administering Immigration and Resettlement in Israel and the United States

Before 1968 immigration to Israel and subsequent resettlement were the responsibility of the Jewish Agency, a nongovernment body that had served as the political body for Jews in Palestine and Zionists abroad and had survived the creation of the state. Long after military, employment, and educational functions had been transferred from the agency and other nongovernment organizations to the Israeli government, immigration remained in the hands of the agency, except for a brief period soon after the formation of the state. Between 1948 and 1967 most of the immigrants were refugees, either from the displaced person's camps of Europe or from Islamic countries. As such, they were often bereft of capital, education, and skills and were quite dependent on the Jewish Agency and whatever arrangements it could make for them.

Between 1948 and 1951 half the immigrants were from Asia and Africa, and between 1952 and 1957 over three-quarters were from those two continents. Following the 1967 Six-Day War nearly three-quarters of the immigrants came from the United States, Europe, and Oceania, the first time in Israeli history that so many immigrants had come from the Western world. They brought capital, education, and skills and were not as dependent on the agency. The change in the character of the immigrants and the perception that the agency was not capable of dealing successfully with the new breed created pressure for bringing immigrant resettlement under the aegis of the government, regularizing procedures, and establishing rational, bureaucratic, and less politicized bodies to take over the functions of the agency. A successful political counterattack by the agency resulted in a compromise whereby the agency retained responsibility for "initial absorption" of immigrants and the newly created Ministry for Immigrant Absorption (MIA) was in charge of "permanent absorption."[4] Ironically, most of the staff of the new ministry came from the agency, despite the fact that a major argument for creating the ministry had been alleged incompetence of the agency employees.

The new ministry was weak from the start because it was dependent on other ministries—housing, labor, treasury—for the goods and services it was supposed to provide its clients. As soon as the MIA lost its political clout as a result of cabinet reshuffles, it could no longer exert pressure on the other ministries and therefore found it harder to provide services and supplies for immigrants. Moreover, the great bulk of the MIA's budget comes from the Jewish Agency, whose funds are raised outside Israel. Thus, the agency retains financial power over the ministry. Finally, the agency has never reconciled itself to the existence of the ministry and has carried out a long sniping campaign against it, apparently with the aim of restoring its sole jurisdiction in immigration matters. For the immigrant this adds up to duplication of effort, confusion, blurring of jurisdictional lines, evasion of responsibility, and multiplication of paperwork.

Along with the administrative reorganization, the Israeli government adopted measures designed to ease the transition from higher standards of living to Israeli conditions. These included tax breaks, import privileges, rental subsidies, housing mortgages at favorable rates, and small business loans on terms better than the average citizen could obtain, though the government cut back these benefits in the mid-1970s.

Ironically, the largest group of immigrants in the 1970s came from the USSR, where standards of living were generally lower than those in Israel. In the 1970s about 160,000 Soviet immigrants arrived in Israel, constituting nearly half of all immigrants in that period. In 1972 and 1973, peak years of Soviet immigration, they comprised nearly 60 percent of all immigrants.[5] The political, social, and economic impact of this immigration was tremendous, and it became an important issue within the Soviet Union as well as in Soviet-U.S. relations. Not since the 1920s had the Soviet government permitted so many people to emigrate, and never had Israel received as many highly educated and skilled immigrants in so short a period, and from a country whose Jews were assumed by many to be thoroughly assimilated and, in any case, unable to leave. Soviet Jewish emigration became a major human rights issue even for U.S. administrations and for international meetings on human rights.

When large numbers of Soviet émigrés began to come to the United States, the Jewish community reacted with ambivalence. On the one hand, getting the Jews out of the USSR was seen as a worthy aim since they would now enjoy freedom and the possibility of choosing a Jewish way of life. On the other hand, their choice not to go to Israel presumably reflected unfavorably on that country, as well as on the Jewish commitment of the émigrés. Some argued that the struggle had been for aliyah (immigration to Israel), not for emigration, and that *neshira* (dropping out) was a betrayal of the aliyah activists who had sacrificed so much in the USSR. Moreover, said some, it was both immoral, since Jews left the USSR with the stated intention of going to Israel, and politically dangerous, since the Soviet authorities could use *neshira* as an excuse to cut off further emigration. The Israeli government and the Jewish Agency demanded that HIAS and other U.S. Jewish organizations stop "seducing" Soviet émigrés. Other U.S. Jews argued that it would be immoral to deny Soviet Jews the freedom to choose a country of immigration. In the end HIAS made a few weak gestures in the direction of appeasing the Israelis, but only when Soviet emigration had trailed off considerably. Whatever the merit of the arguments for and against welcoming Soviet Jews in the United States, they continued to come. By 1980 nearly 80,000 Soviet Jews had immigrated to the United States.[6]

Unlike Israel, where government or quasi-governmental agencies took charge of resettlement, in the United States private communal organizations, such as Jewish Family Services, Jewish Vocational Services, and Jewish Community Centers, took responsibility for immigrants. Moreover, Soviet immigrants were generally more educated and had more industrial skills and experience than those coming to the United States from Asia and the Caribbean. This enabled them to find urban employment and residence relatively rapidly. They also had the assistance of an affluent, socially conscious host community spread throughout the country. The impressive resources of both the immigrants and the U.S. Jewish community combined to provide for a generally smooth resettlement. In addition to the different methods of organizing resettlement, Israel and the United States have received different kinds of Soviet immigrants. While the sex, age, and educational profiles of the two immigrations have been remarkably similar, the geographical composition has not. The great majority of Georgian and Central Asian Jews have gone to Israel, as have most of those from the Baltic and other areas absorbed by the USSR between 1939 and 1944. Only about 30 to 35 percent of the *olim* (Israeli immigrants) were from the USSR's European heartland. By contrast about 87 percent of the U.S. immigrants came from Russia, the Ukraine, and, to a lesser extent, Byelorussia, the three Slavic republics. Put another way, about 72 to 75 percent of the émigrés from Russia and the Ukraine did not go to Israel, whereas only 6 percent of the Georgians and 13 percent of the Central Asians did not.[7]

Those from the Slavic heartland have lived longer under Soviet rule, have been without Jewish schools, newspapers, and other cultural facilities for a generation or two longer, and therefore have a different kind of Jewish identity than those who managed to cling more closely to Jewish tradition and culture. These geographical-cultural differences help to explain why one stream went to Israel and another to the United States.

The variables of geographical-cultural background and methods of resettlement are likely to produce, and account for, different behaviors in the resettlement process. Personality, expectations, previous image of the country of immigration, and hierarchy of individual values are other factors determining reactions to resettlement. In addition, one must bear in mind that in Israel the government is more heavily and directly involved in the economy, housing, and employment than it is in the United States, and this is true not only in the case of immigrants. Therefore one can expect that discontent will be directed toward the government, which will be seen as the cause of the blame. In the United States, blame, like responsibility, will be more diffused.

It may also be that in a Jewish state, Jews feel less inhibited about criticizing the authorities than they do in other countries, where, despite official egalitarian ideologies, they still defer to "his honor, the 'goy' " in Aaron Zeitlin's phrase.

My own observations among immigrants in Israel and the United States leave me with the impression that in Israel there is a kind of folklore of immigrant complaints, which is reinforced in discussions among immigrants and passed on from earlier arrivals to later ones. Folkways seem to have emerged where immigrants vie for the honor of relating the most dramatic bureaucratic story or claiming the greatest injustice done to an immigrant. In the United States, while complaints are not lacking, they do not seem so widely bruited about, nor do they appear often in the general media, as they do in Israel.

Comparing Resettlement in Israel and the United States

One cannot easily establish which system of immigrant resettlement, that of Israel or the United States, is "better." Each system has developed within the overall context of national traditions, the purposes attached to immigration, and the ideologies that have developed around it. The way in which a country treats immigrants is an organic outgrowth of its national history and values. Still, parts can be transposed from one system to another, and a comparison of systems may shed light on problems or advantages characterizing them.

The success of resettlement may be measured in both objective and subjective terms. Objective measures might include the proportion of immigrants in the work force who are actually employed at a specified time after immigration, their incomes, linguistic capabilities, and rates of reemigration. Even such measures may be hard to compare across systems because of differences in those systems themselves. For example, certain societies value facility in the dominant language much more than others do. The difficulties in making such comparisons are multiplied when one uses subjective measures of resettlement, those involving immigrants' own perceptions of their new country, their feelings about their situations, and their evaluations of resettlement procedures and agencies. There may also be significant variation in the social mores of expressing satisfaction or dissatisfaction.

Moreover, in different systems reactions will be focused differently. In Israel, where so much resettlement activity is concentrated in the Jewish Agency and Immigrant Absorption Ministry, one would expect discontent to be rather sharply focused on those two targets. In the United States, on the other hand, where resettlement activities and responsibilities are more diffuse, the targets are more numerous and less sharply in focus. Moreover, there may be a greater proclivity to voice dissatisfaction when one is in a secure, majority situation than when one is a minority (immigrants) within a minority (Jews).

It is useful, nevertheless, to compare subjective perceptions of immigrants. It allows us to observe differences among groups *within* each of the two countries; for example, do immigrants from a particular region or of a particular age have consistently different perceptions from those of other groups? Country comparisons also allow identification of the salient problems and successes in each country and highlight the characteristics of each group of immigrants as well as of the host society. We can also determine relationships among variables that remain constant in different countries and those that vary with the country of immigration. For example, in one country the more educated immigrants may be likelier to obtain employment commensurate with their training, whereas in another country they may not be as easily employable as those with less education. These are issues that can be illuminated by analyzing data collected on the process of resettlement in the course of a study of bureaucratic encounters in the Soviet Union. Some data from other studies also shed light on resettlement experiences.

In my own study a group of 1,161 ex-Soviet citizens who left the USSR between 1977 and 1980 were interviewed during 1980–81 in Israel (N = 590), the Federal Republic of Germany (N = 100), and the United States (N = 471). Here the groups in Israel and the United States were compared. The sample was drawn as a quota, nonprobability sample, in line with hypotheses that led to a certain distribution of age, sex, education, nationality, and republic of residence. On some variables, such as age and sex, the proportions in the sample approximated those in the Soviet adult population rather closely. But nearly half the respondents have had higher education (about 40 percent of all Soviet immigrants to Israel and the United States have had higher education), 38 percent had secondary education, and only 15 percent had grade school education or less—a higher educated percentage than is normally found in the USSR.

Seventy-seven percent, or 889 people, had been registered as Jews on their internal Soviet passports. The areas in which the respondents had lived most of their lives are as follows: RSFSR, 330; Ukraine, 247; Moldavia, 120; Baltic, 174; Georgia, 120; and Central Asia, 165. (The area of residence of 5 respondents was not clear.)

The men and women were quite evenly distributed in the age and regional categories, but men dominated the blue-collar professions and females the white-collar ones, despite very similar educational levels (48 percent of the men and 46 percent of the women have had higher education). Educational levels were highest among those from the RSFSR. The lowest educational levels were found among people from Central Asia (only 18 percent have had higher education) and from Moldavia (23 percent).

These people were interviewed in Russian or Georgian by native speakers. There were remarkably few refusals to be interviewed. The average interview lasted between two and three hours.

Objective Indicators of Immigration Absorption. Most studies of Soviet immigrants in Israel conclude that they have done very well in resettling, if measured by objective indicators such as employment, housing, income, and acquiring fluency in the Hebrew language. According to official statistics, by the end of two to three years nearly all those who had been employed in the USSR were working in Israel, but about 15 percent of those with higher education had to change their vocations and about one-third of those over fifty-five years old failed to find employment.[8]

Industrial workers and technicians had the least difficulty in finding employment, generally within Israel's burgeoning defense, electronics, metallurgical, and food-processing industries. Scientists, physicians, artists, and athletes presented greater employment challenges, but Israeli authorities were quick to realize that they were invaluable assets. In some cases special programs were launched to ease their transition into their professions in Israel. Israel's artistic, musical, and scientific-academic life has been greatly enhanced by the absorption of these immigrants.[9] By 1977 immigrants constituted one-third of all physicians in the country, and of these more than half were from the USSR.[10]

Housing is a more difficult problem, as it is for Israeli society as a whole. It takes as long as five years for immigrants to find what the government classifies as permanent housing, but proportionately more Soviet immigrants found such housing within one year than did other immigrants. Moreover, they tended to cluster in the major population centers of the country, especially in the highly desirable central region.[11]

The incomes of Soviet immigrants are generally higher than Israeli averages, especially among women. Within about three and a half years of their arrival, the family income of Soviet newcomers was a full third above the average of all Jewish families in Israel and 20 percent above the average for Ashkenazi families.[12]

Studies of the immigrants' knowledge and use of the Hebrew language reveal that, although very few of them arrive knowing any Hebrew, Soviet immigrants read Hebrew newspapers sooner than U.S. immigrants, and by the end of three years most have acquired fluency.[13] *Ulpanim* (intensive Hebrew language courses) enable immigrants to acquire the language quickly and efficiently. Immigrants with higher education are granted a period of at least six months' stay in an immigrant hostel where there are daily intensive Hebrew courses. They are granted this advantage on the theory that Hebrew facility is more important to their professional lives than it is to that of workers and clerks. Insofar as these measures of absorption are concerned, one can agree with Theodore Friedgut that, "however painful—and sometimes needlessly painful—the absorption process may have been, it has nevertheless been largely successful."[14]

Information on similar measures of Soviet immigrant absorption in the United States is more fragmentary. There have been quite a few studies of absorption in individual communities[15] and a fourteen-city survey of 900 immigrants taken in 1981 for the Council of Jewish Welfare Federations.[16] The general impression is of somewhat lower levels of employment than among the Israeli immigrants but also of rather high income levels, low rates of dependence on public assistance, and few housing problems. In my sample 41 percent of the Israeli immigrants and 59 percent of the Americans were employed. The fourteen-city CJF survey found that 84 percent of the men and 72 percent of the women had been employed full-time in the USSR, and it took about two to three years for them to reach "equilibrium level" in their American employment. Within a year the age-adjusted proportion employed is the same for Soviet immigrants as for other American men, but it is higher for women than for other American women.[17]

There is not much information on language acquisition by Soviet newcomers to the United States; however, in my study 13 percent of the Americans, but only 4 percent of the Israelis, identified language acquisition as the problem that vexed them most in their new country. In the CJF study 75 percent mentioned English as a major problem, and 74 percent mentioned finding a job.

In our sample the Israeli and American groups have similar educational profiles. Of those in Israel 16.3 percent had completed elementary education, 35.9 percent had completed secondary education, and 47.8 percent had completed higher education. The percentages for Soviet immigrants to the United States were 10 percent elementary education, 37.6 percent secondary education, and 52.4 percent higher education. Roughly similar educational levels were reported in the CJF study. Statistics supplied by HIAS and by the Israeli government indicate that the educational levels of the two immigrations are very similar, and this similarity appears also in our sample. However, the proportion of immigrants with higher education is slightly larger in our sample than in the immigration as a whole, and the U.S. group has somewhat higher levels of education. In both groups those from the RSFSR have the highest levels of education, the Moldavian Jews have the lowest, and younger people tend to have more education than older ones. The migrations to Israel and the United States are not differentiated by education. It is not that the more educated come to the United States, leaving the others to seek their fortunes in Israel. In fact, since the great majority of Central Asians—who have lower levels of education than all the European groups except the Moldavians—go to Israel, the educational profile of all other Israeli immigrants is at least as high as that of Americans.

In spite of the differences between the two societies that they enter, both groups of highly educated people experience at least a temporary loss of status and a shift in their self-image. When asked to define their social class, 44 percent of both Israelis and Americans chose to describe themselves as new immigrants. Only 22 percent in Israel and 16 percent in the United States called themselves "intelligentsia," which is the group almost all identified with in the USSR.

One might suppose that the immigrants to Israel are more religious or at least have stronger Jewish backgrounds than those who choose the United States. This is not the case among the respondents, and other evidence suggests that it is not the case among the immigrants generally (see table 8.1), though there seems to be a higher proportion of immigrants

Table 8.1. Religious Identity of Soviet Jewish Emigrants (in percentages)

	Israel	United States
Religious	8.3	13.6
Traditional*	37.9	34.8
Neither religious nor traditional	51.0	46.7
Antireligious	2.0	0.2
Don't know/no answer	0.0	4.7

* Traditional is a term widely used in Israel and is generally taken to mean that one observes certain holidays, customs, and traditions, but selectively and occasionally, usually without imputing too much religious significance to the observance. In the CJF study over 16 percent defined themselves as "somewhat," "fairly," or "very" religious in the USSR, but in the United States fully 42 percent placed themselves in these categories. In a recent study among Soviet immigrants in New York, respondents rated the synagogue more positively than any other Jewish institution.[19]

with non-Jewish spouses in the United States.[18] When Jewish immigrants were asked to define themselves religiously, the results shown in table 8.1 were obtained.

The higher proportion of religious immigrants we found in the United States is even more surprising when we realize that two-thirds of those who define themselves as religious in Israel are Georgians and Central Asians. Among the Israelis from the European USSR, who are culturally similar to U.S. immigrants, only 2.7 percent call themselves religious. Moreover, when asked to describe the Jewish atmosphere of their parents' homes, European respondents in both countries gave similar answers. As expected, over three-quarters of the Central Asians and nearly as many Georgians define the homes in which they grew up as strongly Jewish, while only 38 percent of those from the RSFSR do so. In both countries, but especially in Israel, religious identification is positively correlated with low educational levels.

Respondents were asked whether they had owned eight consumer durables in the USSR and whether they owned them in Israel or the United States. The two groups did not differ in the number of consumer goods possessed in the USSR. Immigrants to the United States do own more consumer durables than do Israelis, especially televisions and automobiles; however, this should not be taken as an indication that Americans have prospered more than the Israelis. Israelis still living in immigrant hostels are not likely to own televisions; automobiles are not as necessary in Israel, where public transportation is better than in the United States; and the cost—both absolute and relative to earnings—of many of the consumer durables is much higher in Israel.

There has been a shortage of housing in the USSR, but it has been far more pronounced in the European areas. The forms of housing also differ. Cooperatives are more popular in Europe, and private houses are fairly common in Central Asia but rare in European urban areas. Thus, over half the Georgian and 65 percent of the Central Asian respondents owned private houses in the USSR, whereas only 4 percent of the others did. This explains why those from Europe had a modal living space of 30 to 39 square meters, whereas among Georgians and Asians it was over 100 meters.

While Israelis express their envy of the housing provided for immigrants, housing ranks high on the list of complaints by Israeli immigrants, including Soviet ones.[20] The most severe complaints might presumably come from those who had large living quarters in the USSR and were now in the typical immigrant apartment of sixty or so square meters. But according to the sample, those who had the smaller Soviet state-owned apartments list housing first or second in the list of basic causes of dissatisfaction in Israel. By contrast, housing is low on the list of complaints of those who had private housing in the old country. This may be due to the fact that housing density is often quite high in Central Asia because extended families tend to live under one roof. Even if the roof is large, the family is usually larger, and a move to Israel might mean a gain in per person space.[21] It is also likely that housing complaints do not pertain so much to the size or quality of housing as they do to the long waiting lists for apartments and the fact that immigrants often spend a year or two in immigrant hostels waiting for an apartment. For the CJF study, by contrast, 64 percent of the respondents felt that their American housing was better than their Soviet housing, only 17 percent thought it was worse, and 19 percent judged it to be about the same.[22]

Subjective Perceptions of Absorption. The objective conditions surrounding an immigrant undoubtedly influence that person's assessment of his or her situation, but the same living conditions may be evaluated differently by different persons. It is one's subjective evaluation that determines satisfaction or dissatisfaction in the new country, and rational arguments about the objective situation will probably do little to change such an evaluation.

Table 8.2. Motivation for Emigration (in percentages)

	Israel	United States
Political reasons, desire for freedom	14.0	15.7
Desire to live among Jews	26.5	12.3
To join relatives	30.9	14.2
Education, vocational opportunities	2.9	8.5
Anti-Semitism	11.3	19.3
Economic improvement	2.9	5.9
Other	12.1	21.9
Don't know/no answer	0.2	2.2

In probing the immigrants' subjective responses to their host countries, one should begin with their motivations for leaving the USSR, since those logically influence their expectations and judgments of the new country. Motivations for emigration are numerous and complex, but respondents were urged to identify the main reasons for their decision to leave the USSR. In order to capture the full flavor of their reasoning and its nuances, the question was posed in an open-ended way and then coded (see table 8.2).[23] ("Other" includes responses such as "Soviet life had become boring"; "I thought the Israeli climate would be good for my daughters' asthma"; "Everyone was going, so we went too"; "I did not want to leave, but my children did, so what could I do?" These responses should alert us to the heterogeneity and idiosyncrasies of decisions to emigrate.)

Understandably, those who have a strong desire to live among Jews tend to go to Israel, whereas those who wish to escape anti-Semitism are just as likely, or more so, to go to the United States. Among the Israelis 75 percent of the Central Asians and 72 percent of the Georgians, the most traditional Jewish groups, cite their desire to live among Jews. Those going to the United States emphasize educational, vocational, and economic opportunities. The far greater size and wealth of the United States make it more sensible for them to choose that country. The fact that there is a significantly greater proportion of Israeli immigrants whose motivation is to join relatives is attributable largely to Georgian and Central Asian respondents, 35 to 38 percent of whom cite this reason for leaving, whereas only 17 percent of the other Israelis give this reason. This is explained by the extended and often patriarchal nature of the Georgian and Central Asian families, which are more closely knit than the European families.

Because of the potential in this question for respondents to tell interviewers what they thought was socially acceptable or politically judicious, they were asked to indicate why *others* had emigrated. Interestingly, both groups saw their fellow émigrés in a less idealistic light than that in which they had portrayed themselves. Over half the U.S. respondents, for example, attributed the migration of others to the desires to escape anti-Semitism and to better themselves economically. Still, the differences between the Americans and the Israelis remained much as indicated in describing their own motivations for departing the USSR.

The Israeli immigrants do seem to gain a new identity more easily than the Americans. When asked whether they felt Russian (or Georgian) in Israel or the United States, more than half of the Americans but only 28 percent of the Israelis said they always felt Russian or Georgian; a third of the Israelis said they never felt this way, but less than 10 percent of the Americans made that claim. In both Israel and the United States those with only elementary education said they never feel Russian more often than the others. The people with higher education feel Russian more frequently than the others in the United States, but this is not true in Israel.[24]

The émigrés were asked to judge whether their standard of living had gone up, down, or remained the same as a consequence of their emigration (see table 8.3). The obvious conclusion would be that the standard of living in the United States is considerably higher than in Israel, so the immigrants to the United States experience a sharper rise. Indeed, the Americans possess more consumer durables (televisions, tape recorders, automobiles, and so on) than the Israelis. Further analysis reveals, however, that much of the downward mobility experienced by Israelis is a reflection of the Central Asians' experience. Over half (52 percent) of the Central Asians feel their standard of living declined, but only 33 per-

Table 8.3. Changes in Emigrants' Standard of Living (in percentages)

	Israel	United States	*CJF* Study
Standard went up	29.8 (31.6)*	56.1	75
Standard stayed the same	29.6 (25.6)	28.5	10
Standard went down	36.9 (33.4)	12.3	13
Don't know/no answer	6.6 (9.4)	3.2	2

* Figures in parentheses show results for Israelis excluding Central Asians.

cent of the other Israelis feel this way (still more than twice as many as the Americans). The Moldavians in Israel perceive the most dramatic rise in their living standards, as might be expected of people from one of the least developed European areas. In the United States there is no differentiation by republic of origin on this question (it should be remembered that there are no Central Asians in the U.S. sample). Among the Americans those with less education experience a greater rise in their standard of living, perhaps because the more educated do not yet have jobs commensurate with their education and skills; therefore, the gap between them and the others is not significantly widened. In Israel perceptions of change in the standard of living are not consistently related to education. No doubt the real difference between U.S. and Israeli living standards explains most of the difference between the two groups' responses, but the Americans might be prone to exaggerating the improvement in their living standards since this was a prime reason for many of their departures from the USSR.

The Americans evaluate resettlement agencies more positively than the Israelis. Asked who had helped them most in settling in the new country, over 40 percent of the Israelis pointed to their own families, and only a quarter of the respondents mentioned either the Jewish Agency or the Ministry for Immigrant Absorption, despite the fact (or perhaps because of it) that the latter play such large roles. In the United States, by contrast, over 40 percent named a Jewish Family Service or equivalent organization. Three times as many people in Israel said no one had helped them in resettlement, though in both countries only small minorities made such a claim.

Some of the surprising results among Israelis are due to the family orientation of Georgians and Central Asians who would instinctively turn to family first and to official agencies only later, if at all.[25] Over half the Georgians and 46 percent of the Central Asians see the family as having helped them most, but only 36 percent of the immigrants from the European sections of the USSR see it this way. Those from the Baltic are most inclined to mention the Jewish Agency and MIA, perhaps lending credence to the cynical complaint of one Central Asian that those agencies favor the Yiddish-speaking Ashkenazim (the highest proportion of Yiddish speakers in the Soviet Union are in the Baltic republics). Twice as many Israelis as Americans maintain that the resettlement agencies are unfair and treat different categories of immigrants differently. The Israelis claim that people have *protektsiia* (pull) or people who raise a fuss, threaten, or have connections get preferential treatment. Georgians and Central Asians, especially, charge that "they don't like the Sfardim" and even some Ashkenazi immigrants sometimes complain that they favor *olim* from the Western countries. Several Central Asians point out that none of the officials themselves are Central Asians. "In the Jewish Agency there are no Bukharan Jews (Central Asians) among the employees. They favor the Ashkenazim. . . . Everywhere in the agency the Bukharan Jews stand on line. They shout, they cry, they speak everywhere about injustice."[26]

The U.S. immigrants took a more favorable general view of the resettlement agencies than did the Israelis. Respondents were asked, "How well does the Jewish Agency/Jewish Family Service (or equivalent) work?" (A separate question was asked of Israelis about the MIA and the results are very similar to those provided in table 8.4.) Three-quarters of the Americans but fewer than half of the Israelis have a generally positive view of the organizations. In both countries the least educated have the most favorable views, perhaps because their expectations of any bureaucracy may be lower. Not surprisingly, the Central Asians take the dimmest view of the Jewish Agency and MIA, 63 percent of them rating these organizations poorly. Among the Americans there is not much difference when measured by republic of origin.

Immigrants in both countries may be projecting their experiences with absorption agencies on to other government offices. Moreover, experiences in the country of immigration may color their views of Soviet government offices. Sixty percent of Israeli immigrants say that most government offices in Israel do not work as they should, but only a quarter of the Americans feel this way about U.S. government offices. Over 30 percent of the Israelis believe that Soviet government offices are run more efficiently than their Israeli counterparts (only 2 percent of the Americans think so), and only 17 percent said the Israeli offices work better

Table 8.4. Emigrant Evaluations of Resettlement Agencies (in percentages)

	Israel	United States
Very well	1.2	5.1
Well	10.7	33.5
Not badly	32.4	41.8
Poorly	40.2	14.0
Don't know/no answer	15.6	5.5

(the rest give other answers or do not have any opinion).[27] As might be expected, the Central Asians are the most critical of the Israeli bureaucracy, 63 percent of them saying that Soviet offices are better administered. These feelings seem to radiate back to the USSR, since Americans are far more negative about the way Soviet offices operate than are Israelis (still, 52 percent of the latter say Soviet offices do not work well; only among the Central Asians is there a majority—61 percent—who say they work well). Since there is no reason to assume that the Israeli and U.S. immigrants had very different experiences with government offices in the USSR, it seems likely that their different evaluations of those offices reflect their contrasting experiences in the countries of immigration. Those who have a negative view of the more recent experience tend to look back more favorably on the bureaucracies they left behind and vice versa.

Feelings about Israeli and U.S. officials are not only tied to evaluations of Soviet offices but also seem linked to feelings about the host societies in general. Israeli immigrants are considerably more inclined than U.S. ones to say that their fellow countrymen would take advantage of them if they had the chance. Again, the Central Asians are more cynical than the other Israeli groups, but even without them four times as many Israelis as Americans feel this way. U.S. immigrants are also more inclined to see Americans helping each other rather than thinking of themselves, though even among the Israelis more immigrants see people in Israel helping each other rather than thinking of themselves. Only among the Central Asians do a greater number of people take the cynical view, but interestingly the Central Asians have a far more positive world view than any other group of people in the USSR, being altruistic rather than egotistic.

Some of the differences between the two host societies and their ways of dealing with immigrants are brought to light by what disturbs the immigrants most about their new countries. For the Israelis it is the cost of living and rampant inflation, with Israel's security situation second. Surprisingly, the Americans are also most concerned about security, but of a different sort. Domestic crime and what they see as U.S. weakness regarding the USSR worry them more than anything else. Respondents speak of U.S. unawareness of the true dimensions of the Soviet threat to the whole world, the defenselessness of American democracy in the face of totalitarian regimes, the inability of the United States to take firm decisions, and political carelessness, myopia and ignorance, the rise of liberalism, and unthinking attitudes of American youth. The second most disturbing thing to the Americans is the necessity of knowing English and the difficulties in learning it. Probably because Israel is a more multilingual society and has more efficient and comprehensive ways of teaching language, language acquisition is not as important a problem to the Israeli immigrants. In both countries unemployment ranks high on the list of things that disturb the immigrants, especially among the highly educated. Both groups miss friends more than anything else in the Soviet Union. Around 10 percent of each group say they miss nothing from the USSR, but almost that many among the Israelis say they miss everything (only 2 percent of the Americans do)—further testimony to the greater dissatisfaction of the Israelis.

All of these sentiments meld in general feelings of satisfaction or dissatisfaction in Israel and the United States (see table 8.5). In both countries the satisfied constitute a majority, but there is a greater proportion of them among the Americans. If one sets aside the Central Asians, nearly 60 percent of whom fall into the dissatisfied categories, the Israeli-U.S. difference is considerably reduced. The Israeli European sample exhibits nearly the same levels of satisfaction as the American sample. There are no significant differences in satisfaction between those with higher and secondary education, but satisfaction is highest among the least educated groups, excluding the Central Asians. There is no statistical correlation between income and satisfaction or between whether one is employed and satisfaction. What, then, are the causes of dissatisfaction among those who express it? The answers are widely scattered, but housing, inflation, and unemployment are often cited by Israelis, whereas Americans complain more about unsuitable jobs and language

Table 8.5. Emigrant Satisfaction in Israel and the United States (in percentages)

	Europeans	Israel		Israel	United States
		Georgians	Central Asians		
Very satisfied	16.9	11.1	4.0	11.2	18.0
Satisfied	40.3	53.0	35.0	43.0	48.0
Dissatisfied	28.3	24.0	35.0	28.1	27.4
Very dissatisfied	8.6	6.0	24.0	10.5	3.2
Don't know/no answer	5.8	5.1	2.0	7.1	3.4

difficulties. There is a strong correlation between dissatisfaction and perception of a decline in standard of living (gamma $= .57$, tau $= .39$). Men are more satisfied than women, and older people are more satisfied than those in their late twenties and early thirties, probably because the latter have strong aspirations and higher expectations. When asked whether other Soviet immigrants are satisfied, both groups impute less satisfaction to others than they have expressed for themselves. This may reflect the possibility that immigrants gripe to each other more often than they express satisfaction.

In both countries the great majority would leave the USSR if they had it to do over again. The only exceptions are the Central Asians, 46 percent of whom would "definitely" or "probably" not emigrate again. Both groups are also happy with their choice of Israel or the United States, and over three-quarters would choose those countries again. Of those who would not, the Israelis would head mostly for the United States, and the Americans would go to Canada, Western Europe, and, to a smaller extent, to Israel.[28] In short, then, these Soviet Jews are happy they left the USSR and satisfied with the immigration choices they made.

Soviet Jewish Identity in the United States

Critics of *neshira* (dropping out) have argued that by not going to Israel, Soviet émigrés run the risk of losing their Jewish identities and disappearing into the American melting pot. Indeed, many American Jews, including those not particularly observant or Jewishly active, have been critical of Soviet immigrants for supposedly making excessive demands on the Jewish community but giving it nothing in return, failing to attend religious services, and not joining Jewish organizations. Whereas before emigration began many American and Israeli Jews assumed that for understandable reasons Soviet Jews were highly assimilated and uninterested in Jewish culture, they now act as if Jewish émigrés should have rushed into the synagogues and Jewish institutions immediately upon their arrival. Unfortunately, we do not have sufficient information to assess the transformation of the Jewish identity of the émigrés nor to evaluate the effectiveness of the various "Jewish acculturation" programs designed for them in many communities.

However, several studies convey the impression that a high proportion of the émigrés see themselves as Jews. In fact, though their formal, public Jewish affiliations are generally fewer than those of many American Jews, their sense of Jewish identity, and pride in it, may well be stronger than what is generally found among American Jews. As would be expected among immigrants, their social contacts are very largely within their own community. In my study 62 percent said their closest friends were Soviet Jews, and only 2.3 percent said they were non-Jews. Nearly three-quarters of those interviewed in the CJF study said all their close friends were Jews, and 55 percent identified them as Soviet immigrant Jews. The New York study found 90 percent identifying their three closest friends as Jews, 79 percent being other Soviet immigrants.[29]

The CJF study found that 90 percent would want to be born Jewish. Only 7 percent said that being Jewish did not matter to them.[30] We have already noted the rise in religious identification when they moved from the USSR to the United States, and synagogue attendance, measured in different ways by the three studies cited here, seems to be at least as frequent as that among other American Jews. According to both CJF and New York studies, nearly 70 percent attend synagogue or temple services on the High Holidays; other holidays, rituals, and customs are observed to varying degrees.

When asked to describe themselves, respondents in all three studies were strongly inclined to identify as Jews. In my survey nearly half identified themselves as "Jews" or "American Jews"; in the CJF study 43 percent said that "Jewish" described them "very well." Only 6 percent said it did not describe them at all. The New York study found over 70 percent ascribing to themselves a "primary identity" as Jews, either alone or with an adjective such as "American" or "Russian" Jew. That study said its "primary conclusion" is "that Soviet Jewish immigrants strongly and positively identify as Jews."

On the other hand they do not express that identity in public, institutionalized activity. Over half the respondents in my survey rarely or never participate in organized Jewish activity. In the CJF study only eight people said they were active in Jewish organizations. This pattern— strong identity, weak affiliation—is probably a carryover from Soviet conditions where Jewish identity is official and hard to escape, but public Jewish activity is almost unheard of in recent decades and would be regarded as subversive. Americans are "joiners"; Soviet immigrants of the first generation may not be. It is reasonable to expect that the second generation will come closer to dominant American modes in this and in other spheres. Meanwhile, there does seem to be a strong sense of identity which carries with it the potential for Jewish activity and continuity.

The great majority want their children to remain Jewish and marry Jews. All the studies show about a third of the children attending a Jewish day school, although there is a substantial drop in attendance when tuition subsidies are ended. Nevertheless, the potential for Jewish continuity and growth seems to be at least as great among the immigrants as it is among the American Jewish community at large.

Conclusion

Soviet émigrés in both Israel and the United States seem to be fundamentally satisfied and well resettled. Satisfaction may be greater in the United States, but it is hard to know whether to attribute this to objective conditions in each country, the methods of immigrant absorption, the differences in the composition of each migration stream, or even the different mores that have developed among the immigrant subcultures of each country. U.S. immigrants clearly perceive themselves better off materially than do the Israeli ones, but the Israelis are more comfortable with their new culture and identities.

The vastly different economic and political situations of the host societies have produced a different order of concerns among the immigrants. Israeli newcomers are disturbed by economic problems, and, like all other Israelis, they seem to be constantly aware of the immediate and tangible threats to Israel's existence. U.S. immigrants from the USSR appear to be troubled by a perceived Soviet threat and U.S. laxity in the face of it, a danger that seems less tangible and imminent to most Americans. U.S. immigrants are also more disturbed by their inadequacies in learning the English language. Both groups have faced aspects of capitalist society that they had not experienced in the USSR, such as the prospect or reality of unemployment and the importance of money as a criterion of success as well as a means to it.

Both, but especially the Americans, have generally favorable views of the people in their new societies; however, a significant number of the Israelis are highly critical of the Jewish Agency and Ministry for Immigrant Absorption, whereas U.S. views of the roughly parallel but nongovernmental agencies in the United States are more benign. The negative feelings toward the Israeli agencies seem to have suffused the immigrants' feelings toward Israeli government offices in general, whereas the Americans have no particular complaints concerning U.S. government offices.

It cannot be determined from the evidence at hand whether this results from real and profound shortcomings in the Jewish Agency and the MIA in contrast to more efficient voluntary agencies in the United States. An alternative explanation might be that the U.S. agencies have more resources to deal with the problems and needs of their clients. They satisfy the immigrants more, not because their operations are inherently better, but because they are able to say "yes" more frequently and more generously. Then again, the politically engendered duplication, waste, and sheer irrationality of the dual Israeli agency structure rather than a lack of resources may have caused immigrants' frustrations. It is also possible that the Israeli immigrants are more inclined to complain because that is more acceptable in Israeli society as a whole and in immigrant subgroups in particular. They are not constrained by fears of standing out as a discontented minority. They see themselves not as guests of an alien society that has condescended to admit them but as people for whom the state exists and who are badly needed by it. Some may feel that while the United States is doing the Soviet Jews a favor by allowing them in, Soviet Jews are doing Israel a good turn by choosing to come there.

Whatever the explanations may be for the observed differences, the Central Asians clearly stand out from the others as a group with special problems. The mass media in Israel have usually focused on the Georgians as the problematic *olim,* especially since the Georgians arrived in larger numbers and more concentrated groups during the early 1970s, when Soviet immigration was still a sensation. The Central Asians arrived later, in smaller numbers, and generally adopted a lower profile, or were given it, than the Georgians. But this study demonstrates that their resettlement has been more difficult than that of the other Soviet groups. More research is required in order to understand why the Central Asians have fared as they report they have and to suggest ways in which their difficulties may be alleviated.[31]

The emigration of over a quarter-million Soviet Jews in the 1970s was a dramatic and unforeseen development that had a great impact on the Soviet Union, Israel, and American Jewry. These Jews had been cut off from world Jewry for at least thirty years and in most cases for half a century; they had no access to Jewish education, Zionist emissaries, or positive information about Israel; and finally, they made an extremely rapid transition from a closed, nominally socialist society to open capitalist ones. Considering these factors, their absorption in both Israel and the United States has been a remarkable achievement, mainly by the immigrants themselves but also by their receiving countries.

Should Soviet emigration policy change to allow substantial emigration once more, it is likely that the great majority of Jewish émigrés would want to come to the United States. The largest reservoirs by far of potential émigrés are in the RSFSR and the Ukraine, the two republics where Jews are most acculturated and from where more than three-quarters of the American immigration has come. If the American Jewish community wishes to increase the likelihood that such émigrés identify with it, a serious, comprehensive study of the experiences of the 1970 immigrants must be undertaken so that the community can learn what are the effective means of absorption and Jewish acculturation, which programs make a difference, and why. Understandably, the community was not fully prepared to deal with the immigration of the 1970s, but there are lessons to be learned from that experience that many hope will be relevant in the not too distant future.

9. Soviet Jewish Artists in the USSR and Israel: The Dynamics of Artistic Resettlement

Stephen Feinstein

One of the lesser studied areas of the recent Soviet Jewish emigration involves the resettlement of artists. This is a highly problematic area as painting and sculpture as a medium of expression for Soviet Jewish national culture or dissent is not as well known as the written literature. Literature, even one of dissent, can be transmitted through the medium of samizdat (illegal copying of manuscripts, usually by typing, and their circulation), whereas art is not as portable. On top of this is the dual complication of the nature of art in the USSR, broken into two categories in recent years by art historians, the "official" and "unofficial" schools of art, and the general problem of remoteness of artist training in the USSR from the most recent tendencies in the West.

On the immigration end of the spectrum, artists coming to Israel have experienced the same turbulence that other Soviet (and non-Soviet) newcomers have found, perhaps even more so. This situation relates in particular to the institutionalized nature of art as a profession in the USSR compared with the West.

Art in the USSR tends to be divided generally between two forms—official and unofficial. This generic difference became visible only in the 1960s, when the thirty-year old policy of "Socialist Realism" began to wear thin. Socialist Realism, a policy begun in 1932, had decreed that art must be realist in form and socialist in content and thus ended any experimentation in avant garde or abstract art. When the new nonconformist art began appearing, it was only occasionally for open exhibition purposes and more often only in the artist's studio. However, the difference between official and unofficial artists is quite significant in terms of financial and job security. Official artists are given studios and supplies, have exhibitions and sales of their works arranged by the Union of Artists, and are paid salaries. An official artist may also be unofficial in terms of the type of art he produces outside of his job as an artist for the state. An artist who plays both the official and unofficial game has the advantage of access to supplies and access to peers who might provide support for his endeavors. The purely unofficial artists, however, especially an individual without formal artistic training, would generally have extreme difficulties obtaining studio space, access to supplies including paints, and would find it extremely difficult, if not absolutely impossible, to market his works.

Some of the Jewish artists in the USSR have fallen into the official category, painting socialist themes, theater sets, and even Jewish themes. The Leningrad artist Anatoly Kaplan, who died in 1979, not only painted Jewish themes but was allowed to sell them internationally through the Artist's Union and USSR state export agencies. Others were artists not by profession but by avocation.

But there was something missing when Jewish art appeared with an official character. The subject was usually that of Yiddish culture and therefore that of a world which had been destroyed within the Soviet context. Despite the fact that he produced massive numbers of lithographs in series form to illustrate the works of writers like Sholom Aleichem, I. L. Peretz, and Mendele Mokher-Sephorim, Kaplan never had a large public showing of his Jewish works. One of his great hopes was that the State Russian Museum in Leningrad, which owns one copy of every one of his lithographs, would provide a retrospective exhibition. However, that show has yet to materialize.[1] Nor, however, did Kaplan do anything to help fledgling Jewish artists. He was clearly in the official school, and in certain respects he was better known in Jewish circles outside the Soviet Union than in the country itself. More than one critic has suggested that he became the "court Jew" for the Soviet regime in the realm of art.

The issue of emigration to Israel poses many practical and ideological problems for artists. First, while Soviet artists tend to understand artistic trends in the West, they are at a serious disadvantage because of the lack of interchange with Western artists directly or with the art itself. Most Soviet artists learn about contemporary art from large format art books brought into the USSR. Whatever the technical level of Soviet artists (which is usually quite high), from a practical level they are removed from the trends in the artistic marketplace. The result of this is almost an automatic critical response by Western viewers attesting to the "inferiority" of the Soviet artistic product. Secondly, with only a handful of exceptions, the subject matter and style of Soviet artists is usually misunderstood by Western audiences. The expressionism or the pure realism of many Soviet artists is seen as awkward and dated, rather than artistic styles with deep regional roots in Eastern Europe.

Third, Soviet artists find that in Israel, like other capitalist countries, there is no soft floor for artists. Being a small country, the Israeli art market may be described as having a narrow band of sophisticated art buyers, but a large majority of the population with a very provincial outlook and a lack of appreciation of the use of original works of art. Another part of the Israeli art market caters to Jewish tourists from the West, often with less than sophisticated tastes. The issue perhaps becomes clearer when one notes that the most important contemporary Israeli artists like Yaakov Agam and Mordechai Ardon live abroad because of the reality that art and artists must seek an international market. In Israel, as in Western art markets, there is also a very high demand for Jewish ceremonial objects and manuscripts but less of a demand for Israeli art.

Fourth, a very significant issue that affects the immigrant artist is the problem of exhibiting. The ability to exhibit is hardly guaranteed in any Western country, and Israel is no exception. Many Israeli art galleries are reluctant to exhibit Soviet newcomers, and even if an exhibition is arranged, the artists may have to pay a fee to the gallery as well as print his own brochures and catalogue for the show. And, of course, the most interesting issue faced by immigrants from the Soviet Union is that of trying to deal with the questions about the nature of international art, Jewish art, and Israeli art. What may be a highly appreciated and thoughtful work of art in the USSR may be brushed aside as irrelevant in Israel.

Connected to these issues is the very important issue of pricing works of art. An underlying concern of many immigrant artists is that art is insignificant if it is priced cheaply. Alternately, for the few artists who have managed to come with their own art, they have established prices based on the highly inflated values established by Soviet customs when they left the country. Generally speaking, it can be said that many works of art by Soviet newcomers are overpriced, not out of greed, but simply because of a lack of knowledge of the mechanics of pricing, along with the large commissions taken out of sales by dealers.

Perhaps the most difficult issue to deal with, however, whatever the problems of Soviet art itself, are the questions of "what is Jewish art?" and "what is the relationship between Jewish art and Jewish artists?" These are essentially international questions that have been debated for a long time. For example, how does one classify the late Marc Chagall—as Russian, as Jewish, or as French? Attributions tend to vary. On another level one may ask if the awareness of Jewish questions plus the painting of Jewish themes are the sole criteria for identification as a "Jewish artist." This might not be the case if one examines the works of certain American Jewish painters such as Louise Nevelson and Anthony Caro but might be identifiable in the paintings and sculptural works of Larry Rivers and George Segal. In Israel itself a "national" style has yet to evolve in painting, although a more positive achievement has occurred in the area of crafts because of the historic success of the Bezalel School.

These issues, complex in nature to begin with, assumed even more importance as individual Soviet Jewish artists began to paint Jewish themes and attempted to exhibit their works during the 1960s and 1970s. The art movement became one small but significant component of the attempt to revive Jewish culture in the Soviet Union. The issue was not a moot one, as was explained by Mikhail Borgman, who wrote part of the catalogue for the American version of the "Group Aleph" Leningrad show of Jewish artists in 1975:

> We proposed showing a group of works in one way or another linked to the spirit and life of the Jewish people and its national and cultural tradition. Once the idea took definite shape and the artists were chosen, the contours of the exhibit became clearer. Attempting to avoid casual speculation in searching for the guiding principle, we demanded of ourselves an answer to the question: "what specifically gives any one of us the right to call his work Jewish. What features of Jewish art are reflected in the works chosen for the exhibit?" . . . This much is certain: the artists themselves consented to the exhibit, by so doing, demonstrating, whatever the consequences, their desire to be identified as Jews.[2]

Alexander Okun, another member of the Leningrad Aleph group, also recalled that the most difficult issue discussed before the show was the issue of what made one a Jewish artist. Was the issue of nationality the sole criteria, or was content an important aspect of the issue? To some individuals, art became a vehicle for the expression of issues connected with the Jewish national problem during the late 1960s and early 1970s, an artistic identity that would rapidly change after migration to an environment of artistic freedom. For others, however, a stronger consciousness existed from an earlier era. Mikhail Grobman, for example, has written of the strength of the Jewish images around him from earliest times, which led him to paint Jewish themes as early as the 1960s and in turn has led him to continue with strong Jewish themes in his most recent art: "The spiritual milieu in which my consciousness crystallized consisted of my mother's memories of Jewish life in the Ukraine, of the years of revolution and civil war, of pogroms against the Jews, of small psychological events and of feelings of hope. Jewish legends and bible stories made a deep impression on me. My imagination absorbed Pushkin's poems as mysterious stories from Jewish life."[3] For a few artists, however, there would be another extreme—that of noninvolvement personally or artistically in the Jewish national or religious movement, with the result that the art was produced with an international style that would not change much with the process of emigration. It is entirely possible to argue, however, that abstract expressionism does convey Jewish values in its own way by providing an avenue for the artist's psychological subconscious.

The result of these polarities generally led to a group of themes to be found in the works of Soviet Jewish artists, while they lived in the Soviet Union. These themes may be divided into the following categories:

1. Paintings or sculptural works done in an international style, with no Jewish content but generally expressionist, possibly with subtle or overt criticisms of Soviet reality.

2. Active Jewish themes, such as illustrations for stories in an official or unofficial context, themes of wandering in a search for roots and culture, Biblical themes used in an allegorical sense, and some art with direct reference to the problems of emigration and aliyah.

3. Morbid and tragic themes, reflective of aspects of Soviet life itself, as well as personal experience, usually illustrated through an expressionist motif.

4. Memorials, often the product of the experience of emigration, usually produced by artists who have gone through a prison experience or who have never had the opportunity to artistically examine the sense of the injustice of Soviet Jewish history. Such memorials might be the artistic equivalent of written testimony and provides some new avenues of documenting the history of dissent.

5. Utilization of Jewish and Russian primitive elements as a thematic element. This "primitivism" may be drawn from old Russian broadsides (Lubky—primitive works with cartoonlike fig-

ures and textual explanations in the work), synagogue art and architecture, especially decorations on Torah arks, Jewish ceremonial art, and calligraphy.

6. The Holocaust, if treated, usually found entirely in an unofficial format for artists who painted in the Soviet Union and occasionally in a format which links the Holocaust to World War II. For Jewish artists, however, there is a real problem in dealing with this subject, since the official Soviet policy is to deny that Jews suffered more than other nationalities. After emigration many artists try to deal with the Holocaust in the open environment of Israel.

7. Satire and irony. Jews are often associated with anecdotes and humor in the Soviet Union. Some of this humor and satire has crept over into the realm of the unofficial art. The best examples of this can be found in the works of the Moscow-New York artists Vitaly Komar and Aleksandr Melamad, who work in a pop-art style now as they did in the Soviet Union.

If all of the above elements may be present in the work of Soviet Jewish artists to some degree, there is also one element that was generally obscured while they lived in the USSR—that of the linkage of Jews to Israel and the Israeli landscape. Very few works were published in the Soviet Union dealing with Israel through the artist's vision. One such work was a folio done by the Lithuanian artist Samuelis Rozinas (now Shmuel Rosen in Israel), which features a series of Israeli landscapes, Israeli and Arab figures, as well as block prints of the Great Patriotic War and the life of Lenin. These works, however, were done during the 1960s.

In assessing the situation of Jewish artists while they resided in the Soviet Union, it is important to point out that unofficial Soviet art may be called the freest art in that the artist may have no intention to exhibit and the art may be generated only for the artist himself. The individualized "freedom," however, becomes troublesome if artists begin to group together for exhibition purposes.

The Legacy of the Group Aleph Show

A new direction took place in the unofficial art movement in Leningrad on November 23 1975, when a group of nonconformist artists, predominately Jewish but with some non-Jewish associates, opened an underground show in the apartment of artist Yevgeny Abezgauz (now Abeshaus). The show was called "Aleph" after the first letter of the Hebrew alphabet, which also signified the first totally Jewish show in modern Soviet history. Since aleph was the first letter, there was a presumption that more Jewish shows might follow if Soviet officialdom permitted it. There were sixteen nonconformist artists associated with putting the show together but the more characteristic identity of this unofficial exhibition came to be associated with twelve Jewish artists. More than four thousand people saw the show during the week it was open in Leningrad, and five thousand more saw it in Moscow. Of the artists represented in the exhibition, one, Oscar Sidlin, was already deceased. Sidlin's works were held in special regard as he was the first teacher for many of the young artists and was generally regarded as a father figure by them. The most significant of the non-Jewish associates, according to Anatoly Basin, was Aleksandr Arefiev, long one of the leaders of the nonconformist movement in Leningrad. Basin and Aleksandr Okun both suggest that Arefiev was the individual who raised the idea of a Jewish show.

Of the participants who were alive when the show took place, six emigrated to Israel and one (Alex Rapoport) to the United States. Of the six who came to Israel, one, Yuri Kalenderov, has since departed to Italy. Those who remain in Israel are Yevgeny Abezgauz, Anatoly Basin, Aleksandr Okun, Sima Ostrovsky, and Tanya Kornfeld. Abezgauz, Basin, and Okun were probably the most significant ideological leaders for the Aleph show.

Abezgauz's work figured prominently in the exhibit because of its intensive Jewish and political character, plus his leadership. The painting *Aliyah Shelanu* (Our Aliyah) became a symbol of the show. It depicted the remains of a Star of David, smashed into an almost unrecognizable form, in the middle of a wasteland. From Leningrad's St. Isaac's Cathedral in the background emerge a flock of birds abandoning their nest for the Jewish symbol. (Ironically, recent interpretations of this painting have taken a reverse meaning, given the problems connected with Jewish resettlement. The "wasteland" depicted in the work has been taken by some immigrants to symbolize the sterile intellectual environment in Israel and all of the hopes that have been dashed by the emigration process.)

In *Little Israel Roamed Russia in Search of Happiness* the artist placed himself in the position of wandering Jew, amidst the cold Russian landscape. *It Was Quiet in Our Town after the Pogrom* depicted the aftermath of a barbaric episode often repeated in Russian Jewish history. This image, usually not treated in Soviet art, stood in direct contrast to the dreamlike scenes of Chagall or the nostalgic mood created by the works of Kaplan. *Judith Was Proud But Sorrowful* was a work drawn from the classical theme of Judith and Holofernes. The ironic difference in Abezgauz's work was that Judith was his wife, and she held the head of the artist. Abezgauz also painted a series of self-portraits in the style of the eighteenth century, with each subject adorned with a medallion bearing the face of a refusenik friend.

Since emigrating in 1977, Abezgaus has undergone some significant changes, including his name, to Abeshaus. His early works in Israel continued some of the same thematic ideas developed in Leningrad, but with a greater primitiveness and satirical element. These paintings and etchings, like his earlier works, were strongly suggestive of the influence of Russian *Lubky,* or broadsides, with their characteristic naive style and textual explanations written in Hebrew. In a certain sense all of these works remain self-portraits or personal history in one form or another.

Later, the artist moved into some surrealistic motifs but returned to the naive form, with an amusing overtone, perhaps in reaction to the reality of Zionism being far from the vision that existed among the Jewish artists when they resided in Leningrad. This series, entitled *Vanities,* with the name taken from the opening of the Book of Ecclesiastes, shows various figures, some identified as Israeli, some as nondescript individuals, engaged in all sorts of vain activities. Vanity is expressed by large bubbles moving through each work. The works seem less engaging than the works produced by the artist when he was in Leningrad, although they have become the basis for a series of book covers for the works of various Russian and Yiddish writers in New York and Paris. Nevertheless, the works appear humorous to those who understand some of the social conflicts of contemporary Israeli society.

Okun was one of the younger (born 1949) members of the Aleph group, but nevertheless emerged as one of the significant thinkers in the realm of Jewish art and culture. When he lived in the USSR, Okun was an art teacher, having graduated from the Leningrad Academy of Fine Arts in 1972. He was refused entry into the Association of Artists of the USSR a year later on the grounds that his paintings were "formalist," the Soviet term used to describe any work that does not follow the guidelines of Socialist Realism. Before leaving the USSR, however, Okun traveled to Armenia several times and helped in arranging an exhibition of Leningrad artists at the Museum of Modern Art in Yerevan. The nonconformist movement generally found kindred spirits in Armenia, where the officially painted art came very close to the nonconformist tendency in Leningrad. The difference, however, lay in the Soviet government's toleration of some artistic forms as examples of Armenian national culture. Okun's supporter in these endeavors was Genrikh Ijitian, director of the museum in Yerevan.

During his Soviet period Okun painted works that were cubist and expressionist in style, utilizing bright shades of color. While Okun always considered himself a Jewish artist, the influences on his art as such were Russian icons and some eighteenth-century Russian painters, especially Rokotov. The iconographic influence can be seen in all of his works, including those done in Israel. Faces and color textures evoke features found in the classical Russian icons, especially those of the schools of Theofanes the Greek and Rublev. *Girl with a Toy Whistle,* painted in 1967, suggests some of this iconographic influence in the positioning of the figure, but to this is added cubist dimensions and more vibrant and shaded color indicating influences of some turn-of-the-century artists like Malevich and Goncharova. The result is a work which, at first glance, appears to be a product of an earlier period, yet modern because of subtle "textual" additions to the canvas. A large untitled work completed in 1978, the artist's last work painted in Leningrad, contains an amalgam of images from the Russian past and present—a self-portrait, iconographic images, street scenes, faces, and buildings ablaze.

Since arriving in Israel, Okun has intensified his interest in trying to establish a universal Jewish content to his art, without forcing himself into the provinciality of a singular Israeli environment. Okun accepts the principle that although Israel may be rich in history and archaeology, both it and Jewish culture generally are essentially barren of an artistic tradition before the twentieth century. Okun also takes the view that Jewish life is a balance between smiles and tears, and his art tends to reflect these polarities.

In *Kinnerret* (Sea of Galilee) the artist shows a family bathing in deep green water, backed by a red sky. The iconlike figures are painted with great delicacy of texture and color. The rocks that surround the Kinnerret appear like the rocks of the Holy Land as depicted in Russian icons, simplified yet jagged. The red sky, according to the artist, was not inspired by any preconceived ideas, but evolved as did the painting itself.

Okun interprets the red to be the blood of the Jews, shed in Roman times, and a reminder of the role that art plays in evoking a Jewish national imagery.[4] *Crying Man,* on the other hand, is more direct in its attempt to show a Jewish, yet universal response to grief.

During 1982 Okun painted a series of works inspired by the Mahane Yehuda Market in Jerusalem. These include works of high color and a pleasant expressionism that are microscopic views, in a sense, of not only Israeli, but also Jewish life. The audience finds not only fish sellers and butcher shops in these paintings, but also a total spectrum of Jewish elements integrated into the symbolism of the works. *Hamsin,* for example, shows two distorted human figures holding a slaughtered chicken, a symbol of sacrifice, while in the background the desert outskirts of Jerusalem can be seen with the inference of heat and emotion.

From 1983 through 1985 Okun began an intellectual and artistic search for lost Jewish traditions. The artist believed that since Jewish history was linked to so much destruction, along with religious limitations on artistic expression, Jewish life never developed normal artistic traditions. His reaction, therefore, was to "reconstruct" a series of large, mixed-medium works to illustrate these missing episodes from Jewish art history. For example, *Empire* is a large work done with oil on wood and provides some universal images from Jewish life in an apparent nineteenth-century type of opulence. In the upper right and left are found the priestly hands with the traditional sign of benediction. Below are three ears of corn and a necklacelike braid of garlic cloves. On the bottom right and left are two small images from Jewish life—*tefilah,* an inscription from a mezuzah, and a shopping list (both look the same). All of this is set against a rich red background with gold borders to suggest the nineteenth-century style. There is both a touch of irony and satire found in this work, but one cannot escape its Jewishness. Other works, such as *Amulet* and *Shopping List,* are rich in symbols from Jewish life— from the challah for Shabbat, to old clothes in a wardrobe, to visions of Jerusalem.

Okun's most monumental work is a large wooden structure painted with oil entitled *Self-Portrait, 1949–1984.* The format of the work is half-sculpture, half-painting, in the shape of what appears to be at first a design for a *bima* (altar) in a synagogue. However, the symbolism found in the work is personal, Jewish, and Christian. A hand appears at the top center in a curved panel, evoking the Christian image of creation. On each side of a center curtain below are found nine self-portraits, indicating the artist's experiences. In the center there is a white, closed curtain, indicating perhaps the uncertainty of the future, or perhaps, the ancient holy of holies in the Temple of Jerusalem.

That these works are not entirely Jewish does not bother the artist, as his goal is to create a "normal" Jewish art that focuses not on purely religious themes or the kitsch expressions of Jewish culture, but is based on the everyday reality of Jewish life. And since Jewish life is multidimensional, bringing together the experiences from other cultures as well as Jewish, the artist finds no difficulty in pulling together mixed images. This is not a new Hellenism, but a reflection of Jewish, especially Israeli, reality.

Anatoly Basin, another member of the Aleph group has not undergone any change in his style of painting since coming to Israel. His works are expressionistic, especially centered on nudes, in a motif not unlike Matisse, utilizing a rich and heavy application of color and outline. While his paintings are clearly international in appeal, the artist nevertheless feels that his ability to express himself on canvas has been enhanced by the freedom of Israel. Basin, however, is important because before coming to Israel he amassed a large photographic and historical archive of the entire nonconformist art movement in Leningrad. More recently, he has delved into Jewish philosophy and poetry and hopes to direct himself to a thorough analysis of the relationship of philosophy to painting.

Tanya Kornfeld, the fourth member of the Aleph group in Israel, painted canvases in the 1975 show that contained substantial Jewish content. In *Shabbos* she painted a Modigliani-like woman, in greenish hues, her hands raised as before beginning the Shabbat prayer over candles. *On the Floor,* another work from the Leningrad exhibition, depicted two large shuttered Leningrad style windows, deeply recessed from the wall. Around these dominant windows the viewer finds small mementos of Jewish life that appear as mysterious symbols: on the wall between the two windows a small cameolike family portrait; on the bottom right a small figure that appears to be a man, seated and hunched over, wrapped in a prayer shawl; and in the center a shadowed figure appears sleeping before two Shabbat candles. This work creates a mysterious image of the Soviet Jewish world, as if one is viewing a shadow box filled with antiquated objects.

Tanya Kornfeld has actually emigrated to Israel twice. During her initial absorption in the country she met and married an American and wound up living in Anaheim, California. There she continued her painting and established good gallery connections. Most significantly, living in Anaheim provided her with easy access to the American Southwest desert landscape not unlike Israel. During 1985 Kornfeld and her family returned to Israel as permanent residents. The artistic result of this double migration process is impressive, for Kornfeld's works now appear to have achieved a sophisticated universalism, with strong influences from the American Southwest as well as from the landscape of Israel. Her latest works, done mainly in acrylic, emphasize soft desert tones and varying subjects. *Still Life* (1985) integrates a still life scene into a desert environment, with great effectiveness through delicate brush work. *Safari,* a series of six works, depicts various animals in movement. The animals appear not in a realistic form, but with a primitivism that makes them appear as book illustrations, with refined line and color.

Kornfeld's most interesting works, however, possess a Jewish "national" quality in that they can be best understood within the context of her being an Israeli artist. *Angel* (1985) depicts an extended, feminine form as an angel, with faint wings of white, with a flame emerging from her hand. This is a highly interesting work because it appears to be entirely unique in its inspiration, without the implied artistic references of iconography or other forms from the Western tradition. *Girl on a Goat* (1985) depicts a nude girl riding on a goat. This is a theme not unknown to the Middle East. But Kornfeld has managed to create new life into these subjects and provides a mild level of eroticism in both works. In her series of illustrations from the Bible, she integrates a Hebrew text into her interpretation of Old Testament figures, who appear almost like Bedouins within a desert environment. The results are highly effective, as Biblical personages become human beings that share the same experience as contemporary humanity.

Boris Penson—The Legacy of Prison

Boris Penson was best known not as a refusenik artist but as one of the accused in the Leningrad Hijack trial of 1970. Penson had been raised in Riga and studied with Semyon Gelberg and then at the Art Academy in Riga. He had his first encounter with the Soviet judicial system when he was eighteen years of age, in 1964, when he was falsely accused of rape. He was sentenced to five years in prison, serving three and a half. After the hijack group was caught by the KGB, Penson was sentenced to ten years at hard labor.

Being an artist as well as a prisoner, Penson became a special kind of prisoner for the Jewish world. Some of his art works, mainly expressionist themes, some experiments in cubism, and some prison scenes from an earlier time were smuggled out of the Soviet Union and became the basis for several shows in Israel and the West. Penson always considered himself a Jewish painter but never exclusively dealt with Jewish themes.

In April 1979 Penson and others connected with the hijacking were freed in a spy exchange, and he came to Israel. Having been "adopted" by the city of Netanya, he decided to reside there. In the seven years since his resettlement in Israel, Penson's style has gone through significant changes. His main focus now is on analytical abstraction and cubism, mixed with a dramatic change in his use of light and color. This change is not unexpected, as the more somber blues and gray colors characteristic of the Baltic gave way to the more sun-washed colors of the Mediterranean. Thematically, however, abstraction holds the upper hand in his works, and for Penson this seems logical. The artist sees himself, as do most other Jewish artists, as part of an international style but subjectively possessing the potential to evoke Jewish themes.

Penson has gone out of his way to create two folios of etchings which can be best classified as "memorials" to his former existence. A folio of seven etchings, entitled *Prison Views,* was produced in 1979. Dark and somber, these etchings evoke visions of human suffering and deprivation from the past. One is forced to recall that the references are more contemporary, based on the artist's familiarity with the Soviet prison system.

Penson's latest "memorial" (1985) is an album of fourteen etchings entitled *The Land of Women.* It is again based on the prison experience, but one of a peculiar nature. During his years in prison Penson met and spoke on several occasions with women prisoners who were being transported to another region. From these discussions, and from his knowledge of the Soviet prison system, he learned of the special impact that prison has on women—what he termed the "erotic aspect of female convicts' existence . . . and the extreme sexual hunger caused and aggravated by particular prison conditions."[5] Penson described this bleak mood in the introduction to his album: "Humbled in unflattering convict's clothes, suffering from deprivation, victimized by guards and wardens, without family, love, or men's affections, a tribe of women is fenced off from their usual life by barbed wire and dogs. They create their special monstrous unisexual world, where everything that is inherent in a human being—love, dreams, hatred, hope, jealousy, and violence finds its own particular aspect of expression."[6] The etchings in the album are exceptionally interesting and cannot be classified as usual prison art. Penson examines in the fourteen etchings, each done with exacting detail, the isolation and alienation of searches as well as daily routines, the sense of helplessness of a young prisoner speaking to an older woman inmate, the sexual demands at the hands of the warden, the embarrassment and coldness of a conjugal visit from a husband, the visions of Satanic figures which intrude into the life of those who feel helpless. Penson's art does not provide the viewer with easy images to digest. Although blatantly political, the artist felt compelled to compose these images, just as other writers have written of their prison experiences as a memorial to those who did not survive.

As an Israeli artist, Penson comprehends well the confinement of Israel as an environment for the artist. Nor does living in Netanya provide him with easy access to the circles of artists in Tel Aviv or Jerusalem. Despite the attractions of Western art capitals, Penson feels compelled to remain in Israel because of what the state means to him as a Jew. Thus, there are always conflicting elements in his outlook, because his own Zionism conflicts with a realistic appraisal of what his artistic capability might be in a more accepting artistic environment.

Aharon April—Light and Color

Aharon April's art is an example of a Soviet Jewish artist who underwent an immense transition in style insofar as use of color and light is concerned while he lived in the Soviet Union, as opposed to the usual experience of a postimmigration change. With his immigration to Israel was added the potential for utilizing Jewish, specifically Biblical themes in a highly impressionistic mode.

April was born in Lithuania but raised in Yakutia as a result of his family's deportation. He came to Moscow twice, the second time in 1954 to study at the Surikov Art Academy. Until 1966 his art focused around realistic landscapes, which had been painted mainly in Siberia. These works are highly reminiscent of the landscapes of the Russian-Jewish turn-of-the-century painter Isaac Levitan—realistic, yet highly evocative because of the natural balances of the Siberian setting and use of color. Some of these works were used as illustrations for articles in Soviet periodicals. A few of the paintings went beyond realism to portray official socialist motifs. One, *On the Ob River,* is exceptionally large and at first strikes the viewer as another work of Socialist Realism. However, a closer look, especially after viewing April's later works, reveals an intense level of experimentation with color. Most of April's scenes are painted on sunny days, thus intensifying the depth of each dark color and lightening of the brighter ones. This is the type of experimentation with lighting that one might expect from the Mediterranean region, but not from Siberia.

April was able to have two one-man shows in Moscow during 1963 and 1970 and because of his official status traveled to India, Jordan, and Egypt in 1967. It was this contact with more southerly climates and sunny atmospheres that intensified his interest in the use of color and light. Seeing the Israeli port of Elath from Aqaba also stimulated his interest in Israel. After the mid-1970s most of his works are dominated by the interplay of these elements, plus the addition of nude forms, which provide a modest, and later a more dramatic, eroticism.

April immigrated to Israel in 1972. Because he was one of the early émigré artists in the country, and was endowed with considerable artistic skills, he was able to find employment in teaching positions at Haifa University, the Hebrew University of Jerusalem, and the Bezalel Art Academy. Since 1975 he has had numerous one-man shows.

Since his arrival in Israel April's style has not changed in terms of his interplay of color and light, but he has developed a higher level of abstraction. During the past several years he has produced a series of water colors, entitled *Song of Songs.* April pointed to the logic of an alliance between art and the Bible when he indicated that "without having mastered the Code of Art, one may say that neither the painter's brush nor the sculptor's chisel can express better than what was written in the Book of Books."[7] Based on the Bible, the series is a grouping of forty-three works, many with highly erotic qualities, yet done with a high standard of taste. In producing these April takes a particular view of the task of the Jewish artist. While acknowledging that Jews are historically perceived more as a bookish than as an art-oriented people, April sees an understanding of art just as important to Judaism as is the study of the Talmud:

There is something in the fact that the written word is closer to the Jews than an image. There is an attitude that art's function is mainly decorative.

Just as there is a code for those reading the Holy Scriptures, so is there a code for the understanding of genuine art.

Well known artists, the foremost members of the ultra-modern groups and ensembles, leave them to study the holy scriptures in the retreat of the Yeshivot. Famous Rabbis analyze painting and sculpture so expertly and perceptively that it is regrettable that the general public is unaware of it.[8]

For the artist the Song of Songs provides a potential format for a biblically based "internationalist" art form. The evocative passages of love and naturalism have been used by April to their maximum potential. The product is improvisational and sensuous.

Mikhail Grobman—The Search for a National Jewish Art

If there is a single artist among the émigrés who can be identified as a member of the avant-garde, it is Mikhail Grobman. Grobman is not only a painter, but also an art collector, archivist of the Jewish art movement in the Soviet Union, poet, and essayist. Born in 1939, he was affected both by a strong Jewish home environment and loss of his extended family during the Holocaust. From 1955 to 1959 Grobman received his higher art education in Moscow at the Mukhina Institute. In 1959 he had his first one-man exhibition and also became involved with the "Leva (Left) Group" of Moscow avant-garde artists and poets. Of the fifteen members of this group, which included some of the most significant nonconformist artists of the period (Rabin, Zveryev, Kulakov, Kropivinsky, Masterkova, Veisberg [Weisberg], Neizvestny), 70 percent, according to Grobman, were Jews. Most, however, were cosmopolitan and were not concerned with the creation of a Jewish national art. Much of the work produced by the "Leva Group" was political, and some artists, like Vladimir Yankilevsky, went out of their way to avoid subjects connected with Jewish themes.

In 1964 Grobman was sent to Yerevan to design a commissioned work with a socialist realist theme. There, however, he was heavily influenced by the environment of Armenia and came back with designs for Jewish themes. The official reaction was one of "disbelief," with accusations that the artist was creating Jewish "fairly-tales." Grobman's response, however, was to plead that he was interested in painting the Jewish life that was dying in the USSR. In this respect he considers himself to have been the first official Jewish artist in the Soviet Union as he became involved with themes outside of the shtetl motif.

In 1965 Grobman held what he termed the "first Jewish exhibition" since the death of Stalin, and possibly since the closing of the Yevsektsiia (Special Section for Jewish Affairs in the Communist Party, 1918–30, eliminated by Stalin), at the Artist's House (Dom Khudozhnik) in Moscow. This was a two-week long exhibition with two non-Jewish painters. Grobman's contributions featured works such as the pastel, *Death of a Jewish Soldier* (1963), which depicted an abstract tomb, set against a black desert background and dark, expressionist sky with two moons. In the foreground was a large menorah. According to the artist, the actual title of this work was *Death of an Israeli Soldier.* But no matter how daring the exhibit in its exhibition of Jewish themes, the Israeli motif could not be tolerated. Another work exhibited in the same show was entitled *Babi Yar,* which depicted the small monument which then stood at the Kievan massacre site, flanked by six lit menorahs. Grobman also exhibited a series of old Jewish people done in watercolor and monotype. One of these works was *Talmudist* (1964) which depicted a rabbi.

Grobman tells the story of meeting an elderly Jew at the exhibit who did not know what to make of what he was seeing and who became very flustered and anxious. The unexpected nature of the exhibition actually scared him. There was great discussion about the exhibit, according to Grobman, but no reviews or catalogs were printed. *Sovietische Heimland,* however, mentioned the existence of the show, and both Moshe Taife, the official Jewish poet and publisher of the journal, and Aaron Vergalis, its editor, came to Moscow for the event. Four years later, in 1969, *Sovietische Heimland* published a picture of one of the works of Grobman and Yuri Kuperman, another Moscow artist.

Grobman did not limit his works to Jewish themes. Many ironic and satirical works emerged by 1967, utilizing the form of the collage. *Winter Festival* (1966) is a work that may mark a transition into a more heavily Jewish style for the artist. The gouache and tempera work has a high blend of colors done in a style that appears like pointillism (a post-impressionist form of painting perfected by Seurat which applied the paint to the canvas in small dots). The bird form appears to be a mythical creature, surrounded by other supernatural elements. The result is a fairylike construction. *Mediterranean Sea* (1967) was a simplified watercolor showing a Jewish man wearing tefillin, with abstract forms of an angel wing, the sun, and the sea in the background. *Desert* of the same year depicted a bearded angel in a thinly constructed desert environment, while *Kabbalist* depicted a Jewish man walking with a Bible toward an outdoor altar, a Star of David at the top and a fiery glow around it. This is a particularly interesting work in light of Grobman's move toward Kabbalistic themes after his immigration to Israel in 1971. In 1968 Grobman painted *Broken Palm,* a work that showed a crowned, semi-abstract bird holding a broken palm. The form of the bird evokes the image of the Russian *Lubky* (broadsides) or primitive Jewish art. More specifically, however, the work was dedicated to the Israeli military victory in the Six-Day War.

In 1969 Grobman decided to leave the Soviet Union, and he received permission to emigrate in September 1971. He brought with him more than a hundred paintings of his own as well as the works of other artists, plus a huge library of art books (because of changes in Soviet customs regulations, it is now impossible for such materials to be carried out of the country). Grobman was quickly recognized as an artist of international merit and had no trouble exhibiting, not only in Israel, but also in Europe and the United States. His works from 1971 through 1977 became increasingly complex and heavily laden with Jewish symbolism. By the late 1970s a special quality which differentiated Grobman's works clearly from all other artists became visible. These traits included primitive animal forms mixed with Biblical symbolism, Hebrew calligraphy, and extensive documentation of the painting itself, written in Russian, with such extensive detail as indications as to the day and hour when the painting was completed. *Kaddish* (1977), for example, shows a dramatically formed birdlike devilish figure in yellow, against a deep red background. Across the body of the bird are Kabbalistic symbols from the Zohar built into a "tree of life," with symbols of black and white indicating the forces of good and evil and other symbols of God's name. Across the front of the figure is the phrase in Hebrew from Genesis, "And the earth was without form." Around the outer edge of the painting is the text of the Kaddish, the Hebrew prayer for the dead as well as a praise of the power and majesty of God, written in Russian. Most of Grobman's later works continue to contain such symbolism and Biblical referencing.

In 1975 Grobman was influential in bringing together a group of talented Soviet émigré artists to form the avant-garde group called Leviathan. The group included Shmuel Ackerman, Boris Yuchvetz, Lena Rabinovitch, Dina Blich, Ilia Zundelevitch, Lev Nussberg (who lives in the United States), Grigoriy Patlas, and Avraham Alajem-Ofek, the only member of the group not from the Soviet Union (having emigrated from Bulgaria in 1949). The main purpose of Leviathan was not simply to exhibit, but to have an amalgam of émigré aritsts help in the creation of what Grobman called a "Jewish national art."

Leviathan was an avant-garde movement reminiscent of the best that the Soviet avant-garde of the 1920s could offer. It came complete with manifestos, a newspaper handwritten on an occasional basis by Grobman, art exhibitions, outdoor sculptural events, and "happenings." The ideological basis of Leviathan was "Death to Realism," which is described as an art form which itself pollutes all attempts to create true art. Not only is realism per se the culprit, but also all hybrid forms of realism, from surrealism to conceptual art. Most significantly, the prevalence of the public's taste for realism turns the artist into something unappealing: "The artists willingly attired in domestics' uniforms the path of spiritual grave-diggers, offering themselves for sale with a deep bow and the flattery of an eunuch. The contemporary artist is a crossbreed of a grocer and a prostitute. Such is the outcome of blind obedience to Realistic principles in art, principles of illusionism and imitations of nature."[9] According to Grobman, who was the major ideologist of Leviathan, the alternative to realism was "the way of apprehension and of adhesion with the spiritual."[10] Grobman emphasizes the need for "transgenerational memory" and "magic symbolism" as a way of comprehending the world. In particular his statements in the Leviathan manifestos suggest a way for interpreting his own works:

Magic Symbolism is a system that enables intuitive comprehension of the world by following visual means. An object that conforms to the standard of Magic Symbolism, appears as a visual-static form. The interpretation and comprehension of that object is a world view. Meditation upon a magic symbolic object leads man into the circle of Kabbalistic concepts, to a mystical religious experience of the soul and from there to wisdom and love, that is to say, happiness. The words of Kabbalah are directed toward the initiates of Kabbalah. Magic Symbolism sees in form a rare possibility of conveying mystical knowledge to wide circles without desecrating it.[11]

The practical manifestation of this ideology was the production of several outdoor "happenings" in the Dead Sea area, which featured theaterlike events with Grobman playing the angel of death in a costume he had made. In addition, the group developed outdoor landscape sculptures in the desert and the idea of painting rocks with Kabbalistic symbols and statements of the presence of God. In 1978 Grobman illustrated the first English and German translations of *The Book of Bahir,* a twelfth-century Kabbalistic manuscript.

While some viewers found it difficult to comprehend the "purpose" of the Leviathan group, the art forms developed at these events were serious and aspired to higher levels of artistic formation. In a certain sense it was way beyond what the Israeli public was capable of comprehending artistically.

During 1982 Grobman temporarily abandoned Kabbalistic directions for a retreat into Pop Art. He produced an outrageous series of fourteen works entitled *Leniniana,* which took an iconoclastic view toward the founder of the Soviet state that only an émigré could possibly dare touch. The works included an icon of the "virgin birth of Lenin," scenes from the life of young Lenin (produced in cartoon form), a "dead Lenin" as a statue talking to school children (after the infamous Socialist Realist painting by Serov), Lenin's personal paintings (similar to Hitler's own watercolors, suggesting that a dictator can be identified by his own art works!), Lenin photographed at the time of his first arrest for writing "don't forget your mother's birthday" across the front of his own head, and Lenin having Krupskaya executed and then taking out his sexual energies on peasant women in the countryside. This satirical approach to the Soviet "cult of the personality" that surrounds Lenin in a religiouslike aura can only be described as delicious humor that is all too often hidden in the Soviet Union. Grobman produced a similiar series about himself, as well as one on Maxim Gorky.

Mikhail Grobman, therefore, appears to represent a more dynamic force in the artistic world of Israel in that he has not only managed to produce his own unique form of art, directed toward the Kabbala as an inspiration for a Jewish national style, but has also managed to galvanize other artists together into a movement that has a specific direction. This is a difficult momentum to maintain in Israel because the main support for such art comes from a very narrow base.

Mark Zhitnitsky—The Presence of the Jewish
Past and the Holocaust

One of the most interesting personalities among Soviet émigré artists is Mark Zhitnitsky. Zhitnitsky, who emigrated to Israel in 1971, now lives in Jaffa. His personal history in a certain sense mirrors the fate of many Jewish artists and writers who have lived since the Communist Revolution in 1917. Born in 1903 in Moghilev, Zhitnitsky received a modest education until he joined the Red Army cavalry in 1918 at age fifteen. He served in the Red Army for five years and afterward, from 1925 to 1932, was a student at the Moscow Art Institute.

After graduation Zhitnitsky worked as a book illustrator and official artist, with several exhibitions until his arrest in 1936. Caught in the Stalin purges with other revolutionary artists, he was sentenced to a twenty-five year term in the Pechora prison and later to exile in the Komi Autonomous Republic of the Soviet Union. Although a prisoner, Zhitnitsky continued to paint official posters, Socialist Realist paintings, and set designs for the stage. His wife and son were both killed during the German occupation of Minsk. Zhitnitsky stayed in prison until he was pardoned in 1946.

From 1946 to 1949 Zhitnitsky returned to Minsk and to his art, producing a series of anti-Nazi drawings for public exhibition. During this period he also remarried. In 1949, however, he was rearrested during the anti-Cosmopolitan campaign and given another ten-year sentence in the region of the Yenesey River in Siberia. The artist was rehabilitated after the 20th Party Congress in 1956 and became a member of the Union of Artists. Before emigrating in 1971, he produced many works on themes related to World War II, as well as satirical cartoons.

Zhitnitsky is an interesting artist for many reasons. First, he represents a high level of artistic talent combined with what was a high level of Jewish consciousness that was never lost, despite substantial time spent in prison. His prison drawings, done during his prison experiences of the 1940s and 1950s, convey the full range of human tragedy and human waste that resulted from such incarcerations. Later, Zhitnitsky produced personalized art works as memorials to Jewish artists and writers who perished during the "Black Years" of Soviet Jewry. One such drawing memorializes in a joyous sense of "Freilech," one of Solomon Mikhoels' last stage plays. Zhitnitsky also produced a series of drawings to illustrate several poems and narrative works by the Yiddish writer Moshe Kulbak, who died in prison in 1940.

Secondly, Zhitnitsky as an "official" artist managed to produce anti-Nazi works as official propaganda which came very close to being "Jewish art," as themes often dealt with massacres and the fate of the Jews during World War II. Although never exhibited as "Holocaust art," in essence that was the theme. According to the artist, the Soviet government was on the verge of planning an exhibition of these graphics in 1969 when plans were scrapped. The reaction of the Union of Artists board was to tell Zhitnitsky that "these works should be exhibited in Tel Aviv."

Zhitnitsky brought 140 works with him when he left the USSR in 1971, and they formed the core of a collection that was well received by the Israeli public. An exhibition in April 1972 in Tel Aviv exhibited drawings of the fall of Fascism, the Holocaust, the world of Shalom Aleichem, and satirical drawings. Twenty-one of the drawings from the world of Shalom Aleichem were published in book form during 1977.[12] Since that time Zhitnitsky has produced illustrations for the works of I. B. Singer and Alexandr Solzhenitsyn, although none have been published or reproduced. One of the most interesting drawings was a revision of a satirical cartoon that Zhitnitsky himself had done as official art during the antireligious campaign of the early 1920s. At that time he drew a widely circulated cartoon that showed two rabbis holding an unrolled torah scroll around a shtetl, vainly trying to keep the population within the boundaries of the old ways. Two emancipated Jews managed to jump the wall of the "Torah wall" and flee to the confines of the new Socialism. Forty-five years later Zhitnitsky redrew the same work, this time showing Brezhnev and other Soviet authorities holding a barbed wire circle around the Jewish community, while within the wire, a bulldozer demolishes a Jewish cemetery and a group of Jews cynically read a decree from Birobidzhan (the Jewish "Autonomous" Republic in Siberia established by Stalin), while others are controlled by armed guards. Amid this scene two young Jews jump the barbed wire to freedom carrying an Israeli flag.

Since the mid-1970s Zhitnitsky has been aggressively painting oil works illustrating varying events of the Holocaust. Some of these have been done on commission from Yad VaShem and Lochamei HaGetaot, museums of the Holocaust in Israel. While these works are visually interesting, they are less dramatic and less well artistically conceived compared to earlier works. In any case Zhitnitsky's themes from the immediate Jewish past loom as significant, and in his case immigration to Israel has permitted a full artistic flowering, even at a late age.

Haim Kapchits—Themes of Orthodoxy

Haim Kapchits represents another model of an artist in transition, one that moved from heavy involvement with expressionistic works during most of his life in the Soviet Union to paintings with strong Jewish overtones after emigrating to Israel in 1981. On a more interesting level, Kapchits, who possessed substantial experience in constructing monumental mosaics and murals, moved into rather esoteric areas for a Soviet émigré artist—designing religious ritual items such as mezuzahs and spice boxes and the interiors of synagogues.

Kapchits was born in Byelorussia in 1937 and studied at the Leningrad Academy of the Arts between 1957 and 1963. Between 1963 and the time of emigration in 1981 he was successful by Soviet standards, being a member of the Union of Artists, participating in shows across the USSR and in Bulgaria, and receiving major commissions for wall engravings, frescos, mosaic panels, textile panels, and wood reliefs for various cultural centers and sports palaces in the Perm region of the Urals.

A major change in his art appears to have occurred around the time of his father's death in 1974, which in turn led to a higher level of Jewish consciousness generally. Kapchits felt impelled to build an elaborate oversized memorial at his father's grave site. Carved from stone by the artist, the work is striking as a monumental tombstone, completely covered with Jewish artistic motifs and Hebrew calligraphy. On the top of one side of the monument is a large star of David, flanked on each side by Shabbat candles, and beneath are carved hands in a position of prayer. The reverse side is heralded by a menorah. The memorial to the artist's mother was fashioned in a similar way in 1979. That such works could be produced in the USSR is amazing in itself given the technical problems involved. However, Kapchits went beyond production and had them installed at the grave sites.[13]

A work from 1977 titled *Grief* also indicated a change in the direction of the artist's drawing. While still expressionist, the work has clear suggestions of Jewish symbols—a girl, her head bowed in reverence and surrounding her, hands, a book, and a candle. From this point forward Kapchits has indulged heavily in Jewish subjects, particularly of Jewish faces in his paintings. The more intense use of color after emigration from the USSR is striking.

Being one of the few émigré artists who was religiously observant, Kapchits became involved in religious projects of great diversity in

Israel, much in keeping with the secular diversity of his murals and decorative motifs in the USSR. Recently, he produced a frescoed *bima* (altar) for a Georgian synagogue in Jerusalem, moving then into design and mass production of mezuzahs (small prayer boxes installed in doorways) and ritual spice boxes. Kapchits has also been successful in developing a career as a book illustrator, recently illustrating a cover and text drawings for a Western edition of Bulgakov's *The Master and Margarita* and a memoir by Leib Rokhman.

The transition of Kapchits is particularly interesting because of the direction which he took religiously and which he chose to integrate into his art. From his art production before 1977 there is little to indicate an intense turn toward Jewish themes. To be sure, not all of this was due to the Israel experience—but much of it is linked to a new tie with land and people.

Lev Podolsky—"Living in Israel But Residing in Moscow"

Lev Podolsky (b. 1923) emigrated from Moscow in 1972, leaving behind a long career as an official Soviet artist. His prime area of work in the USSR was as a wood engraver and book illustrator. Podolsky's transition to Israeli society has been difficult. Another émigré artist characterized him as "living in Israel but residing in Moscow." This statement was generated by the fact that Podolsky has been reluctant to learn Hebrew and still converses mainly in Russian or Yiddish. Artistically, his works seem to evoke scenes that could only be conceived of in a Russian environment. However, this explanation may be deceptive, for Podolsky's works have tremendous artistic merit and are striking in their plasticity of form.[14]

The subjects of Podolsky's works are lonely bedrooms and hallways of Moscow apartments. The scenes themselves create a certain nostalgia about Soviet life and a feeling of intense isolation, as the works are devoid of any human forms, except an occasional cameo on the wall. The production method for these works is also important, for process in this case is part of the product. Podolsky utilizes his own updated version of a wood engraving by making the prints from an engraving cut into Perspex (Plexiglass) plates. This is an exceptionally tedious process, more like a contemplative craft, where the process helps remove the artist from the outside world.[15] Podolsky prints these works in a gray gouache on white format, thus providing an evenness to all works, and only one print can be made from each plate.

The result is an art form with high technical qualities, but not a subject that places the work beyond time and space, as the artist might prefer. The uniformity of color, and the concentration on subjects such as sofas, beds, hallways, and the like do provide some universal forms. But the isolation of the scenes themselves suggest they are definitely Russian, aspiring perhaps for a greater universalism.

The Case of Yefim Ladyzhensky

Of all of the Soviet Jewish artists who emigrated to Israel, perhaps the most tragic case is that of Yefim Ladyzhensky. Ladyzhensky had a long career as a scenery painter and set designer in the USSR for various Moscow theaters, including the Taganka, Mali, and Satirical Theaters. He was a member of the Union of Artists and enjoyed many privileges from this position, including a large studio. Unofficially, Ladyzhensky painted large canvases depicting scenes of Jewish life in the USSR, especially in his home town of Odessa.

In 1978 Ladyzhensky decided to emigrate to Israel to follow his daughter to Jerusalem. At age sixty-eight Ladyzhensky assumed that he would be welcomed in Israel as a Jewish artist of great repute. In fact, his arrival was treated with as much fanfare as one could hope for in a country where the artist is not king. A major retrospective of his works was shown at the Israel Museum in Jerusalem in 1979 and another show at the University of Haifa Art Gallery in 1980. He was, in fact, the only newly arrived Soviet immigrant to be given a show at the Israel Museum. The artist, however, took these achievements not as examples of progress but of disinterest. As David Shipler has noted, Ladyzhensky was never able to grasp the notion of a capitalist art market and the problems that surround the economic and artistic fate of painters: "He could never accept or even grasp the concept of a free market in art. He didn't want to sell his paintings, but he did want people to be willing to pay huge amounts for them. He didn't want to hang them in private galleries for sale, but he did want them seen constantly and widely."[16] Ultimately, Ladyzhensky fell into a protracted depression and hung himself.

There are at least two interesting aspects to the life and work of Yefim Ladyzhensky. The first relates to the content and style of his art and the second to the dramatic change in his artistic content just before his death. The artist's official works from the 1930s through the 1960s, all painted for the most part in the realist style, bear no distinctive traits of greatness. They are genre scenes of churches, still lifes, portraits, and landscapes. However, the unofficial canvases of the later period depict a remarkable array of Jewish themes, especially of life in Odessa during the 1920s. These works are painted in a deliberate "primitive" style as a way to evoke some of the nostalgia for Jewish life as it was in a pre-dominantly Jewish city.

Ladyzhensky was able to bring many of his Odessa and Jewish thematic works with him to Israel when he emigrated. Others that were not taken out of the USSR were redone in Israel. The Odessa works in particular are exceptionally interesting because of the dynamic and cos-mopolitan life he showed in the city. There is a lyrical and highly colorful quality to all of these works, which have a natural attraction to the viewer. In *Restaurant of the Hotel London,* there is a crowded scene in an outdoor garden, with all of the human subjects dressed in wonder-ful turn-of-the-century white attire. Some of those at the restaurant are standing, while others appear to sit. But on a closer look the artist has neglected to put in the chairs! On these canvases the viewer also sees the same subjects made famous in the Isaac Babel short stories: Bernie Krik, the Odessa bank robber, in a carriage drawn by a white horse after a job, going to a house of prostitution. *Turn,* which strikes the viewer as a work with exceptional detail focusing on a turning trolley track actually is directed toward a commentary on the food situation during the 1920s, for parallel to the tracks, almost surrounding the canvas, is a queue for bread. *To Mecca: Through My City,* documents what was presumably an annual event in the Imperial period—the large group of Muslims coming to the port of Odessa on their Hajj to Arabia. *The Funeral of Vera Kholodnaya,* captures the intensity of the funeral of a popular fig-ure, with the effect of a crowded canvas intensified by a primitivist style. And, of course, Ladyzhensky also paints Jewish life, the crowded syna-gogues on the high holidays, which are part of the dead past. In all of these works there is both a special quality because of the intensity of the work and a simplicity from a genre aspect:

In between the highs and lows of Odessa life are the traditional genre scenes of people going about the prosaic business of day to day life. Women, hanging laundry in a quiet courtyard, proudly ex-hibit their wash like banners of proletarian innocence while children play contently nearby. The busy fishermen bringing in their daily catch are a reminder both of Odessa's proximity to and dependence upon the sea as well as a personal remembrance of the artist's father, who was a fish salter by profession.[17]

During 1980 and up to the time of his death, Ladyzhensky became increasingly ill at ease in Israel. He was never able to identify with the country and developed an increasing self-pity. What is most remarkable, however, is that Ladyzhensky placed all of his feelings on canvas—and it was this psychological outpouring of grief through the artist's brush that made Ladyzhensky's wife and daughter not suspect the gravity of his depression. Two large triptychs, plus a series of self-portraits, demonstrate the depth of the problem.

In *Unfinished Chronicle*, painted in 1981, Ladyzhensky seems to suggest the frustrations of Jewish life and perhaps those of a Jewish artist. A Chagall image rests in the center of the first canvas, surrounded by sixteen men in *tallesim* (prayer shawls), as if they are in mourning. The second work depicts an inverted Chagall-life folk figure carrying a torah. He is set against a dark blue sky and is surrounded by forms similar to the Jews wearing *tallesim* in part one, only these figures are Arabs wearing kaffiyehs on their heads. The third part of the triptych shows the twentieth-century Russian ruling class seated at a table, with representations of everyone from Tsar Nicholas II through Lenin and Stalin to two faceless leaders. Beneath the table are three inverted Jews carrying torah scrolls. The message here seems clear—that the fate of the Jews is never to be resolved, either in one's own land of birth or in one's homeland.

The triptych of 1982, *I am in Israel,* is more devastating than the first. Part one of the series shows the artist clad only with a white cloth around his waist, set against the backdrop of his studio, with an arrow in his chest. The imagery of the martyrdom of St. Sebastian is inescapable in this work. In part two the artist sits in the center, his hand against his face in despair, mourning his own body that rests in a coffin below him. An array of one hundred and twenty *yartzeit* (memorial) candles glow in the background, cut off from the artist by a barbed wire fence. Above this scene towers a partial view of the Knesset (Israel's Parliament building). In this work the artist obviously saw himself as a prisoner and as a condemned man, with the Knesset allegorically being represented as the Sanhedrin (hence the 120 candles), having passed a death sentence on the artist by their failure to provide recognition for his achievements. Part three of the triptych shows the artist as orchestra conductor, surrounded by ever-changing images from his Jewish past, particularly Odessa, and ending with a funeral scene on the bottom right corner of the canvas. The conductor appears to be losing control of the events that surround him.

The last self-portraits are as disturbing as the triptychs. These works show a gradually fading image of the artist, whose face evokes an expression of despair and entrapment. A later self-portrait shows the artist holding two of his own heads, one in his left hand at his side, the other by the hair. A final portrait shows four heads of the artist in various degrees of agony, surrounded by barbed wire. The intensity of these works cannot be overlooked, for their effectiveness is twofold: one, because of the high level of realism in the work and, secondly, because of the personal pain so effectively conveyed by the artist.

The complex message of these works, and of Ladyzhensky's fate, was well summarized in an art review in 1982 by Meir Ronnen: "The sad message . . . seems to be: you can't win. It has nothing to do with the spirit that has kept Judaism alive or which built up this country (Israel). The artist's self-pitying view is an intensely personal one, perhaps the result of his being "ignored" by the authorities . . . or being sent to live in a shikun box among people whose language he refuses to cope with."[18]

Conclusions

This paper has attempted to survey a small sampling of the Soviet émigré artists in Israel to determine the spectrum of artistic and personal responses to the emigration process and its implications for their art work. The artists discussed in this paper represent only a portion of the artists in Israel. However, while a modest group numerically, they must be identified as some of the most significant intellectually to the new Israeli art movement. Abezgauz, Okun, Basin, Grobman, and April, for example, all see themselves in search of new avenues to express Jewish values and their own sense of Jewishness, avenues that include philosophical statements as well as painted canvases.

The main lesson which seems to emerge from the study of émigré art is that despite the legacy of Socialist Realism, a genuine spectrum of experimental art did emerge in the USSR during the 1960s and 1970s. This was an art of dissent and was only infrequently seen by both insiders and outsiders. Yet the very fact that it was produced and still exists is a good example of the potential vibrancy of Jewish culture in the USSR. Despite certain educational and visual limitations, the Jewish artists who chose the road to emigration and wound up in Israel have done remarkably well in establishing themselves in individual or group traditions. Like all other aspects of the Soviet emigration to Israel, there are people who are dissatisfied and who will never fit into the system. Some émigré artists have come to Israel only to find themselves restricted intellectually and practically by what they term the country's provincialism. There are also artists who have not been inspired and have reduced their production. Such dropouts or changes in career, however, are probably to be expected in the normal course of the emigrant experience, since migration always provides hopes but no guarantees.

If there is anything that seems to guarantee success for the artist, however, it is an optimistic appraisal of what he is capable of doing in the creative realm and satisfying himself with a minimal amount of public support. Real failure, as in the case of Ladyzhensky, appears to come when expectations, exacerbated by status in the USSR and age, are significantly beyond the reality of the new Israeli homeland.

Appendix 1. Jewish Emigration from the USSR

October				
1968–1970	4,235	1977	16,736	
1971	13,022	1978	28,864	
1972	31,681	1979	51,320	
1973	34,733	1980	21,471	
1974	20,628	1981	9,447	
1975	13,221	1982	2,688	
1976	14,261	1983	1,314	

	1984	1985	1986	1987	1988
January	88	61	79	98	687
February	90	88	84	146	697
March	51	98	47	470	951
April	74	166	72	717	1,020
May	109	51	49	877	1,061
June	72	36	55	796	1,394
July	85	174	31	819	1,371
August	83	29	88	787	1,734
September	69	93	126	724	2,003
October	29	124	104	912	2,068
November	55	128	102	910	2,327
December	91	92	77	899	3,652
Total	896	1,140	914	8,155	18,965

From October 1968–December 1987, 274,726 persons left the Soviet Union with Israeli visas. Approximately 165,817 of them went to Israel.
Source: National Conference on Soviet Jewry.

Appendix 2. The Jackson Amendment, H.R. 6767

93rd Congress—1st Session

In the Senate of the United States
April 10, 1973
Ordered to lie on the table and to be printed (by unanimous consent)

Amendment

Intended to be proposed by Mr. Jackson (for himself, Mr. Ribicoff, Mr. Magnuson, Mr. Javits, Mr. Buckley, Mr. Gurney, Mr. Bayh, Mr. Percy, Mr. Kennedy, Mr. Tunney, Mr. Williams, Mr. Roth, Mr. Scott of Pennsylvania, Mr. Taft, Mr. Allen, Mr. Baker, Mr. Beall, Mr. Bentsen, Mr. Bible, Mr. Biden, Mr. Brock, Mr. Brooke, Mr. Harry F. Byrd, Jr., Mr. Robert C. Byrd, Mr. Cannon, Mr. Case, Mr. Chiles, Mr. Church, Mr. Clark, Mr. Cook, Mr. Cotton, Mr. Cranston, Mr. Domenici, Mr. Dominick, Mr. Eagleton, Mr. Fannin, Mr. Fong, Mr. Goldwater, Mr. Gravel, Mr. Hansen, Mr. Hart, Mr. Hartke, Mr. Haskell, Mr. Helms, Mr. Huddleston, Mr. Hughes, Mr. Inouye, Mr. Johnston, Mr. McClellan, Mr. McGee, Mr. McGovern, Mr. McIntyre, Mr. Mathias, Mr. Mondale, Mr. Montoya, Mr. Muskie, Mr. Nunn, Mr. Pastore, Mr. Pell, Mr. Proxmire, Mr. Randolph, Mr. Schweiker, Mr. Sparkman, Mr. Stennis, Mr. Stevens, Mr. Stevenson, Mr. Symington, Mr. Talmadge, Mr. Thurmond, Mr. Tower, Mr. Weicker, and Mr. Young) to H.R. 6767, a bill to promote the development of an open, nondiscriminatory, and fair world economic system, to stimulate the economic growth of the United States, and to provide the President with additional negotiating authority therefor, and for other purposes, viz: At the end of title V of the Act, add the following new section:

East-West Trade and Freedom of Emigration

Sec. 507.(a) To assure the continued dedication of the United States to fundamental human rights, and notwithstanding any other provision of this Act or any other law, after October 15, 1972, no nonmarket economy country shall be eligible to receive most-favored-nation treatment or to participate in any program of the Government of the United States which extends credits or credit guarantees or investment guarantees, directly or indirectly, during the period beginning with the date on which the President of the United States determines that such country—

(1) denies its citizens the right or opportunity to emigrate; or

(2) imposes more than a nominal tax on emigration or on the visas or other documents required for emigration, for any purpose or cause whatsoever; or

(3) imposes more than a nominal tax, levy, fine, fee, or other charge on any citizen as a consequence of the desire of such citizen to emigrate to the country of his choice,

and ending on the date on which the President determines that such country is no longer in violation of paragraph (1), (2), or (3).

(b) After October 15, 1972, a non-market-economy country may participate in a program of the Government of the United States which extends credits or credit guarantees or investment guarantees, and shall be eligible to receive most-favored-nation treatment, only after the President of the United States has submitted to the Congress a report indicating that such country is not in violation of paragraph (1), (2), or (3) or subsection (a). Such report, with respect to such country, shall include information as to the nature and implementation of emigration laws and policies and restrictions or discrimination applied to or against persons wishing to emigrate. The report required by this sub-section shall be submitted initially as provided herein and semiannually thereafter so long as any agreement entered into pursuant to the exercise of such authority is in effect.

Appendix 3. The 1987 Soviet Decree on Emigration

Text of USSR Council of Ministers Resolution
"On Addenda to the Regulations on Entering and Leaving the USSR"

Source: (Moscow) *Sobraniye postanovleniy pravitel'stva SSR: Otdel pervyy*, No. 31, 1986, pp. 563–66.

The USSR Council of Ministers resolves:

To introduce the following addenda to the regulations on entering and leaving the USSR ratified by USSR Council of Ministers Resolution No. 801 of 22 September 1970 (*Sobraniye postanovleniy pravitel'stva* SSR, 1970, No. 18, p. 139):

After Article 19 of the regulations add the following new section:

"Consideration of applications to enter or leave the USSR on private business."

20. Soviet citizens, foreign citizens, and stateless persons may enter or leave the USSR irrespective of their provenance, social standing, property status, race, nationality, sex, education, language, or religious beliefs.

21. Applications to enter or leave the USSR on private business (reunification with family members, meetings with close relatives, marriages, visits to seriously ill relatives, visits to close relatives' places of burial, settlement of inheritance questions, and other valid reasons) shall be made to the relevant USSR diplomatic missions or consulates or USSR internal affairs organs at the place of residence of the citizen or stateless person.

The procedure for examining applications and formalizing entry to and departure from the USSR on private business is laid down by the present regulations, by other acts of USSR legislation, and by instructions issued in accordance with them by the USSR MVD (Internal Affairs Ministry) and Foreign Ministry, and also—for questions connected with marriages—by the USSR Ministry of Justice Instruction on the Procedure for Registering in the USSR Marriages between Soviet Citizens and Foreign Citizens or Stateless Persons.

22. Applications to invite to the USSR citizens domiciled abroad or to travel abroad on private business may be made by persons who have reached the age of 18.

Children under 18 may travel abroad only on receipt of an application from their lawful representatives and, as a rule, when accompanied by them. Children between 14 and 18 may only leave the USSR to travel abroad for permanent residence following presentation of their duly notarized written consent.

23. Applications to leave the USSR temporarily on private business shall be examined following presentation of the relevant documents.

The length of temporary stay in the USSR or abroad on private business shall be determined with regard to the purpose of the trip. The period may be correspondingly extended by USSR internal affairs organs and diplomatic missions or USSR consulates by agreement with the other state.

24. Applications to travel abroad from the USSR for family reunification shall be examined on presentation of an invitation duly certified by the competent authorities in the corresponding foreign state from a husband, wife, father, mother, son, daughter, brother, or sister, and of substantively certified statements from the family members remaining in the USSR and from the former spouse (if there are children under the age of majority from this marriage) showing that the traveler has no outstanding obligations toward them under the USSR law.

The question of other relatives and dependents leaving the USSR with the traveler who are unable to work shall be examined on application from the traveler if they live together as a household.

If the person applying to leave has no family members in the USSR the application may be considered on presentation of an invitation from another relative.

25. Soviet citizens shall not be permitted to leave the USSR on private business:

(a) If they are privy to state secrets or if there are other reasons of state security—until the circumstances preventing departure no longer obtain;

(b) If this will result in the infringement of the basic rights and legal interests of other citizens of the USSR;

(c) If they have outstanding obligations to the state or property obligations that affect the material or legal interests of state, cooperative, or other public organizations—until these obligations have been honored;

(d) If there are legal grounds for instituting criminal proceedings against them—until the proceedings are completed;

(e) If they have been convicted of a crime—until completion of or release from the sentence;

(f) If it is established that the person issuing the invitation is abroad in violation of the procedure for leaving the USSR or living abroad—until the situation is rectified.

Soviet citizens may be refused permission to leave the USSR on private business:

(a) In the interests of safeguarding public order or the population's health or morality—until the circumstances preventing departure no longer obtain;

(b) If during a previous trip abroad they acted in violation of state interests or if it is established that they violated customs or foreign exchange legislation;

(c) If they provide false information when applying to leave.

26. Entry into the USSR by a Soviet citizen permanently domiciled abroad

may be temporarily refused only in exceptional cases when it is necessary to safeguard state security, to ensure public order and the population's health and morality, or to protect the rights and legitimate interests of Soviet citizens and other persons.

27. Foreign citizens and stateless persons may be refused entry to or exit from the USSR on the grounds laid down by Articles 24 and 25 of the USSR law "On the Legal Status of Foreign Citizens in the USSR."

28. Applications to temporarily enter or leave the USSR on private business shall be examined as quickly as possible, and, as a rule, within no longer than one month, and within three days if the trip is in connection with a relative's serious illness or death.

Applications for entering or leaving the USSR shall be examined within one month; if additional examination is necessary this period may be extended, but for no more than six months.

The applicant shall be informed of the results of the application and, should it be refused, of the reasons for the refusal.

Authorization to enter or leave the USSR shall be valid for six months.

29. In the event of an application to enter or leave the USSR on private business being refused, repeat applications, as a rule, shall be examined no sooner than six months following the refusal. Previously submitted documents shall be taken wholly or partially into account if there have been no changes that could be of substantive importance for the examination of the application.

30. Questions of entering or leaving the USSR on private business may also be regulated by bilateral agreements between the USSR and other states.

This resolution to become effective as of 1 January 1987.

N. Ryzhkov, Chairman of the USSR Council of Ministers
M. Smirtyukov, USSR Council of Ministers Administrator of Affairs Moscow, The Kremlin, 28 August 1986. No. 1064.
(translated by the U.S. Department of State)

Appendix 4. Prominent Anti-Semitic Propagandists and Activists Identified with Pamyat

Vladimir Yakovlevich Begun, member of USSR Writer' Union; senior research worker at Byelorussian Academy of Sciences' Institute of Philosophy and Law; author of a number of anti-Semitic books in the 1970s; most recent book (second ed., 1986) devoted to Freemasonry.

Valery Nikolaevich Emelyanov, linguist; former lecturer, Znanie Society; in 1970s wrote samizdat tracts on Judeo-Masonic conspiracy which would take over the USSR by the year 2000; July 1979 reprimanded by party for drunkenness and hooliganism; March 1980 expelled from party; April 1980 murdered his wife, subsequently placed under psychiatric treatment.

Evgeny Evseev, most prolific anti-Zionist propagandist of early 1970s; most well-known work—"Fascism under the Blue Star"; in early 1980s dismissed from post at Philosophy Institute of Academy of Sciences; has worked since then as translator of Arabic texts.

Aleksandr Zakharovich Romanenko, author of virulently anti-Semitic book *The Class Essence of Zionism* (Leningrad, 1986), which claims that the "Zionists" aim at global supremacy; book condemned by authoritative party journal "Questions of CPSU History," January 1987.

Dear Senator Jackson:

I am writing to you, as the sponsor of the Jackson Amendment, in regard to the Trade Bill (H.R. 10710) which is currently before the Senate and in whose early passage the administration is deeply interested. As you know, Title IV of that bill, as it emerged from the House, is not acceptable to the administration. At the same time, the administration respects the objectives with regard to emigration from the U.S.S.R. that are sought by means of the stipulations in Title IV, even if it cannot accept the means employed. It respects in particular your own leadership in this field.

To advance the purposes we share both with regard to passage of the trade bill and to emigration from the U.S.S.R., and on the basis of discussions that have been conducted with Soviet representatives, I should like on behalf of the administration to inform you that we have been assured that the following criteria and practices will henceforth govern emigration from the U.S.S.R.

First, punitive actions against individuals seeking to emigrate from the U.S.S.R. would be violations of Soviet laws and regulations and will therefore not be permitted by the government of the U.S.S.R. In particular, this applies to various kinds of intimidation or reprisal, such as, for example, the firing of a person from his job, his demotion to tasks beneath his professional qualifications, and his subjection to public or other kinds of recrimination.

Second, no unreasonable or unlawful impediments will be placed in a way of persons desiring to make application for emigration, such as interference with travel or communications necessary to complete an application, the withholding of necessary documentation and other obstacles including kinds frequently employed in the past.

Third, applications for emigration will be processed in order of receipt, including those previously filed, and on a nondiscriminatory basis as regards the place of residence, race, religion, national origin and professional status of the applicant. Concerning professional status, we are informed that there are limitations on emigration under Soviet law in the case of individuals holding certain security clearances, but that such individuals who desire to emigrate will be informed of the date on which they may expect to become eligible for emigration.

Fourth, hardship cases will be processed sympathetically and expeditiously; persons imprisoned who, prior to imprisonment, expressed an interest in emigrating, will be given prompt consideration for emigration upon their release; and sympathetic consideration may be given to the early release of such persons.

Fifth, the collection of the so-called emigration tax on emigrants which was suspended last year will remain suspended.

Sixth, with respect to all the foregoing points, we will be in a position to bring to the attention of the Soviet leadership indications that we may have that these criteria and practices are not being applied. Our representations, which would include but not necessarily be limited to the precise matters enumerated in the foregoing points, will receive sympathetic consideration and response.

Finally, it will be our assumption that with the application of the criteria, practices, and procedures set forth in this letter, the rate of emigration from the U.S.S.R. would begin to rise promptly from the 1973 level and would continue to rise to correspond to the number of applicants.

I understand that you and your associates have, in addition, certain understandings incorporated in a letter dated today respecting the foregoing criteria and practices which will henceforth govern emigration from the U.S.S.R. which you wish the President to accept as appropriate guidelines to determine whether the purposes sought through Title IV of the trade bill and further specified in our exchange of correspondence in regard to the emigration practices of non-market economy countries are being fulfilled. You have submitted this letter to me and I wish to advise you on behalf of the President that the understanding in your letter will be among the considerations to be applied by the President in exercising the authority provided for in Sec. 42* of Title IV of the trade bill.

I believe that the contents of this letter represent a good basis, consistent with our shared purposes, for proceeding with an acceptable formulation of Title IV of the trade bill, including procedures for periodic review, so that normal trading relations may go forward for the mutual benefit of the U.S. and the U.S.S.R.

Best regards,
Henry A. Kissinger

* Statutory language authorizing the President to wave the restrictions of Title IV of the Trade Bill under certain conditions will be added as a new (and as yet undesignated) subsection.

October 18, 1974

Dear Mr. Secretary:

Thank you for your letter of October 18 which I have now had an opportunity to review. Subject to the further understandings and interpretations outlined in this letter, I agree that we have achieved a suitable basis upon which to modify Title IV by incorporating within it a provision that would enable the President to waive subsections designated (a) and (b) in Sec. 402 of Title IV as passed by the House in circumstances that would substantially promote the objectives of Title IV.

It is our understanding that the punitive actions, intimidation or reprisals that will not be permitted by the government of the U.S.S.R. include the use of punitive conscription against persons seeking to emigrate, or members of their families; and the bringing of criminal actions against persons in circumstances that suggest a relationship between their desire to emigrate and the criminal prosecution against them.

Second, we understand that among the reasonable impediments that will no longer be placed in the way of persons seeking to emigrate is the requirement that adult applicants receive the permission of their parents or other relatives.

Third, we understand that the special regulations to be applied to persons who have had access to genuinely sensitive classified information will not constitute an unreasonable impediment to emigration. In this connection we would expect such persons to become eligible for emigration within three years of the date on which they last were exposed to sensitive and classified information.

Fourth, we understand that the actual number of emigrants would rise promptly from the 1973 level and would continue to rise to correspond to the number of applicants, and may therefore exceed 60,000 per annum. We would consider a benchmark—a minimum standard of initial compliance—to be the issuance of visas at the rate of 60,000 per annum; and we understand that the President proposes to use the same benchmark as the minimum standard of initial compliance. Until such time as the actual number of emigrants corresponds to the number of applicants, the benchmark figure will not include categories of persons whose emigration has been the subject of discussion between Soviet officials and other European governments.

In agreeing to provide discretionary authority to waive the provisions of subsections designated (a) and (b) and Sec. 402 of Title IV as passed by the House, we share your anticipation of good faith in the implementation of the assurances contained in your letter of October 18 and the understandings conveyed by this letter. In particular, with respect to paragraphs three and four of your letter, we wish it to be understood that the enumeration of types of punitive action and unreasonable impediments is not and cannot be considered comprehensive or complete, and that nothing in this exchange of correspondence shall be construed as permitting types of punitive action or unreasonable impediments not enumerated therein.

Finally, in order adequately to verify compliance with the standard set forth in these letters, we understand that communication by telephone, telegraph and post will be permitted.

Sincerely yours,
Henry M. Jackson

Gromyko's Letter

October 26, 1974

Dear Mr. Secretary of State:

I believe it necessary to draw your attention to the question concerning the publication in the United States of materials of which you are aware and which touch upon the departure from the Soviet Union of a certain category of Soviet citizens.

I must say straightforwardly that the above-mentioned materials, including the correspondence between you and Senator Jackson, create a distorted picture of our position as well as of what we told the American side on that matter.

When clarifying the actual state of affairs in response to your request, we underlined that the question as such is entirely within the internal competence of our state. We warned at the time that in this matter we had acted and shall act in strict conformity with our present legislation on that score.

But now silence is being kept precisely about this. At the same time, attempts are being made to ascribe to the elucidations that were furnished by us the nature of some assurances and, nearly, obligations on our part regarding the procedure of the departure of Soviet citizens from the U.S.S.R., and even some figures are being quoted as to the supposed number of such citizens, and there is talk about an anticipated increase of that number as compared with previous years.

We resolutely decline such an interpretation. What we said, and you, Mr. Secretary of State, know this well, concerned only and exclusively the real situation in the given question. And when we did mention figures—to inform you of the real situation—the point was quite the contrary, namely about the present tendency toward a decrease in the number of persons wishing to leave the U.S.S.R. and seek permanent residence in other countries.

We believe it important that in this entire matter, considering its principled significance, no ambiguities should remain as regards the position of the Soviet Union.

A. Gromyko
Minister of Foreign Affairs
of the U.S.S.R.

Notes

1. Passing Eclipse: The Exodus Movement in the 1980s

1. See Brezhnev's speeches in *Pravda,* October 22, 1980, and November 17, 1981.
2. The riots in Kazakhstan in December 1986 were only one symptom of this. Soviet spokesmen later referred to such tensions in Moldavia and in the Baltic states. Returning travelers told of witnessing disorders with an ethnic background in such out-of-the way places as Yakutsk.
3. Gorbachev has spoken extensively on this theme both before the Central Committee of the Communist party and at the Party Congress, using the term "crisis" and referring to "phenomena of social corrosion."
4. In addition to these three factors that can be closely linked to immediate and prominent regime concerns, there may be other interests for and against Jewish emigration that marginally press upon the decision. One such element that awaits analysis is the locus and influence of a political current based in nationalism that sees Russia better off without Jews. As we will discuss at a later point, it is no secret that such an element exists and has some influence within the Soviet leadership. There is, however, no documentation of this view playing a part in the opening or closing of emigration.
5. The six Jews elected at the 26th Party Congress in 1981 were Alexander Chakovsky, Georgii Tsukanov, Lev Volodarsky, Lev Shapiro, and David Dragunsky. At the 1986 Congress only Chakovsky, Shapiro, and Dragunsky were reelected.
6. See *Khronika tekushchikh sobytii* (New York), no. 52, 1979, p. 127.
7. The numbers of new invitations requested were: 1980—32,335; 1981—10,922; 1982—3,159; 1984—1,140. See Benjamin Pinkus, "National Identity and Emigration Patterns Among Soviet Jews," *Soviet Jewish Affairs,* November 1985, p. 18.
8. The Soviet newspaper *Sovetskaia Rossiia,* April 3, 1987, confirmed that a total of 680,000 people were covered by *vyzovy* issued. Only about 300,000 have been used.
9. For a detailed analysis of this period see Theodore H. Friedgut, "Soviet Anti-Zionism and Anti-Semitism: Another Cycle," *Soviet Jewish Affairs,* February 1984, pp. 3–22.
10. The spokesman for the Soviet Foreign Ministry, Gennadi Gerasimov, later categorized Gorbachev's limitation of the duration of secrecy as mistaken. This was taken up by other Soviet spokesmen whose reaction as expressed to refuseniks and to non-Soviet journalists and other visitors ranged from a statement that Mr. Gorbachev had no right to speak on this issue to a denial that he had ever limited the duration of secrecy.

11. The decree was published in *Sobranie postanovlenii pravitel'-stva SSRa*, no. 31, 1986, pp. 563–566. For the text of the decree see Appendix 3 of this book.
12. See article 30 of decree in Appendix 3.
13. A detailed analysis of the decree, its flaws, and its merits will be found in F. J. M. Feldbrugge, "The New Soviet Law on Emigration," *Soviet Jewish Affairs* 17, no. 1 (1987), pp. 9–24.
14. See "Permission to Leave," *Novoe Vremia* (Russian), no. 28 (1987), pp. 24–26. The interview was subsequently broadcast on Radio Moscow's foreign broadcasts in both English and Russian and so was undoubtedly meant to be known and tested.
15. This conversation was repeated, with even greater openness regarding the issue of Jewish emigration, when the two men, this time both of them foreign ministers, met again in the autumn of 1987.
16. Formation of the commission was reported in the *Manchester Guardian Weekly* 136, no. 1, for the week ending January 4, 1987, p. 1.
17. *Pravda,* January 19, 1987, p. 6.
18. *New York Times,* January 17, 1987, p. 3.
19. Zivs's remarks appear in the *New York Times,* January 16, 1987.
20. The need for care in checking the factual accuracy of both public and private statements by Soviet officials was reemphasized in mid-November 1987. A delegation of refuseniks protesting the fact that answers on their emigration requests were not being received in the time period stipulated by the regulations were told by the deputy director of OVIR that in the preceding days 100 permissions had been granted. When challenged he read off a list of names that proved to be members of families granted permission to leave over the previous seven months.
21. As this was being written, news came that Magarik had been informed that he may leave the USSR. Zelichonok received permission at the end of 1988.
22. *Vecherniaia Moskva,* February 12, 1987.
23. See the statement of Y. B. Kashlev in the *New York Times,* January 17, 1987. Kashlev and others have repeated this opposition to free emigration on a number of occasions.
24. See the report of Gorbachev's speech for the seventieth anniversary of the revolution in *New York Times,* November 3, 1987.
25. The interview was broadcast by NBC on November 30, 1987. Extensive commentary and excerpts appeared in the *New York Times,* December 1, 1987.
26. See the report of his speech before Soviet writers on June 29, 1986, as reported in *Materialy samizdata* (Munich), no. 33 (October 24, 1986), AS 5785.
27. See references to such a phenomenon in an interview with freed dissident Sergei Grigoriants in the *New York Times,* Sunday, February 22, 1987, section 4, p. 1.

2. The Soviet Public Anti-Zionist Committee: An Analysis

1. See Aleksander Solzhenitsyn, *The Gulag Archipelago,* vols. 1–2 (New York, 1973), p. 92.
2. *Morning Freiheit,* May 4, 1985.
3. *Pravda,* March 5, 1970; *Izvestia,* March 6, 1970.
4. Ibid.
5. See, for example, *Pravda,* March 12, 14, 15, 18, 19, 20, and 21, 1970.
6. E. L. Sol'mar, "Protokoly antisionistsikh mudretsov," *Yevreiskii Samizdat* 16 (1978), pp. 128–143.

7. Ibid., pp. 134–135.
8. Ibid.
9. *Pravda*, April 1, 1983.
10. Ibid. See also the *New York Times*, April 2, 1983.
11. See, especially, articles by B. Kravtsov in *Leningradskaia Pravda*, April 19–20, 1983.
12. *Radio Peace and Progress* (Moscow), April 28, 1983. (In Hebrew)
13. *Tass*, June 4, 1983.
14. *Pravda*, April 22, 1983; *Sovetskaia Litva*, May 6, 1983.
15. For details on the officers, see *Literaturnaia gazeta*, June 22, 1983; concerning Zivs, see the *New York Review of Books*, July 21, 1983.
16. See the author's article on this subject in *Midstream*, August–September 1985, p. 12.
17. Ibid.
18. Ibid.
19. See *Sovetskaia Litva*, May 6, 1983, and *Literaturnia gazeta*, June 22, 1983.
20. *Sovetskaia Litva*, May 6, 1983.
21. Ibid.
22. For an analysis see *Insight: Soviet Jews* (London), vol. 9, no. 5 (September, 1983).
23. *Izvestia*, June 4, 1983.
24. *Novosti* provided detailed coverage. See *APN*, June 7, 1983. See also *Literaturnaia Gazeta*, June 22, 1983.
25. *APN*, June 7, 1983.
26. Ibid.
27. On this point see Robert O. Freedman, "Soviet Jewry and Soviet-American Relations," in *Soviet Jewry in the Decisive Decade, 1971–1980*, ed. Robert O. Freedman (Durham, N.C.: Duke University Press, 1984).
28. For details see *Human Contacts, Reunion of Families, and Soviet Jewry* (London, 1986), p. 27.
29. Ibid.
30. *APN*, June 7, 1983.
31. Ibid.
32. Ibid.
33. Lev Korneyev, *Klassovaia sushchnost' sionizma* (Kiev, 1982). See reviews in *Izvestia*, January 29, 1983, and *Sovetskaia kul'tura*, April 28, 1983.
34. *Sovetskaia Litva*, May 6, 1983.
35. *New York Times*, June 7, 1983.
36. Ibid.
37. Ibid.
38. *New Times* (Moscow), no. 21 (May 1983); *Izvestia*, August 6, 1983.
39. *Pravda*, July 28, 1983, carried an article by Dragunsky, and *New Times*, no. 28 (July 1983) carried an essay by Krupkin.
40. *Radio Damascus* (in Arabic), October 29, 1983.
41. Ibid.
42. *Supported by the Soviet People* (Novosti, 1983) and *Anti-Zionist Committee of Soviet Public Opinion* (Novosti, 1983).
43. For details see Zvi Gitelman, *Jewish Nationality and Soviet Politics* (Princeton, 1972).
44. Yehoshua Gilboa, *The Black Years of Soviet Jewry* (Boston, 1971).
45. *Jews in the USSR* (London), November 3, 1983.

46. *Agence Telegraphique Juive* (Paris), January 3, 1984.
47. *Radio Damascus* (in Arabic), October 29, 1983.
48. *New Times,* no. 46 (November 1983).
49. *Pravda,* January 17, 1984.
50. *Tass,* January 19, 1984.
51. For details, see *Literaturnaia Gazeta,* May 23, 1984.
52. Radio Moscow, May 15, 1984.
53. *Literaturnaia Gazeta,* May 23, 1984.
54. Ibid.
55. Only 896 Jews were given exit visas in 1984.
56. Yuri Kolesnikov, *The Curtain Rises* (Moscow, 1979).
57. *Pravda,* September 5, 1979.
58. Valentina Mal'mi, *Ogonyok,* May 19, 1984. For the press conference see *Tass,* May 15, 1984, and *Literaturnaia Gazeta,* May 23, 1984.
59. *Sovetskaia Kultura,* March 1, 1984.
60. *Vechernaia Moskva,* June 5, 1984. This local newspaper was the only one that carried the story.
61. *Tass,* May 15, 1984; *Literaturnaia Gazeta,* May 23, 1984.
62. *Literaturnaia gazeta,* October 17, 1984.
63. Ibid.
64. Ibid.
65. See, especially, *Komsomol'skaia Pravda,* October 31, 1984, and *Izvestia,* January 13, 1984.
66. Ibid.
67. *Tass,* January 17, 1985. Excerpts appeared in *The Times* (London), January 19, 1985.
68. *Tass,* January 17, 1985. Excerpts appeared in *The Times* (London), January 19, 1985.
69. Ibid.
70. A copy of the telegram is in the author's possession.
71. *Belaia kniga: novye fakty, svidetel'stva, dokumenty* (Moscow, 1985).
72. *Pravda,* August 10, 1985, and *Literaturnaia Gazeta,* August 21, 1985.
73. *Belaia kniga: svidetel'stva, fakty, dokumenty* (Moscow, 1979).
74. *Tass,* August 15, 1985.
75. See *Insight: Soviet Jews* (London), vol. 11, no. 6 (November 1985).
76. Ibid.
77. Professor Glazer provided the author with details of this episode.
78. Ibid.
79. Ibid.
80. *Argumenty i fakty,* no. 47 (November 19, 1985).

3. Soviet Anti-Semitism Unchained: The Rise of the "Historical and Patriotic Association, Pamyat"

This chapter first appeared as an Institute for Jewish Affairs (London) Research Report.

1. On the slogans of the demonstrators see Andrey Kiselev and Aleksandr Mostovshchikov, "Let's talk on equal grounds: Boris Eltsin talks to members of the Pamyat Association," *Moscow News,* May 17, 1987; G. Alimov and R. Lynev, "Where is Pamyat heading?" *Izvestia,* June 3, 1987; Julia Wishnevsky, "El'tsin meets with members of 'Pamyat'," *Radio Liberty Research* (Munich), RL

191/87, May 19, 1987. For the background to the current Soviet reforms and their effect on the Jewish position see Lukasz Hirszowicz, "Gorbachev's *perestroyka* and the Jews," *Institute of Jewish Affairs (IJA) Research Report*, no. 1, (May 1987).

2. On Eltsin's apparent position in the current Soviet political constellation see, for example, Andrew Wilson, "Key round in Gorbachev's power game," *Observer* (London), June 7, 1987.

3. *Moscow News*, May 17, 1987.

4. *Izvestia*, June 3, 1987.

5. Andrew Wilson, *Observer*, June 7, 1987.

6. Soviet press organs which have condemned Pamyat and associated organizations are: *Moscow News*, May 17, 1987; Anatoly Golovkov and Aleksey Pavlov, "What Is All the Noise About?" *Ogonyok*, no. 21 (May 1987); E. Losoto, "Oblivion—Where the Leaders of the So-called 'Pamyat Association' Are Going," *Komsomolskaya Pravda*, May 22, 1987; G. Alimov and R. Lynev, "Where Is 'Pamyat' Heading?" *Izvestia*, June 3, 1987; Andrey Cherkizov, "Genuine Values and Imaginary Enemies," *Sovetskaya Kultura*, June 18, 1987; I. Lugovsky, "What 'Pamyat' Has Forgotten," *Komsomolskaya Pravda*, June 24, 1987 (a selection of readers' letters both for and against Pamyat).

7. Data on the origins and development of Pamyat are derived from *Ogonyok*, no. 21 (May 1987), and Dominique Dhombres, "The 'Memory' of Patriots," *LeMonde*, June 24, 1987.

8. *Ogonyok*, no. 21 (May 1987).

9. See *Sovetskaya Kultura*, June 18, 1987.

10. *Komsomolskaya Pravda*, May 22, 1987.

11. Ibid.

12. Ibid.

13. Ibid.

14. Paul Quinn-Judge, "Right-Wing Russians," *Christian Science Monitor* (Boston), June 18, 1987.

15. *Sovetskaya Kultura*, June 18, 1987.

16. Ibid.

17. V. P., "The Defense of Russian Culture or a Struggle Against 'Yids and Masons'? Antisemitic Speeches at the Central Artists' House," *Russkaya mysl*, May 15, 1987.

18. Paul Quinn-Judge, "Right-Wing Russians," *Christian Science Monitor*, June 18, 1987.

19. *Komsomolskaya Pravda*, May 22, 1987.

20. "Pagans?" *Russkaya mysl*, March 27, 1987.

21. *Komsomolskaya Pravda*, June 24, 1987.

22. Xan Smiley, "Nazi-Style Gangs Take to Russian Streets," *Daily Telegraph* (London), June 15, 1987.

4. Soviet Jewry As a Factor in Soviet-Israeli Relations

1. J. B. Schechtman, "The USSR, Zionism and Israel" in *The Jews in Soviet Russia Since 1917*, ed. Lionel Kochan (New York: Oxford University Press, 1978), p. 108.

2. Cf. Zvi Y. Gitelman, *Jewish Nationality and Soviet Politics* (Princeton: Princeton University Press, 1972), pp. 280–218.

3. Stalin is reported to have commented, in reference to the large percentage of

Jews in the Menshevik Faction at the Russian Social Democratic Party Congress of 1907 (as compared with the Bolshevik Faction that was primarily Russian): "It would not be a bad idea for us, the Bolsheviks, to organize a pogrom in the Party." Cited in William W. Orbach, *The American Movement to Aid Soviet Jews* (Amherst, Mass.: University of Massachusetts Press, 1979), p. 14.

4. Gitelman, *Jewish Nationality*, pp. 280–281, and ch. 8.
5. The best discussion of the origin and development of the Jewish Anti-Fascist Committee is found in Yehoshua Gilboa, *The Black Years of Soviet Jewry* (Boston: Little, Brown, 1971), ch. 2.
6. Ibid., p. 42.
7. Ibid., p. 51.
8. For a study of U.S. policy in the 1947–49 period, see Herbert Feis, *The Birth of Israel* (New York: W. W. Norton, 1969).
9. Cf. Zionist Archives (Jerusalem), particularly documents S/25/9299 (July 31, 1947); S/25/9299 (September 11, 1947); S/25/486 (September 9, 1947); and S/25/9299 (October 10, 1947). See also document S/25/6600 (April 5, 1947).
10. For an analysis of possible Soviet goals in aiding Israel in the 1947–49 period see Yaacov Ro'i, *Soviet Decision-Making in Practice: The USSR and Israel 1947–1954* (London: Transaction Press, 1980); Arnold Krammer, *The Forgotten Friendship: Israel and the Soviet Bloc 1947–1953* (Chicago: University of Illinois Press, 1974); and the archival documents cited in note 9 above.
11. For an "insider's" view of Stalin's growing paranoia see Milovan Djilas, *Conversations with Stalin* (New York: Harcourt Brace and World, 1962).
12. Schechtman, "USSR, Zionism and Israel," p. 125.
13. Cf. Gilboa, *Black Years*, chs. 7–10.
14. Ibid., p. 295.
15. The cause was a bomb explosion in the garden of the Soviet legation in Tel Aviv. For an analysis of Soviet-Israeli relations during this period see Avigdor Dagan, *Moscow and Jerusalem* (New York: Abelard-Schuman, 1970), pp. 68–69.
16. *Jerusalem Post*, February 3, 1961. Cited in William Korey, *The Soviet Cage* (New York: Viking Press, 1973), p. 35.
17. For a description of the Matzo ban see Korey, ibid., pp. 46–47, and Joshua Rothenberg, *The Jewish Religion in the Soviet Union* (New York: Ktav, 1971), pp. 85–88. The Brezhnev regime lifted the ban in 1969, although Soviet Jews still have difficulty getting sufficient Matzoth.
18. It should be noted that the book was published at a time when many Jews were being given the death penalty for alleged "economic crimes." For a description of these "crimes" see Korey, ibid., pp. 80–81.
19. Cited in Dagan, *Moscow and Jerusalem*, p. 163.
20. See the description by Elie Wiesel, *The Jews of Silence* (New York: Holt, Rinehart and Winston, 1966).
21. For a description of Moscow's changing policies in the Middle East at this time see Robert O. Freedman, *Soviet Policy Toward the Middle East Since 1970* (New York: Praeger, 1982), 3d ed., ch. 2.
22. Cf. Nasser's speech to the Egyptian national Assembly, May 29, 1967, reprinted in *The Israel-Arab Reader*, edited by Walter Laqueur and Barry Rubin (New York: Penguin Books, 1984), p. 188.
23. A description of the Leningrad trial is found in Korey, *Soviet Cage,* and

Leonard Schroeter, *The Last Exodus* (New York: Universe Books, 1974), chs. 10 and 11.

24. For a description of the events in Poland see A. Ross Johnson, "Polish Perspectives, Past and Present," *Problems of Communism* 20, no. 4 (July–August 1971), pp. 59–72. Ironically, Gomulka had blamed the student demonstration of 1968 on "Zionists" and as a result had expelled the vast majority of Poland's Jews by 1970 so that they were no longer available to be blamed for the December 1970 riots. For an analysis of Gomulka's policies toward Poland's Jews see Paul Lendvai, *Anti-Semitism Without Jews* (Garden City, N.Y.: Doubleday, 1971), part 2.

25. Marvin Kalb and Bernard Kalb, *Kissinger* (New York: Dell, 1975), p. 245.

26. Leonid Brezhnev, "Report of the Central Committee of the Communist Party of the Soviet Union to the 24th Congress of the CPSU," *The 24th Congress of the Communist Party of the Soviet Union, March 30–April 19, 1971* (Moscow Press Agency Publishing House, 1971), p. 50.

27. For a detailed description of Soviet policy at this point see John Newhouse, *Cold Dawn: The Story of SALT* (New York: Holt, Rinehart and Winston, 1973), p. 215.

28. For a description of the sit-in see Korey, *Soviet Cage,* pp. 179–182.

29. Perhaps due to poor American intelligence, or possibly because of Kissinger's desire to encourage trade as a means of ensuring détente, the Russians were able to buy up a great deal of American grain at a very low price. For an excellent analysis of the grain deal, and other Soviet-American economic agreements, see Marshall Goldman, *Détente and Dollars* (New York: Basic Books, 1975), especially ch. 7.

30. For a description of the background of Sadat's expulsion decision see Freedman, *Soviet Policy,* ch. 3.

31. For a description of the head tax, see Korey, *Soviet Cage,* pp. 315–320.

32. Marquis Childs, *Washington Post,* March 13, 1973. Cited in Paula Stern, *Water's Edge: Domestic Politics and the Making of American Foreign Policy* (Westport: Greenwood Press, 1979), p. 65.

33. For studies of the development of American opposition to the proposed inclusion of the head tax in the Jackson-Vanik Amendment, see Stern, *Water's Edge,* and Orbach, *American Movement.* Stern, a former legislative assistant to Senator Gaylord Nelson, is unsympathetic to the role played by Senator Jackson. Orbach takes a more balanced approach. For earlier studies, see Morris Brafman and David Schimel, *Trade for Freedom: Détente, Trade and Soviet Jews* (New York: Shengold, 1975), and William Korey, "The Story of the Jackson Amendment," *Midstream* 21, no. 3 (March 1975), pp. 7–36.

34. Cited in Korey, *Soviet Cage,* p. 320.

35. *American Jewish Yearbook,* 1974–75, p. 211. Cited in Brafman and Schimel, *Trade for Freedom,* p. 41.

36. For an excellent analysis of the Soviet leadership's interest in Western trade at this time see *Foreign Broadcast Information Service Special Report: Pressures for Change in Soviet Foreign Economic Policy* (Washington, D.C.: FBIS, April 5, 1974), report no. 306.

37. For a description of Soviet policy during the Yom Kippur war see Freedman, *Soviet Policy,* ch. 5.

38. Korey, "The Story of the Jackson Amendment," p. 30.

39. For a description of some of the natural gas and oil projects for which the

Soviet leadership was seeking American assistance see John P. Hardt, "West Siberia: The Quest for Energy," *Problems of Communism* 22, no. 3 (May–June 1973), pp. 25–36.

40. Korey, "The Story of the Jackson Amendment," p. 30.

41. Stern argues, not entirely convincingly, that Jackson's quest for publicity and Kissinger's secretiveness doomed the agreement (*Water's Edge*, pp. 162–193).

42. Marjorie Hunter, *New York Times*, August 16, 1974. See also the report by Wolf Blitzer, *Jerusalem Post*, August 16, 1974.

43. Total trade was 742.2 million rubles in 1974, 1,599 million rubles in 1975, and 2,205.5 million rubles in 1976 with the bulk of the increase coming from Soviet imports from the United States. (See *Vneshniaia Torgolvia SSR ZA, 1974 and 1976* [Moscow International Relations Press, 1974 and 1976].)

44. Orbach, *American Movement*, pp. 43–45.

45. Ibid., p. 45. The motivations for the switch in Israel's policy remain unclear. Stern, *Water's Edge*, p. 6, argues that public pressure, seized upon by Menachem Begin, then an opposition member of Israel's first National Unity government (1967–70), forced the government's hand. Arthur Klinghoffer, in his study *Israel and the Soviet Union: Alienation or Reconciliation* (Boulder, Colorado: Westview Press, 1985), asserts that the Golda Meir government deliberately pushed the issue to derail what it saw as an emerging Soviet-U.S. détente relationship that would force Israel to give back the territories it captured in the 1967 war.

46. Cited in Orbach, *American Movement*, pp. 49–50.

47. Ibid., p. 76.

48. For a detailed description of the role of Soviet Jewry as an issue in Soviet-American relations during the Carter presidency see Robert O. Freedman, "Soviet Jewry and Soviet-American Relations," in *Soviet Jewry in the Decisive Decade, 1971–1980*, ed. Robert O. Freedman (Durham, N.C.: Duke University Press, 1984), pp. 47–66.

49. The author of this paper, a member of the Executive Committee of the (U.S.) National Conference for Soviet Jewry, was told by the NCSJ leadership on a Friday morning in early October that the conference was set for Paris, "so that the Soviet Jewish issue will be seen as more than just a U.S.-Israeli political ploy." He received a telegram announcing the postponement of the conference and its relocation to Jerusalem two days later.

50. Personal observations of the author, who attended the conference.

51. Cf. article by Seth Mydans, *New York Times*, November 14, 1984.

52. Cited in article by Aryeh Rubinstein, *Jerusalem Post*, October 25, 1984.

53. *Izvestia*, May 13, 1985.

54. Jerusalem Radio Domestic Service, July 19, 1985 (Foreign Broadcast Information Service [hereinafter FBIS (USSR)], July 19, 1985, p. H-1).

55. For an analysis of Soviet policy during this period see Robert O. Freedman, "Soviet Policy toward the Middle East since the Israeli Invasion of Lebanon," in *The Middle East Since the Israeli Invasion of Lebanon*, ed. Robert O. Freedman (Syracuse: Syracuse University Press, 1986), pp. 54–56.

56. See Radio Liberty Report, no. 197/85, by Daniel Greenberg for an analysis of the negative Soviet reaction to the U.S. statement.

57. Cf. comments by Leonid Zamyatin, head of the International Information Department of the Communist Party Central Committee, as reported in KUNA, July 27, 1985 (FBIS [USSR], July 29, 1985, p. H-1).

58. Cf. Novosti report, cited in *New York Times*, August 7, 1985.

59. Cf. report by Michael Eilan and Joshua Brilliant, *Jerusalem Post,* October 31, 1986. The rumor was renewed after a December 1985 Bronfman visit to the Soviet capital (see the reports in the *Washington Post,* December 23 and 25, 1985). Bronfman, it should be noted, was closer to Prime Minister Peres than to Foreign Minister Shamir, who often took a dim view of the World Jewish Congress president's quasi-diplomatic activities.

60. Cf. report by Thomas Friedman, *New York Times,* October 18, 1985. (A preliminary version of the "agreement-in-principle" was broadcast over Israel radio on October 5, 1985.)

61. Cited in *Jerusalem Post,* October 6, 1985.

62. Cf. report by Walter Ruby, *Jerusalem Post,* November 17, 1985.

63. Cited in report by Asher Wallfish, *Jerusalem Post,* November 19, 1985.

64. Cf. report by Ihsan Hijazi, *New York Times,* November 20, 1985. See also the report by David Ottaway, *Washington Post,* November 8, 1985.

65. For the text of Reagan's speech on this subject see *New York Times,* October 25, 1985.

66. Arafat was particularly suspicious. See report by Ihsan Hijazi, *New York Times,* November 20, 1985.

67. *Jerusalem Post,* December 4, 1985.

68. Cited in *Jerusalem Post,* December 8, 1985.

69. For the text of Gorbachev's speech, see *Pravda,* February 26, 1986. His foreign policy emphasis was on Soviet-American, Soviet-European, and Soviet-Asian relations, in that order.

70. For a background analysis of Soviet-Libyan relations at the time of the U.S.-Libyan clashes see Robert O. Freedman, "U.S.-Libyan Crisis—Moscow Keeps Its Distance," *Christian Science Monitor,* April 24, 1987.

71. Cited in report by Celestine Bohlen, *Washington Post,* March 26, 1986.

72. For an analysis of the events leading up to the Soviet-Israeli talks see the article in the *Jerusalem Post,* August 5, 1986. The Soviet warning to Libya and Syria came during Moscow visits by Syrian Vice President Abdel Khaddam and Libya's number two leader, Abdel Jalloud, in May.

73. Moscow was less happy, however, at King Hussein's crackdown on Jordan's Communist party and his arrest of leaders of the Jordan-Soviet Friendship Society, which the USSR may have feared might be the first step to a deal with Israel (Cf. *Pravda,* May 29, 1986).

74. For the Soviet view of the talks see the *Tass* report, in English, August 19, 1986 (FBIS [USSR], August 20, 1986, p. CC-1). For the Israeli view see Helsinki Domestic Service, in Finnish, August 18, 1986 (FBIS [ME], August 19, 1986, p. I-1) and Tel Aviv, IDF Radio in Hebrew, August 18, 1986 (FBIS [ME], August 19, 1986, pp. I-1, I-2). One effect of Sharansky's coming to Israel had been to raise the political stature of the Soviet Jewry movement, which now had such important politicians as Moshe Arens on its side. Hitherto, the main Knesset activists were fringe politicians, such as Tehiya's Geula Cohen.

75. See the report by Bernard Gwertzman, *New York Times,* September 23, 1986. In his U.N. speech, Shevardnadze noted that Israel owed its existence "to, among others, the Soviet Union," and also reiterated Moscow's call for a preparatory committee "set up within the framework of the Security Council" to do the necessary work for convening an international conference on the Middle East.

76. For the State Department's view of the discussion of human rights in general and the issue of Soviet Jewish emigration in particular at the Reykjavik summit

see *Gist: The Reykjavik Meeting* (Bureau of Public Affairs: Department of State, December 1986).

77. Cited in report by Wolf Blitzer, *Jerusalem Post,* February 20, 1987.

78. See report by Ari L. Goldman, *New York Times,* March 1, 1987. For a perceptive analysis of the issue, see the essay by Edith Frankel, "Don't Squabble Over Refusenik Drop-outs," *Jerusalem Post,* February 18, 1987.

79. Cited in report by Benny Morris, Yossi Lempkowicz, and David Horowitz, *Jerusalem Post,* February 24, 1987.

80. For the text of this document see FBIS (ME), March 23, 1987, pp. I-2, I-3.

81. Cited in Reuters report, *New York Times,* March 20, 1987. Eight hundred and seventy-one Jews, the highest monthly total in six years, left in May 1987.

82. Cited in National Conference on Soviet Jewry Report, April 1, 1987.

83. Cited in report by Walter Ruby and Andy Court, *Jerusalem Post,* April 2, 1987.

84. Cf. Jerusalem Radio Domestic Service interview with Soviet Foreign Ministry spokesman Genady Gerasimov, April 2, 1987 (FBIS [ME], April 2, 1987, p. I-1). See also the article by Henry Kamm, *New York Times,* April 3, 1987.

85. Cf. Jerusalem Radio Domestic Service interview with Yitzhak Shamir, March 26, 1987 (FBIS [ME], March 27, 1987, p. I-1). Shamir also downplayed the importance of the Bonfman-Abram visit (cf. report by Thomas Friedman, *New York Times,* April 1, 1987).

86. Cf. report by Joel Greenberg, *Jerusalem Post,* March 27, 1987.

87. Reuters report, *New York Times,* March 29, 1987. China's permanent U.N. representative Li Luye met with the director general of the Israeli Foreign Ministry, Abraham Tamir. See also the report by David Landau and Walter Ruby, *Jerusalem Post,* March 29, 1987.

88. Cf. Jerusalem Radio Domestic Service interview with Soviet Foreign Ministry spokesman Genady Gerasimov, April 2, 1987 (FBIS [ME], April 2, 1987, p. I-1).

89. Jerusalem Radio Domestic Service interview with Peres, April 2, 1987 (FBIS, April 3, 1987, p. I-1). In the interview Peres noted other changes in Soviet policy including the release of nearly all the prisoners of Zion, the rise in exit permits from 100 to nearly 500 a month, and Soviet statements in diplomatic meetings that they wanted improved relations with Israel.

90. Jerusalem Radio Domestic Service, April 5, 1987 (FBIS [ME], April 6, 1987, p. I-1, and *Jerusalem Post,* April 5, 1987).

91. Cited in report by John Tagliabue, *New York Times,* April 8, 1987.

92. Jerusalem Radio Domestic Service, April 8, 1987 (FBIS [ME], April 9, 1987, p. I-1).

93. Jerusalem Radio Domestic Service, April 9, 1987 (FBIS [ME], April 10, 1987, p. I-3).

94. This information, reported by "sources close to Peres," was discussed in the *Jerusalem Post,* April 10, 1987, in the report coauthored by Wolf Blitzer, David Horowitz, Jonathan Karp, and Robert Rosenberg.

95. Jerusalem Radio Domestic Service, April 7, 1987 (FBIS [ME], April 8, 1987, p. I-3).

96. Cited in report by Lea Levavi and Asher Wallfish, *Jerusalem Post,* April 10, 1987.

97. Jerusalem Radio Domestic Service, April 12, 1987 (FBIS [ME], April 13, 1987, p. I-3).

98. Ibid.

99. Israeli Defense Forces Radio interview with Yitzhak Shamir, April 13, 1987 (FBIS [ME], April 13, 1987, pp. I-4–I-5).

100. For the text of Gorbachev's comments see *Pravda*, April 25, 1987.
101. Cited in *Jerusalem Post*, April 24, 1987. In early March, in another cultural exchange, Moscow had sent its Gypsy Theatre Troupe to play in Israel.
102. Cited in report by Thomas Friedman, *New York Times*, May 8, 1987.
103. Jordan's denial came in a statement by Jordanian Prime Minister Zaid Al-Rifai. The text of the denial was printed in the *Jerusalem Post*, May 5, 1987. According to a report by David Shipler, *New York Times*, May 12, 1987, Jordan had reportedly agreed to a limited role for the USSR in the conference which would be convened by the secretary general of the United Nations based on U.N. resolutions 242 and 338. King Hussein and Peres had reportedly secretly met in Western Europe following Peres's attendance at the Socialist International.
104. Cf. report by Glen Frankel, *Washington Post*, May 15, 1987.

5. The West European Approach to the Soviet Jewry Problem

1. Christopher Walker, "Gorbachev Determined to Separate Europe From U.S.," *The Times*, March 22, 1986.
2. *Conference on Security and Cooperation in Europe: Final Act* (London: Her Majesty's Stationery Office, August 1975).
3. See *The Meeting Held at Belgrade from 4 October 1977 to 9 March 1978 to Follow-Up the Conference on Security and Cooperation in Europe* (London: Her Majesty's Stationery Office, March 1978).
4. See *Concluding Document of the Meeting Held at Madrid from 11 November 1980 to 9 September 1983 to Follow-Up the Conference on Security and Co-operation in Europe* (London: Her Majesty's Stationery Office, October 1983).
5. *The Jerusalem Post*, July 23, 1973.
6. See in particular the report on the situation of the Jewish community in the Soviet Union prepared by Anita Gradin for the Parliamentary Assembly of the Council of Europe, July 6, 1982, doc. 4936 revised.
7. The European Parliament appears to be regarded with some cynicism by the population of Western Europe as "fundamentally a talking-shop without the power to legislate." See Institute of Jewish Affairs, *Research Report*, "The Elections to the European Parliament, June 1984," no. 10 (1984), which also includes a useful description of the functions of the European Parliament and of the structure of the EEC.
8. See, for example, the *Jewish Chronicle*, May 21, 1982; *Agence Telegraphique Juive* (Paris), January 25, 1983; *Jewish Chronicle*, April 27, 1984.
9. *Agence Telegraphique Juive*, May 15–16, 1982.
10. See reports prepared by the Institute of Jewish Affairs for the International Council of the World Conference on Soviet Jewry, *The Position of Soviet Jewry: Human Rights and the Helsinki Accords, 1985*, pp. 5–6, and *Human Contacts, Reunion of Families and Soviet Jewry*, pp. 25–26. (For details of a series of "Helsinki process" reports prepared by the Institute of Jewish Affairs, see note 27 below.)
11. *Le Monde*, June 8–9, 1980.
12. *Jewish Chronicle*, July 13, 1984.
13. Radio Liberty special report, May 26, 1984. The International Parliamentary Group was described as an organization of the CIA and Mossad by Lidiya Modzhoryan, an influential Soviet academic lawyer and author on human rights issues. See *New Times* (Moscow), no. 33 (August 1984).

14. *Jewish Chronicle,* June 14, 1985.
15. See William W. Orbach, "The British Soviet Jewry Movement" in *Forum* (Jerusalem: World Zionist Organization), no. 32–33 (1978), pp. 21–27, and his letter of March 16, 1979, also in *Forum,* no. 35 (1979), pp. 180–184. Orbach appears to be the only author who subjected the Soviet Jewry movement in Great Britain to scholarly analysis. As can be seen from his letter, his *Forum* article did not escape criticism from Soviet Jewry activists. Orbach is, incidentally, the author of a pioneering work on the U.S. struggle on behalf of Soviet Jews. See his *The American Movement to Aid Soviet Jews* (Amherst, Mass.: University of Massachusetts Press, 1979).
16. Letter by Roslind Berman and others, *Jewish Chronicle* (London), April 14, 1978.
17. Orbach, "The British Soviet Jewry Movement."
18. Ibid.
19. *Jewish Telegraphic Agency* (London), February 10, 1976.
20. Emanuel Litvinoff, ed., *Insight: Soviet Jews* (London: European Jewish Library).
21. Emanuel Litvinoff, ed., *Jews in Eastern Europe* (London: European Jewish Library).
22. Nan Griefer, ed., *Jews in the USSR* (London: European Jewish Library).
23. *Jewish Chronicle,* August 23, 1985.
24. Lukasz Hirszowicz, ed., *Soviet Jewish Affairs* (London: Institute of Jewish Affairs).
25. Institute of Jewish Affairs *Research Reports* on the Soviet Jewry question since 1981 include: "Brezhnev's Speech to the 26th Congress of the Communist Party of the Soviet Union," no. 4 (1981); "The Increased Arrests of Soviet Jews in 1981," no. 21 (1981); "Jewish Students in Moscow and the USSR," no. 5 (1982); "Andropov and the Nationalities Question—A New Approach?" no. 1 (1983); "The Soviet Anti-Zionist Committee—Further Developments," no. 13 (1983); "Uni-national and Mixed Marriages in the USSR: Further Statistical Data on Soviet Jewry," no. 19 (1983); *"Pravda* Equates Zionism with Fascism," no. 2 (1984); "Ominous Changes in the Soviet Criminal Code," no. 5 (1984); "Fulfilling a Restricted Role: The Soviet Anti-Zionist Committee in 1984," no. 16 (1984); "The Myth of Zionist-Nazi Collaboration: Some Sources of Soviet Propaganda," no. 2 (1985); "Jewish Issues in the Soviet VE Day Propaganda Campaign," no. 3 (1985); "Trials of Soviet Jewish 'Refuseniks' and Activists, 1980–July 1985," no. 5 (1985); "Jewish Culture in the USSR Today," no. 10 (1985).
26. The IJA published the following books: Jack Miller, ed., *Jews in Soviet Culture* (New Brunswick: Transaction Books, 1984); Jacob Blum and Vera Rich, *The Image of the Jew in Soviet Literature: The Post-Stalin Period* (New York: Ktav, 1984); and Lukasz Hirszowicz, ed., *Proceedings of the Experts' Conference on Soviet Jewry, London 4–6 January 1983,* special issue of *Soviet Jewish Affairs* 15, no. 1 (1985).
27. The following reports were prepared by the Institute of Jewish Affairs for the Presidium and Steering Committee (subsequently International Council) of the World Conference on Soviet Jewry: *Soviet Jewry and the Implementation of the Helsinki Final Act* (1977); *The Position of Soviet Jewry, 1977–1980: Report on the Implementation of the Helsinki Final Act Since the Belgrade Follow-up Conference* (1980); *The Position of Soviet Jewry: Human Rights and the Helsinki Accords, 1985* (1985); *The Problems of Jewish Culture* (pub-

lished on the occasion of the Cultural Forum of the CSCE in Budapest, 15 October–25 November 1985) (October 1985); *Human Contacts, Reunion of Families and Soviet Jewry* (1986). The Institute of Jewish Affairs also published a number of *Research Reports* on Soviet implementation of the Helsinki accords in the Jewish sphere. They include the following: "Madrid Ends and Helsinki Continues: The Agreement at the CSCE Follow-Up Conference (no. 5, 1983) and "Ten Years After Helsinki and the Ottawa Human Rights Stalemate" (no. 6, 1985). For a description by a West European participant of the Third World Conference on Soviet Jewry (15–17 March, 1983) see *Soviet Jewish Affairs*, 13, no. 2 (1983), pp. 71–74.

28. Martin Gilbert is currently preparing a volume on the life of Anatoly Sharansky. His previous book in the field of Soviet Jewry was *The Jews of Hope: The Plight of Soviet Jewry Today* (London: Macmillan, 1984). See review in *Soviet Jewish Affairs* 14, no. 3, (1984), pp. 60–62.

29. See note 26 above.

30. *Jewish Chronicle*, March 27, 1981.

31. Ibid., August 2, 1985.

32. *Hansard* (record of parliamentary debates, November 28, 1984).

33. *Jewish Chronicle*, December 14, 1984.

34. Ibid., February 15, 1985.

35. Ibid., June 15, 1984.

36. Ibid., December 2, 1983.

37. Ibid.

38. *Guardian Weekly*, May 2, 1981.

39. *Jewish Chronicle*, May 1, 1981.

40. *Jewish Chronicle*, March 11, 1983.

41. *Financial Times* (London), December 20, 1984.

42. Solodar's most well-known, and perhaps most characteristic, volume on this subject is his *Dikaya polyn* (Wild Wormword) (Moscow 1977).

6. Jewish, German, and Armenian Emigration from the USSR: Parallels and Differences

The assistance of many individuals and organizations made the preparation of this paper possible. Special thanks are expressed for the support of Colorado State University, the American Philosophical Society, the Research and Development Committee of the American Association for the Advancement of Slavic Studies, the U.S. State Department, and the Deutscher Akademischer Austauschdienst. Responsibility for the contents and opinions of the paper are solely the writer's.

1. This paper is based on research for a full-scale study of the Third Emigration. Both the paper and the larger study draw on information compiled in libraries, archives, and private collections in this country, Europe, and Israel and provided by various specialists, officials, informants, and Soviet emigrants. Much of the data in the paper has never been recorded, used, or published until now.

2. Armenian emigration to the United States is shrouded in obscurity. U.S. government records show that only 17,500 Soviet Armenians have arrived in this country since 1972, whereas other evidence discovered in the research for the larger study indicates that the figure should be approximately 40,000 for many of them entered the United States unidentified as Soviet Armenians as a result of several factors (they came as spouses of Soviet Jews, arrived from third

countries and were counted as refugees from there, etc.). The data concerning Armenian emigration presented here have been compiled from various sources hitherto unused by any other researcher and represent the most comprehensive and accurate statistics available today (that is, the end of 1986; see epilogue for an updating of these figures).

3. The literature on Soviet Jewry and Jewish emigration is voluminous. This section is based on various published accounts including the following: A. Alexander, *Immigration to Israel from the USSR* (Tel Aviv: Faculty of Law, Tel Aviv University, 1977) (reprinted from *Israel Yearbook on Human Rights*, vol. 7, 1977); Joel Cang, *The Silent Millions: A History of the Jews in the Soviet Union* (New York: Taplinger Publishing, 1969); Robert O. Freedman, ed., *Soviet Jewry in the Decisive Decade, 1971–1980* (Durham, N.C.: Duke University Press, 1984); George Ginsburgs, "Soviet Law and the Emigration of Soviet Jews," *Soviet Jewish Affairs* 3, no. 1 (1973); Zvi Gitelman, *Antisemitism in the USSR: Sources, Types, Consequences* (New York: Institute for Jewish Policy Planning and Research of the Synagogue of America, 1974), "Moscow and the Soviet Jews: A Parting of the Ways," *Problems of Communism* 39 (Jan.–Feb. 1980), and "Soviet Jewish Emigrants: Why Are They Choosing America?" *Soviet Jewish Affairs* 7, no. 1 (1977); Ben Zion Goldberg, *The Jewish Problem in the Soviet Union: Analysis and Solution* (New York: Crown Publishers, 1961); Dan N. Jacobs and Ellen Frankel Paul, *Studies of the Third Wave: Recent Migration of Soviet Jews to the United States* (Boulder, Colo.: Westview Press, 1981); William Korey, *The Soviet Cage: Antisemitism in Russia* (New York: Viking Press, 1973); Thomas E. Sawyer, *The Jewish Minority in the Soviet Union* (Boulder, Colo.: Westview Press, 1979); and Victor Zaslavsky and Robert J. Brym, *Soviet-Jewish Emigration and Soviet Nationality Policy* (New York: St. Martin's Press, 1983).

4. There was a Jewish autonomous oblast in the Soviet Far East, created in 1934, but Jews constitute only a very small minority of its population, and it has never developed into a genuine Jewish territorial base down to the present.

5. For details of these developments see the publications listed in note 3 above, particularly titles by Freedman, Korey, and Sawyer.

6. Countries besides Israel and the United States where Soviet Jews have resettled include Canada, various states in Europe and Latin America, Australia, and New Zealand.

7. There is a growing body of literature dealing with the Soviet Germans, part of it available only in German. This section is based on published and unpublished sources including the following: C. C. Aronsfeld, "German Emigration from the Soviet Union," *Research Report* (London: Institute of Jewish Affairs), no. 2 (Sept. 1982); *30 Jahre Lager Friedland* (Hanover, West Germany: Herausgegaben vom Niedersachischen Minister für Bundesgelegenheiten, 1975); CDS/CSU Group in the German Bundestag, *White Paper on Human Rights Situation in Germany and of the Germans in Eastern Europe* (Bonn: CDS/CSU Group in the German Bundestag, 1977); Ingeborg Fleischhauer, *Die Deutschen im Zarenreich: 200 Jahre Deutsch-Russischer Kulturgemeinschaft* (Stuttgart, West Germany: Deutscher Verlag Anstalt, 1986); Ingeborg Fleischhauer and Benjamin Pinkus, *The Soviet Germans: Past and Present* (New York: St. Martin's Press, 1986); Adam Giesinger, *From Catherine to Khrushchev: The Story of Russia's Germans* (Saskatchewan, Canada: Marian Press, 1974); Sidney Heitman, *The Soviet Germans in the USSR Today* (Cologne, West Germany: Bundesinstitut für ostwissenschaftliche und internationale Studien, 1980), and

"Soviet German Population Change, 1970–1979," *Soviet Geography: Review and Translation* 22, no. 9 (Nov. 1981); *Re Patria; Sbornik materialov posviashchennyh istorii, kul'ture i problemam nemtsev Sovietskogo Soiuza* (Moscow: Samizdat, 1974); and *Untersuchung über die Aussiedler in der Bundesrepublik Deutschland—Anpassung, Umstellung, Eingliederung* (Bad Homburg v. d. Hohe, West Germany: AWR-Forschungegesellschaft für das Weltflüchtlingsproblem, deutsche Sektion e.V., 1982).

8. There is not a single publication in any language today dealing with Armenian postwar emigration from the USSR because the subject has been repressed by the USSR and the international Armenian diaspora, for both of whom it is politically sensitive. This section is based on information provided by informants in the Armenian-American community that has never been published until now and on the following written sources: Esther Agabian, "In the Shadow of Ararat, Armenia Revisited," *Christian Science Monitor*, March 5, 1979; Akademiia nauk Armianskoi SSR, *Atlas Armianskoi Sovetskoi Sotsialisticheskoi Respubliki* (Erevan and Moscow: Glavnoe upravlenie geodezii i kartografii, 1961); Ellie Andrassian, "Immigrants from Soviet Armenia Today," unpublished paper, 1985; Michael J. Arlen, *Passage to Ararat* (New York: Farrar, Strause & Giroux, 1975); Elizabeth Fuller and Ann Sheehy, "Armenia and Armenians in the USSR" in *The All-Union Census of 1979 in the USSR; Radio Liberty Research Bulletin* (Munich, West Germany: Radio Free Europe-Radio Liberty, 1980); "Armenians," in *Great Soviet Encyclopedia*, vol. 2 (English trans. of 3d Russian edition; New York: Macmillan, 1973); Robert Mirak, "Armenians," in *Harvard Encyclopedia of American Ethnic Groups* (Cambridge, Mass., and London: Harvard University Press, 1980), and *Torn Between Two Lands: Armenians in America, 1890 to World War I* (Cambridge, Mass.: Harvard University Press, 1983); Richard G. Hovannisian, *Armenia on the Road to Independence, 1918* (Berkeley: University of California Press, 1967), and *The Republic of Armenia*, vols. 1 and 2 (Berkeley: University of California Press, 1971 and 1982); Mary K. Matossian, "Armenia and the Armenians," in *Handbook of Major Soviet Nationalities* (New York: Free Press, 1975), and *The Impact of Soviet Policies in Armenia* (Leiden, The Netherlands: E. J. Brill, 1962, and Westpoint, Conn.: Hyperion, 1981); Claire Mouradian, "L'immigration des Arméniens de la diaspora vers las Rus d'Arménie, 1946–1962," *Cahiers du monde russe et sovietique*, no. 1, (1979); and Ronald Grigor Suny, *Armenia in the Twentieth Century* (Chico, Calif.: Scholars Press, 1983).

9. *Naselenie SSSR po dannym vsesoiuznoi perepisi naseleniia 1979 goda* (Moscow: Izdatel'stvo politicheskoi literatury, 1980) and *The All-Union Census of 1979 in the USSR; Radio Liberty Research Bulletin*.

10. Estimates of the number of Armenians who emigrated to the USSR from France and then returned range as high as 30,000, but the actual number is not known. This paper uses a conservative estimate of 12,000. For brief discussions of this movement see the article by Claire Mouradian cited in note 8 above and Benjamin Pinkus, "The Emigration of National Minorities from the USSR in the Post-Stalin Era," *Soviet Jewish Affairs* 13, no. 1 (1983).

11. The paragraphs that follow are based on several analyses of Soviet emigration and Soviet internal and foreign relations, including Robert O. Freedman, "Soviet Jewry and Soviet-American Relations: A Historical Analysis"; Georg Brunner et al., *Minderheitenschutz in Europa* (Heidelberg, West Germany: C. F. Müller Juristischer Verlag, 1985); Rupert S. Dirnecker, "Between Helsinki and Bel-

grade: A Balance Sheet of CSCE," *Strategic Review* 5, no. 4 (Fall 1977); Robin Edmonds, *Soviet Foreign Policy: The Brezhnev Years* (Oxford and New York: Oxford University Press, 1983); William E. Griffith, *The Ostpolitik of the Federal Republic of Germany* (Cambridge, Mass.: MIT Press, 1978); Wolfram F. Hanreider, ed., *West German Foreign Policy: 1949–1979* (Boulder, Colo.: Westview Press, 1980); John P. Hardt and Donna L. Gold, *Emigration: Soviet Compliance with the Helsinki Accords* (Washington, D.C.: Congressional Research Service, Library of Congress, 1984); William Korey, *Human Rights and the Helsinki Accord: Focus on U.S. Policy* (Headline Series No. 59; New York: Foreign Policy Association, 1983); Benjamin Pinkus, "The Emigration of National Minorities from the USSR"; Donna L. Gold, *Soviet Jewry: U.S. Policy Considerations* (Washington, D.C.: Congressional Research Service, Library of Congress, 1985); and Victor Zaslavsky and Robert J. Brym, *Soviet-Jewish Emigration.* Sources also include a large volume of samizdat material and other published and documentary sources contained in the holdings of Radio Free Europe/Radio Liberty in Munich, West Germany, and New York and in various West German ethnic, human rights, and governmental archives.

12. It should be noted that the publication by Zaslavsky and Brym cited above in note 11 and a related article by John L. Scherer, "Soviet Emigration Policy: Internal Determinants: A Note on Soviet Jewish Emigration, 1971–1984," *Soviet Jewish Affairs* 15, no. 2 (1985), question the linkage between Soviet emigration policy and the foreign relations of the USSR. The authors explore other determinants of Soviet emigration policy, but their thesis is tenuous and unconvincing.

13. This paragraph and the one that follows is based on information provided by informed persons in the American-Armenian community which has not been recorded or published anywhere until now.

14. This campaign consisted of publicizing the difficulties some Soviet emigrants encountered in Israel, the United States, and West Germany. It also consisted of public appearances on Soviet television and radio and accounts in the press by returnees who were permitted to regain Soviet citizenship after unsuccessful efforts to resettle in the West. Though these critical accounts were greatly exaggerated, they were based on actual experiences by Soviet emigrants who found it particularly difficult to adapt to the conditions they encountered in the West. Others sought to return to the USSR because they missed relatives and friends left behind. Of the several hundred who have applied to return, the Soviet government has permitted only a few to do so—presumably those whom they could use to advantage for propaganda purposes.

15. Until the early 1980s persistent demonstrators and agitators who sought to emigrate from the USSR were dealt with surprisingly leniently by the Soviet authorities. Since then, increasingly severe punishments have been meted out to them, including prison sentences, terms in hard-labor camps, and commitment to mental hospitals, and their relatives have also been punished in various ways.

16. In the case of the Germans they have been favored with expanded German language instruction in their schools, the easing of religious restrictions for them, the founding of a German theater in Central Asiatic Russia, where they are today concentrated, and the founding of a semiannual German-language literary journal in 1981—*Heimatliche Weiten,* a politically and ideologically innocuous publication of mediocre artistic merit.

In early 1986 a new chairman of the official Committee for Cultural Relations with Armenians Abroad, which had long been dormant, was appointed—

Garlen Dallakian, formerly the second or third highest ranking member of the Armenian branch of the Soviet Communist party. Whether this was a downgrading of Dallakian or an upgrading of the Committee is not yet clear. Dallakian visited the United States and Canada in June of 1986 to meet leaders of the Armenian communities in both countries, and the writer met him also, but he gave no indication in any of his contacts as to what his future policy may be.

17. The text of the new regulations and their import are discussed in my *The Third Soviet Emigration: Jewish, German and Armenian Emigration from the USSR Since World War II,* prepared for the Office of Long Range Assessments and Research of the U.S. Department of State in 1986 and scheduled to be published by the Bundesinstitut für Ostwissenschaftliche und Internationale Studien in Cologne, West Germany, in 1987.

18. These implications are discussed briefly in the report noted above in the concluding section.

7. Soviet-American Trade and Soviet Jewish Emigration: Should a Policy Change Be Made by the American Jewish Community?

1. Louis Greenberg, *The Jews in Russia: The Struggle for Emancipation,* vol. 2 (New Haven, Connecticut: Yale University Press, 1951), p. 90.

2. R. Ainsztein, "Soviet Jewry in the Second World War," in *The Jews in Soviet Russia since 1917,* ed. Lionel Kochan (Oxford, 1970), p. 271.

3. Yehoshua A. Gilboa, *The Black Years of Soviet Jewry, 1939–53* (Boston: Little, Brown, 1971), pp. 309–313; Salo Baron, *The Russian Jew Under Tsars and Soviets* (New York: Macmillan, 1964), p. 292.

4. Robert O. Freedman, ed., *Soviet Jewry in the Decisive Decade, 1971–1980* (Durham, N.C.: Duke University Press, 1984), p. 4.

5. Meeting with Secretary of Commerce Peter Peterson, Washington, D.C., June 30, 1972.

6. Discussions with Richard Perle, then an assistant to Senator Henry Jackson.

7. Discussions with American businessmen.

8. Discussions with American businessmen.

9. William Korey, "Jackson-Vanik and Soviet Jewry," *World Reports,* International Council of B'nai B'rith (May 1983), p. 7.

10. Ibid.

11. For more detailed description of events in this period see the article by Robert O. Freedman, "Soviet Jewry and Soviet-American Relations: A Historical Analysis," in Freedman, *Soviet Jewry.*

12. A discussion with executives of the New York Conference on Soviet Jewry.

13. Discussions with leaders of various American Jewish groups.

14. Hearings of the Subcommittee on International Economic Policy and Trade, Committee on Foreign Affairs, House of Representatives, February 22, 1979.

15. Correspondence with executives of the American Jewish Congress.

16. Correspondence with Congressman Charles Vanik.

17. Discussion with leaders of American Jewish groups.

18. Discussion with leaders of the Student Struggle for Soviet Jewry.

19. *Business Week,* April 8, 1985, p. 63.

8. Soviet Immigrant Resettlement in Israel and the United States

1. For an elaboration of this argument see Zvi Gitelman, "What Happened?" *Moment* 7, no. 9 (October 1982), p. 37. See also Gitelman, "Soviet Jewish Emigres: Why Are They Choosing America?" *Soviet Jewish Affairs* 7, no. 1 (1977). This section draws heavily on Gitelman, "The Quality of Life in Israel and the United States," in *New Lives: The Adjustment of Soviet Jewish Immigrants in the United States and Israel,* ed. Rita Simon (Lexington, Mass.: Lexington Books, 1985).
2. *Statistical Abstract of Israel,* no. 31 (Jerusalem: Central Bureau of Statistics, 1981).
3. See Zvi Gitelman, *Becoming Israelis: Political Resocialization of Soviet and American Immigrants* (New York: Praeger, 1982), pp. 10–12.
4. For details see Zvi Gitelman and David Naveh, "Elite Accommodation and Organizational Effectiveness: The Case of Immigrant Absorption in Israel," *Journal of Politics* 38, no. 4 (November 1976).
5. Gitelman, *Becoming Israelis,* pp. 70–71.
6. See the HIAS quarterly, *Statistical Abstracts.*
7. See Zvi Gitelman, "Soviet Immigrant Resettlement in the United States," *Soviet Jewish Affairs* 12, no. 2 (May 1982), pp. 5–7.
8. Central Bureau of Statistics, *Monthly Bulletin of Statistics,* supplement 24, no. 6 (June 1973), p. 143. Israel, Ministry for Immigrant Absorption, *Klitat haaliyah,* 1972–1979 (Jerusalem, 1973–1980).
9. See Gitelman, *Becoming Israelis,* pp. 140–148.
10. Attalah Mansour, "Shlish harofim olim, *Haaretz,* February 7, 1977. An excellent study of this group is Judith T. Shuval, *Newcomers and Colleagues: Soviet Immigrant Physicians in Israel* (Houston: Cap and Gown Press, 1983).
11. See *Klitat haaliyah,* and Tamar Horowitz and Hava Frankel, "Olim bemerkazai klitat," Research Report, no. 185, publication no. 538 (Jerusalem: Henrietta Szold Institute, 1975), pp. 130–132.
12. Based on a survey of 400 Soviet families who had come from the European urban centers. See Gur Ofer and Aharon Vinokur, "Consumption Habits of Soviet Immigrants" (Jerusalem: Hebrew University, 1981).
13. See *Klitat haaliyah* and *Monthly Bulletin of Statistics,* 24, no. 9 (1979).
14. Theodore H. Friedgut, "The Welcome Home: Absorption of Soviet Jews in Israel," in *Soviet Jewry in the Decisive Decade, 1971–80,* ed. Robert O. Freedman (Durham, N.C.: Duke University Press, 1984).
15. Some of these studies are collected in Dan Jacobs and Ellen Frankel Paul, *Studies of the Third Wave: Recent Migration of Soviet Jews to the United States* (Boulder, Colo.: Westview Press, 1981).
16. See Rita Simon and Julian Simon, "Social and Economic Adjustment," in Simon, *New Lives.*
17. Ibid., pp. 19, 27.
18. It is possible that immigrants to Israel attempt to conceal the non-Jewishness of spouses in order to avoid complicated citizenship and *halakhic* (religious law, questions. However, there are cases where the decisive factor in leading a couple to choose the United States was the fact that one of them is not Jewish. In 1976–77 a comparative study of *olim* and U.S. immigrants was made by officials of the Ministry for Immigrant Absorption. It found that the *olim* had more positive Jewish reasons for immigrating (desire for Jewish culture), while those going to the United States emphasized economic and professional reasons.

However, the study found that the two groups did not differ significantly in their Jewish backgrounds just as we have observed in our sample. Unfortunately, this study was reported in a public lecture so that few statistical findings were presented and little information was provided regarding the sample. See Elazar Leshem, "Noshrim veolim bekerev yotsai Brit haMoetsot" (Jerusalem: Shazar Library, Institute of Contemporary Jewry, Hebrew University, 1980), pp. 13–15. The sample (about 350 people) is discussed on pp. 58–60. Leshem found that only 0.7 percent of the *olim* in the sample had non-Jewish spouses, whereas 12 percent of those not going to Israel did.

19. "Jewish Identification and Affiliation of Soviet Jewish Immigrants in New York City—A Needs Assessment and Planning Study: Summary of Findings and Recommendations," Federation of Jewish Philanthropies, June 1985, p. 7.

20. See Israeli newspaper reports and opinion surveys cited in Gitelman, *Becoming Israelis,* p. 57.

21. Michael Rywkin, "Housing in Central Asia: Demography, Ownership, Tradition: The Uzbek Example," Kennan Institute for Advanced Russian Studies Occasional Paper No. 82. (Washington, D.C., December 1979), p. 5.

22. Simon, *New Lives,* p. 27.

23. The CJF study, which analyzed motivations for emigration somewhat differently, found anti-Semitism cited more frequently than any other reason, with family reunion and desire to give children a good education and future as other frequently mentioned motivations. Ibid., pp. 14–15.

24. For a study of identity among comparable groups of Jewish émigrés see Michael Inbar and Chaim Adler, *Ethnic Integration in Israel: A Comparative Case Study of Brothers Who Settled in France and in Israel* (New Brunswick, N.J.: Transaction Books, 1977).

25. For a fascinating study of the intricate financial aid arrangements within the Georgian community see Yitzhak Eilam, *Seker antropologi shel hakehilla haGruzinit beAshkelon* (Jerusalem: Research Department of the Ministry for Immigrant Absorption and Department of Sociology and Cultural Anthropology, Hebrew University, 1980).

26. Unattributed quotations in this chapter are comments by interviewees.

27. It is interesting that 95 out of 100 German respondents to a parallel question about German and Soviet government offices said that German offices are run better.

28. In the CJF study, 86 percent stated that they would immigrate to the U.S. again, 5 percent said that they would stay in the USSR, 6 percent would go to Israel, and 1 percent would go elsewhere (1 percent did not answer). Simon, *New Lives,* p. 31.

29. Simon, *New Lives,* p. 30 and "Jewish Identification and Affiliation," p. 7.

30. Simon, *New Lives,* p. 32.

31. One study of Central Asian Jews is by Rinah Ben-Shaul, "Olai Bukhara-Beit Shemesh: Mekhkar Antropologi" (Jerusalem: Ministry for Immigrant Absorption, 1975).

9. Soviet Jewish Artists in the USSR and Israel: The Dynamics of Artistic Resettlement

1. For information on the work of Kaplan, which is not treated in this article, see B. Suris, *Anatolli Lvovich Kaplan* (Leningrad, Khudozhnik RSFSR, 1972).

2. Mikhail Borgman, "The Twelve: The First Leningrad Exhibit," in *Twelve from the Underground* (Berkeley: Judah Magnas Museum, 1976), p. 4.

3. Mikhail Grobman, "The Artist About Himself," in Haim Gamzu, *Michail Grobman* (Tel Aviv Museum Catalogue, 1971), p. 5.

4. Ruth Debel, "Interview with Alexander Okun," in *Debel Gallery Bulletin* (Ein Kerem, Jerusalem), no. 3 (May 1981).

5. Boris Penson, Artist's Introduction to Album, "The Land of Women." Artist's collection.

6. Ibid. For more information on Penson, see Yoav Dagon, *Boris Penson* (Israel: Herziliya Museum, 1984).

7. Aharon April, *Song of Songs Which is Solomon's* (Catalog) (Jerusalem-Tel Aviv: Artist's House and Rosenfeld Gallery, 1983), p. 2.

8. Ibid.

9. "Leviathan Manifesto No. 2," *Leviathan Group* (Jerusalem: Artist's House, 1979), p. 3.

10. Mikhail Grobman, *Leviathan* (Ashdod: Beth Uri and Rami Museum, 1978), p. 2.

11. Ibid.

12. Mark Zhitnitsky, *Shalom Aleichem* (Tel Aviv: Massada Press, 1977).

13. *Haim Kapchits* (Jerusalem: Artist's House, 1982).

14. For an excellent analysis of Podolsky's works see Edna Moshenson, "Lev Podolsky: Works, 1979–1984," in *Lev Podolsky* (Tel Aviv Museum, 1985), p. 3.

15. Ibid. See also Gil Goldfine, "Podolsky's Introvert Interiors," in *The Jerusalem Post*, April 11, 1985.

16. For more on this episode see David K. Shipler, *Russia: Broken Idols, Solemn Dreams* (New York: Quadrangle, 1983), also reprinted as "The Tragedy of Yefim Ladyzhensky" in *Hadassah Magazine*, March 1985, pp. 24–28.

17. Joseph Hoffman, "Ladizhinski and the Iconography of Odessa," in *Yefim B. Ladizhinski: Paintings and Drawings* (Haifa: University of Haifa Art Gallery, 1980), p. 5.

18. Meir Ronnen, "Eternally Displaced," *The Jerusalem Post*, February 19, 1982.

Bibliography

Books

Akademiia nauk Armianskoi SSR. *Atlas Armianskoi Sovetskoi Sotsialisticheskoi Respubliki.* Erevan and Moscow, 1961.

Alexander, A. *Immigration to Israel from the USSR.* Tel Aviv: Faculty of Law, Tel Aviv University, 1977 (reprinted from *Israel Yearbook on Human Rights,* vol. 7, 1977).

Anti-Zionist Committee of Soviet Public Opinion. Moscow, 1983.

Baron, Salo. *The Russian Jew under Tsars and Soviets.* New York, 1964.

Belaia kniga: novye fakty, svidetel'stva, dokumenty. Moscow, 1985.

Brafman, Morris, and David Schimel. *Trade for Freedom: Détente, Trade and Soviet Jews.* New York, 1975.

Brezhnev, Leonid. "Report of the Central Committee of the Communist Party of the Soviet Union to the 24th Congress of the CPSU." *The 24th Congress of the Communist Party of the Soviet Union, March 30–April 19, 1971.* Moscow, 1971.

Blum, Jacob, and Vera Rich. *The Image of the Jew in Soviet Literature: The Post-Stalin Period.* New York, 1984.

Cang, Joel. *The Silent Millions: A History of the Jews in the Soviet Union.* New York, 1969.

CDS/CSU Group in the German Bundestag. *White Paper on Human Rights Situation in Germany and the Germans in Eastern Europe.* Bonn, 1977.

Concluding Document of the Meeting Held at Madrid from 11 November 1980 to 9 September 1983 to Follow-up the Conference on Security and Cooperation in Europe. London, 1983.

Conference on Security and Cooperation in Europe: Final Act. London, August 1975.

Dagan, Avigdor. *Moscow and Jerusalem.* New York, 1970.

Dagon, Yoav. *Boris Penson.* Herzliya, Israel: Herzliya Museum, 1984.

Djilas, Milovan. *Conversations with Stalin.* New York, 1962.

Dreisig Jahre Lager Friedland. Hanover, West Germany: Herausgegaben vom Niedersachischen Minister für Bundesgelegenheiten, 1975.

Edmonds, Robin. *Soviet Foreign Policy: The Brezhnev Years.* Oxford, 1983.

Eilam, Yitzhak. *Seker antropologi shel hakehilla haGruzinit beAshkelon.* Jerusalem: Research Department of the Ministry for Immigrant Absorption and Department of Sociology and Cultural Anthropology, Hebrew University, 1980.

Fleischhauer, Ingeborg. *Die Deuschen im Zarenreich: 200 Jahre Deutsch-Russischer Kulturgemeinschaft.* Stuttgart, 1986.

Fleischhauer, Ingeborg, and Benjamin Pinkus. *The Soviet Germans: Past and Present*. New York, 1986.

Freedman, Robert O. *Soviet Policy toward the Middle East since 1970*. 3d ed. New York, 1982.

Freedman, Robert O., ed. *Soviet Jewry in the Decisive Decade, 1971–1980*. Durham, N.C., 1984.

Giesinger, Adam. *From Catherine to Khrushchev: The Story of Russia's Germans*. Saskatchewan, 1974.

Gilboa, Yehoshua. *The Black Years of Soviet Jewry*. Boston, 1971.

Gist: The Reykjavik Meeting. Bureau of Public Affairs, Department of State, December 1986.

Gitelman, Zvi. *Jewish Nationality and Soviet Politics*. Princeton, N.J., 1972.

Gitelman, Zvi. *Antisemitism in the USSR: Sources, Types, Consequences*. New York: Institute for Jewish Policy Planning and Research of the Synagogue Council of America, 1974.

Gitelman, Zvi. *Becoming Israelis: Political Resocialization of Soviet and American Immigrants*. New York, 1982.

Gold, Donna L. *Soviet Jewry: U.S. Policy Considerations*. Washington, D.C.: Congressional Research Service, Library of Congress, 1985.

Goldberg, Ben Zion. *The Jewish Problem in the Soviet Union: Analysis and Solution*. New York, 1961.

Goldman, Marshall. *Détente and Dollars*. New York, 1975.

Greenberg, Louis. *The Jews in Russia: The Struggle for Emancipation*. Vol. 2. New Haven, 1951.

Griffith, William E. *The Ostpolitik of the Federal Republic of Germany*. Cambridge, 1978.

Grobman, Mikhail. *Leviathan*. Ashdod, Israel: Beth Uri and Rami Museum, 1978.

Hanreider, Wolfram F., ed. *West German Foreign Policy: 1949–1979*. Boulder, Colo., 1980.

Hardt, John P., and Donna L. Gold. *Emigration: Soviet Compliance with the Helsinki Accords*. Washington, D.C.: Congressional Research Service, Library of Congress, 1984.

Heitman, Sidney. *The Soviet Germans in the USSR Today*. Cologne, West Germany: Bundesinstitut für Ostwissenschaftliche und Internationale Studien, 1986.

Hovannisian, Richard G. *Armenia on the Road to Independence, 1918*. Berkeley, Calif., 1967.

Human Contacts, Reunion of Families, and Soviet Jewry. London, 1986.

Inbar, Michael, and Chaim Adler. *Ethnic Integration in Israel: A Comparative Case Study of Brothers Who Settled in France and in Israel*. New Brunswick, 1977.

Institute of Jewish Affairs (London). *Soviet Jewry and the Implementation of the Helsinki Final Act* (1977); *The Position of Soviet Jewry, 1977–1980: Report on the Implementation of the Helsinki Final Act since the Belgrade Follow-up Conference* (1980); *The Position of Soviet Jewry: Human Rights and the Helsinki Accords, 1985* (1985); *The Problems of Jewish Culture* (published on the occasion of the Cultural Forum of the CSCE in Budapest, 15 October–25 November 1985) (1985); *Human Contacts, Reunion of Families and Soviet Jewry* (1986).

Jacobs, Dan N., and Ellen Frankel Paul. *Studies of the Third Wave: Recent Migration of Soviet Jews to the United States*. Boulder, Colo., 1981.

———. *Jewish Identification and Affiliation of Soviet Jewish Immigrants in New*

York City—A Needs Assessment and Planning Study: Summary of Findings and Recommendations. New York: Federation of Jewish Philanthropies, 1985.

Kalb, Marvin, and Bernard Kalb. *Kissinger.* New York, 1975.

Klinghoffer, Arthur. *Israel and the Soviet Union: Alienation or Reconciliation.* Boulder, Colo., 1985.

Kolesnikov, Yuri. *The Curtain Rises.* Moscow, 1979.

Korey, William. *The Soviet Cage: Antisemitism in Russia.* New York, 1973.

Korey, William. *Human Rights and the Helsinki Accord: Focus on U.S. Policy.* Headline Series no. 59. New York: Foreign Policy Association, 1983.

Korneyev, Lev. *Klassovaia suschnost' sionizma.* Kiev, 1982.

Krammer, Arnold. *The Forgotten Friendship: Israel and the Soviet Bloc 1947–1953.* Chicago, 1974.

Ladizhinski, Yefim B. *Paintings and Drawings.* Haifa: University of Haifa Art Gallery, 1980.

Lendvai, Paul. *Anti-Semitism Without Jews.* Garden City, N.Y., 1971.

Leshem, Elazar. *Noshrim veolim bekerev yotsai Brit haMoetsot.* Jerusalem, 1980.

Lev Podolsky. Tel Aviv: Tel Aviv Museum, 1985.

Materialy samizdata. Munich, 1986.

Meeting Held at Belgrade from 4 October 1977 to 9 March 1978 to Follow-up the Conference on Security and Cooperation in Europe. London, 1978.

Miller, Jack, ed. *Jews in Soviet Culture.* New Brunswick, 1984.

Naselenie SSSR po dannym vsesoiuznoi perepisi naseleniia 1979 goda. Moscow, 1980.

Newhouse, John. *Cold Dawn: The Story of SALT.* New York, 1973.

Orbach, William W. *The American Movement to Aid Soviet Jews.* Amherst, Mass., 1979.

Ro'i, Yaacov. *Soviet Decision-making in Practice: The USSR and Israel 1947–1954.* London, 1980.

Rothenberg, Joshua. *The Jewish Religion in the Soviet Union.* New York, 1971.

Rywkin, Michael. *Housing in Central Asia: Demography, Ownership, Tradition: The Uzbek Example.* Kennan Institute for Advanced Russian Studies Occasional Paper no. 81. Washington, D.C., 1979.

Sawyer, Thomas E. *The Jewish Minority in the Soviet Union.* Boulder, Colo., 1979.

Schroeter, Leonard. *The Last Exodus.* New York, 1974.

Shipler, David K. *Russia: Broken Idols, Solemn Dreams.* New York, 1983.

Shuval, Judith T. *Newcomers and Colleagues: Soviet Immigrant Physicians in Israel.* Houston, Tex., 1983.

Solzhenitsyn, Aleksander. *The Gulag Archipelago.* Vols. 1–2. New York, 1973.

Stern, Paula. *Water's Edge: Domestic Politics and the Making of American Foreign Policy.* Westport, Conn., 1979.

Suny, Ronald Grigor. *Armenia in the Twentieth Century.* Chico, Calif., 1983.

Suris, B. *Anatolii Lvovich Kaplan.* Leningrad, 1972.

Wiesel, Elie. *The Jews of Silence.* New York, 1966.

Zaslavsky, Victor, and Robert J. Brym. *Soviet-Jewish Emigration and Soviet Nationality Policy.* New York, 1983.

Zhitnitsky, Mark. *Shalom Aleichem.* Tel Aviv, 1977.

Articles and Chapters in Books

Ainsztein, R. "Soviet Jewry in the Second World War." In *The Jews in Soviet Russia Since 1917,* edited by Lionel Kochan. Oxford, 1970.

"Armenians." *Great Soviet Encyclopedia*. Vol. 2 (English translation of third Russian edition). New York, 1973.

Aronsfeld, C. C. "German Emigration from the Soviet Union." *Research Report*. London: Institute of Jewish Affairs, September 1982.

Ben-Shaul, Rinah. "Olai Bukhara-Beit Shemesh: Mekhkar Antropologi." Jerusalem: Ministry for Immigrant Absorption, 1975.

Dirnecker, Rupert S. "Between Helsinki and Belgrade: A Balance Sheet of CSCE." *Strategic Review* 5, no. 4 (1977).

Feldbrugge, F. J. M. "The New Soviet Law on Emigration." *Soviet Jewish Affairs* 17, no. 1 (1987).

Freedman, Robert O. "Soviet Jewry and Soviet-American Relations." In *Soviet Jewry in the Decisive Decade, 1971–80*, edited by Robert O. Freedman. Durham, N.C., 1984.

Freedman, Robert O. "Soviet Policy toward the Middle East since the Israeli Invasion of Lebanon." In *The Middle East since the Israeli Invasion of Lebanon*, edited by Robert O. Freedman. Syracuse, N.Y., 1986.

Friedgut, Theodore H. "The Welcome Home: Absorption of Soviet Jews in Israel." In *The Decisive Decade: Soviet Jewry, 1971–1980*, edited by Robert O. Freedman. Durham, N.C., 1984.

Friedgut, Theodore H. "Soviet Anti-Zionism and Anti-Semitism: Another Cycle." *Soviet Jewish Affairs* (February 1984).

Fuller, Elizabeth, and Ann Sheehy, "Armenia and Armenians in the USSR." In *The All-Union Census of 1979 in the USSR*. Radio Liberty Research Bulletin. Munich, 1980.

Ginsburgs, George. "Soviet Law and the Emigration of Soviet Jews." *Soviet Jewish Affairs* 3, no. 1 (1973).

Gitelman, Zvi, and Advid Naveh. "Elite Accommodation and Organizational Effectiveness: The Case of Immigrant Absorption in Israel." *Journal of Politics* 38, no. 4 (1976).

Gitelman, Zvi. "Soviet Jewish Emigres: Why Are They Choosing America?" *Soviet Jewish Affairs* 7, no. 1 (1977).

———. "Moscow and the Soviet Jews: A Parting of the Ways." *Problems of Communism* (January–February 1980).

———. "Soviet Immigrant Resettlement in the United States." *Soviet Jewish Affairs* 12, no. 2 (1982).

———. "The Quality of Life in Israel and the United States." In *New Lives: The Adjustment of Soviet Jewish Immigrants in the United States and Israel*, edited by Rita Simon. Lexington, Ky., 1985.

Hardt, John P. "West Siberia: The Quest for Energy." *Problems of Communism* 22, no. 3 (1973).

Heitman, Sidney. "Soviet German Population Change, 1970–1979." *Soviet Geography: Review and Translation* 22, no. 9 (1981).

Insight: Soviet Jews (London), vol. 11, no. 6 (1985).

Institute of Jewish Affairs (London). *Research Reports:* "Brezhnev's speech to the 26th Congress of the Communist Party of the Soviet Union," no. 4 (1981); "The Increased Arrests of Soviet Jews in 1981," no. 21 (1981); "Jewish Students in Moscow and the USSR," no. 5 (1982); "Andropov and the Nationalities Question—A New Approach?" no. 1 (1983); "The Soviet Anti-Zionist Committee—Further Developments," no. 13 (1983); "Uni-national and Mixed Marriages in the USSR: Further Statistical Data on Soviet Jewry," no. 19 (1983); *"Pravda* equates Zionism with fascism," no. 2 (1984); "Ominous

Changes in the Soviet Criminal Code," no. 5 (1984); "Fulfilling a Restricted Role: The Soviet Anti-Zionist Committee in 1984," no. 16 (1984); "The Myth of Zionist-Nazi Collaboration: Some Sources of Soviet Propaganda," no. 2 (1985); "Jewish Issues in the Soviet VE Day Propaganda Campaign," no. 3 (1985); "Trials of Soviet Jewish 'Refuseniks' and Activists, 1980–July 1985," no. 5 (1985); "Jewish Culture in the USSR Today," no. 10 (1985).

Khronika tekushchikh sobytii (New York), no. 52 (1979).

Korey, William. "The Story of the Jackson Amendment." *Midstream* 21, no. 3 (1975): 7–36.

Mirak, Robert. "Armenians." In *Harvard Encyclopedia of American Ethnic Groups.* Cambridge, Mass., 1980.

Mouradian, Claire. "L'immigration des Armeniens de la diaspora vers las Rus d'Armenie, 1946–1962." *Cahiers due monde russe et sovietique,* no. 1 (1979).

Orbach, William W. "The British Soviet Jewry Movement." In *Forum* (Jerusalem, World Zionist Organization), no. 32–33 (1978).

"Permission to Leave." *Novoe vremia* (Russian), no. 28 (1987).

Pinkus, Benjamin. "National Identity and Emigration Patterns Among Soviet Jews." *Soviet Jewish Affairs* 15, no. 3 (1985).

Schechtman, J. B. "The USSR, Zionism and Israel." In *The Jews in Soviet Russia Since 1917,* edited by Lionel Kochan. New York, 1978.

Scherer, John L. "Soviet Emigration Policy: Internal Determinants: A Note on Soviet Jewish Emigration, 1971–1984." *Soviet Jewish Affairs* 15, no. 2 (1985).

Sol'mar, E. L. "Protokoly antisionistskikh mudretsov." *Yevreiskii Samizdat* (Jerusalem), vol. 16 (1978).

Contributors

Steven Feinstein is professor of history at the University of Wisconsin—River Falls. He received his M.A. and Ph.D. degrees from New York University and has contributed a number of articles and chapters to books in the areas of Soviet Jewish resettlement in the United States and Soviet art. A participant in the 1981 Conference on Soviet Jewry at the Baltimore Hebrew University, he contributed the chapter "Attitudes of American Jewry toward Recent Soviet Jewish Immigration" in the conference book, *Soviet Jewry in the Decisive Decade.*

Robert O. Freedman is the Peggy Meyerhoff Pearlstone professor of political science and dean of the graduate school of the Baltimore Hebrew University. He is the author of two books, *Economic Warfare in the Communist Bloc* and *Soviet Policy Toward the Middle East Since 1970.* The latter book, which was recently translated into Japanese, is now in its third edition. Dr. Freedman has also been the contributing editor to five books, including *Soviet Jewry in the Decisive Decade, 1971–1980.* He also serves as a visiting lecturer at the Foreign Service Institute of the Department of State. Dr. Freedman received his M.A., Russian Institute Certificate, and Ph.D. degrees from Columbia University.

Theodore H. Friedgut, a native of Saskatchewan, Canada, is currently chairman of the Department of Russian and Slavic Studies at the Hebrew University in Jerusalem. Dr. Friedgut received his M.A. degree from the Hebrew University and his Ph.D. from Columbia University. He has published numerous books and articles in the field of Soviet studies, including *Political Participation in the USSR,* published by Princeton University Press in 1979. Dr. Friedgut participated in the 1981 Conference on Soviet Jewry held at the Baltimore Hebrew University, contributing the chapter "The Welcome Home: The Absorption of Soviet Jews in Israel."

Zvi Gitelman is professor of political science at the University of Michigan. Dr. Gitelman holds both the Certificate of the Russian Institute and the Ph.D. degree from Columbia University. He is the author of a number of major books in the field of Soviet studies, including *Jewish Nationality and Soviet Politics* and *Becoming Israelis: Political Resocialization of Soviet and American Immigrants.*

Marshall Goldman has been a member of the Wellesley College faculty since 1958 and is the Class of 1919 professor of economics. He is also associate director of the Russian Research Center, Harvard University. He is the author of *The USSR in Crisis: The Failure of an Economic System.* His other books include *The Enigma of Soviet Petroleum: Half Full or Half Empty?, 1980; Detente and Dollars: Doing*

Business with the Russians, 1975; *The Soviet Economy—Myth and Reality,* 1968; and *Soviet Foreign Aid and Trade,* 1967. He received his M.A. and Ph.D. degrees from Harvard University.

Sidney Heitman is professor of history at Colorado State University. He received the Russian Institute Certificate and the Ph.D. degree from Columbia University. An IREX scholar, he has published extensively in the field of Soviet-German affairs and has received research grants from the U.S. State Department, the Ecole Pratique des Hautes Etudes in France, and the Deutscher Akademischer Austauschdienst in Germany.

William Korey is director of International Policy Research at B'nai B'rith and a leading scholar in the fields of human rights and Soviet Jewry. He is the author of *The Soviet Cage: Anti-Semitism in Russia.* He received the Russian Institute Certificate and Ph.D. degree from Columbia University and has recently served as a "public member" of the U.S. delegation to the Helsinki Accord talks in Vienna.

Howard Spier is a research specialist at the London-based Institute of Jewish Affairs, the research arm of the World Jewish Congress. He is also assistant editor of the Institute's journal, *Soviet Jewish Affairs.* He has published many articles on the Jews in the USSR and on Soviet-Middle East relations. He is the translator of Edward Kuznetsov's *Prison Diaries* and the editor of the *Proceedings of the Fifth International Sakharov Hearings* (forthcoming).

Index

Library of Congress Cataloging-in-Publication Data
Soviet Jewry in the 1980s : the politics of anti-Semitism and
emigration and the dynamics of resettlement / edited by Robert O.
Freedman.
    p. cm.
Bibliography: p.
Includes index.
ISBN 0–8223–0906–8
    I. Jews—Soviet Union—History—1917– 2. Antisemitism—Soviet
Union—History—20th century. 3. Jews—Soviet Union—Migrations—
History—20th century. 4. Jews, Russian—United States—
History—20th century. 5. Jews, Russian—Israel—History—20th
century. 6. Soviet Union—Ethnic relations. I. Freedman, Robert
Owen. DS135.R92S655 1989 947′.004924—dc 19   89–1074 CIP